Primer curso de lengua española

THIRD EDITION

Student Activities Manual

BLANCO | DONLEY

VISTA®
HIGHER LEARNING

Boston, Massachusetts

Photography and Art Credits

All images © Vista Higher Learning unless otherwise noted. Fotonovela photos provided by Carolina Zapata.

ISBN: 978-1-61857-996-6

3 4 5 6 7 8 9 BB 19 18 17 16

Contenido

VIDEO MANUAL

Introduction

ESCENAS

FLASH CULTURA

¡VIVAN LOS PAÍSES HISPANOS!

LAB MANUAL

Introduction

The ¡VIVA! Student Activities Manual

Completely coordinated with the ¡VIVA! student textbook, the Student Activities Manual for ¡VIVA! provides you with additional practice of the vocabulary, grammar, and language functions presented in each of the textbook's sixteen lessons. The Student Activities Manual will also help you build your reading and writing skills in Spanish. Icons and page references in the **recursos** boxes of the ¡VIVA! student textbook correlate the SAM to your textbook, letting you know when exercises and activities are available for use. Answers to the Workbook, Video Manual, and Lab Manual are located in a separate answer key booklet.

The Workbook

Each lesson's workbook activities focus on developing your reading and writing skills as they recycle the language of the corresponding textbook lesson. Activity formats include, but are not limited to, true/false, multiple choice, fill-in-the-blanks, sentence completion, fleshing out sentences from key elements, and answering questions. You will also find activities based on drawings, photographs, and maps.

Reflecting the overall organization of the textbook lessons, each workbook lesson consists of **Preparación, Gramática,** and **¡Vivan los países hispanos!** sections. After every four lessons, a **Repaso** section appears, providing cumulative practice of the grammar and vocabulary learned.

The Video Manual

¡VIVA! offers three video programs: **Escenas, Flash Cultura,** and **¡Vivan los países hispanos! Antes de ver el video** offers previewing activities to prepare you for successful video viewing experiences. **Mientras ves el video** contains while-viewing activities that will guide you through each module, targeting key ideas and events. Lastly, **Después de ver el video** provides post-viewing activities that check your comprehension and ask you to apply these materials to your own life.

Escenas Video

The **Escenas** video offers 6–9 minutes of footage for each of the textbook's lessons. Each episode tells the continuing story of a group of college students from various Spanish-speaking countries who are studying in Mexico. Each dramatic episode brings the themes, vocabulary, grammar, and language functions of the corresponding lesson alive. Each module ends with a **Resumen** section.

Flash Cultura Video

This dynamic video is integrated with the **Exploración** section of each lesson. **Flash Cultura** features reporters who interview young people from all over the Spanish-speaking world. In these episodes, you will learn about similarities and differences among Spanish-speaking countries, which in turn will challenge you to think about your own cultural practices and values.

¡Vivan los países hispanos! Video

This video is integrated with the **¡Vivan los países hispanos!** section in each even-numbered lesson of **¡VIVA!** Each segment is 2–3 minutes long and consists of documentary footage from the country of focus.

The Lab Manual

The laboratory activities are designed for use with the ¡VIVA! Lab Audio Program. They focus on building your listening comprehension, speaking, and pronunciation skills in Spanish, as they reinforce the vocabulary and grammar of the corresponding textbook lesson. The Lab Manual guides you through the Lab Audio Program, providing the written cues—direction lines, models, charts, drawings, etc.—you will need in order to follow along easily. You will hear statements, questions, mini-dialogues, conversations, monologues, commercials, and many other kinds of listening passages, all recorded by native Spanish speakers. You will encounter a wide range of activities such as listening-and-repeating exercises, listening-and-speaking practice, listening-and-writing activities, illustration-based work, and dictations.

Each laboratory lesson contains a Preparación section that practices the active vocabulary taught in the corresponding textbook lesson. In Lecciones 1–9, a Pronunciación section follows; it parallels the one found in your textbook, and, offers additional exercises. In Lecciones 10–16, the Pronunciación sections are unique to the Lab Manual and the Lab Audio Program since, in those lessons, your textbook features Ortografía sections instead of Pronunciación. Each laboratory lesson then concludes with a Gramática section.

We hope that you will find the **¡VIVA! Student Activities Manual** to be a useful language learning resource and that it will help you increase your Spanish-language skills in a productive, enjoyable fashion.

The ¡VIVA! authors and the Vista Higher Learning editorial staff

PREPARACIÓN

Lección 1

1 Identificar You will hear six short exchanges. For each one, decide whether it is a greeting, an introduction, or a leave-taking. Mark the appropriate column.

> **modelo**
>
> *You hear:* RAQUEL David, te presento a Paulina.
>   DAVID Encantado.
> *You mark:* Introduction

	Greeting	*Introduction*	*Leave-taking*
Modelo	_____	X	_____
1.	_____	_____	_____
2.	_____	_____	_____
3.	_____	_____	_____
4.	_____	_____	_____
5.	_____	_____	_____
6.	_____	_____	_____

2 Asociar You will hear three conversations. Look at the drawing and write the number of the conversation under the appropriate group of people.

a. _____
b. _____
c. _____

3 Preguntas Listen to each question or statement and respond with an answer from the list. Repeat the correct response after the speaker.

a. Mucho gusto.   c. Nada.   e. Bien, gracias.
b. Chau.   d. Lo siento.   f. Soy de los Estados Unidos.

Lab Manual

PRONUNCIACIÓN

The Spanish alphabet

The Spanish and English alphabets are almost identical, with a few exceptions. For example, the Spanish letter **ñ** (**eñe**) doesn't exist in the English alphabet. Furthermore, the letters **k** (**ka**) and **w** (**doble v**) are used only in words of foreign origin. Examine the chart below to find other differences.

Letra	Nombre(s)	Ejemplo(s)	Letra	Nombre(s)	Ejemplo(s)
a	a	**a**diós	n	ene	**n**acionalidad
b	be	**b**ien, pro**b**lema	ñ	eñe	ma**ñ**ana
c	ce	**c**osa, **c**ero	o	o	**o**nce
ch	che	**ch**ico	p	pe	**p**rofesor
d	de	**d**iario, na**d**a	q	cu	**q**ué
e	e	**e**studiante	r	ere	**r**egular, seño**r**a
f	efe	**f**oto	s	ese	**s**eñor
g	ge	**g**racias, **G**erardo, re**g**ular	t	te	**t**ú
h	hache	**h**ola	u	u	**u**sted
i	i	**i**gualmente	v	ve	**v**ista, nue**v**o
j	jota	**J**avier	w	doble ve	*walkman*
k	ka, ca	**k**ilómetro	x	equis	e**x**istir, Mé**x**ico
l	ele	**l**ápiz	y	i griega, ye	**y**o
ll	elle	**ll**ave	z	zeta, ceta	**z**ona
m	eme	**m**apa			

1   **El alfabeto**   Repeat the Spanish alphabet and example words after the speaker.

2   **Práctica**   When you hear the number, say the corresponding word aloud and then spell it. Then listen to the speaker and repeat the correct response.

1. nada
2. maleta
3. quince
4. muy
5. hombre

6. por favor
7. San Fernando
8. Estados Unidos
9. Puerto Rico
10. España

11. Javier
12. Ecuador
13. Maite
14. gracias
15. Nueva York

3   **Dictado**   You will hear six people introduce themselves. Listen carefully and write the people's names as they spell them.

1. _____

2. _____

3. _____

4. _____

5. _____

6. _____

GRAMÁTICA

1.1 Nouns and articles

1 **Identificar** You will hear a series of words. Decide whether the word is masculine or feminine, and mark the appropriate column.

> **modelo**
> You hear: lección
> You mark: Feminine

	Masculine	Feminine
Modelo	_____	__X__
1.	_____	_____
2.	_____	_____
3.	_____	_____
4.	_____	_____
5.	_____	_____
6.	_____	_____
7.	_____	_____
8.	_____	_____

2 **Transformar** Change each word from the masculine to the feminine. Repeat the correct answer after the speaker. (6 *items*)

> **modelo**
> el chico
> la chica

3 **Cambiar** Change each word from the singular to the plural. Repeat the correct answer after the speaker. (8 *items*)

> **modelo**
> una palabra
> unas palabras

4 **Completar** Listen as Silvia reads her shopping list. Write the missing words.

_____ diccionario
un _____
_____ cuadernos
_____ mochila
_____ mapa de _____
_____ lápices

1.2 Numbers 0–30

1 **Identificar** ¡Bingo! You are going to play two games **(juegos)** of bingo. As you hear each number, mark your bingo card.

Juego 1		
1	3	5
29	25	6
14	18	17
9	12	21

Juego 2		
0	30	27
10	3	2
16	19	4
28	22	20

2 **Números** Use the cue to tell how many there are of each item. Repeat the correct response after the speaker.

> **modelo**
> *You see:* 18 chicos
> *You say:* dieciocho chicos

1. 15 lápices
2. 4 computadoras
3. 8 cuadernos
4. 22 días
5. 9 maletas
6. 30 fotos
7. 1 palabra
8. 26 diccionarios
9. 12 países
10. 3 problemas
11. 17 escuelas
12. 25 turistas

3 **Completar** You will hear a series of math problems. Write the missing numbers and solve the problems.

1. _____ + _____11_____ = _____

2. _____ − _____5_____ = _____

3. _____8_____ + _____ = _____

4. _____ − _____12_____ = _____

5. _____3_____ + _____ = _____

6. _____ + _____0_____ = _____

4 **Preguntas** Look at the drawing and answer each question you hear. Repeat the correct response after the speaker. (*6 items*)

1.3 Present tense of ser

1   **Identificar** Listen to each sentence and mark the subject of the verb.

> **modelo**
>
> *You hear:* Son pasajeros.
> *You mark:* ellos/ellas

	yo	tú	él/ella	nosotros/as	ellos/ellas
Modelo	_____	_____	_____	_____	X _____
1.	_____	_____	_____	_____	_____
2.	_____	_____	_____	_____	_____
3.	_____	_____	_____	_____	_____
4.	_____	_____	_____	_____	_____
5.	_____	_____	_____	_____	_____
6.	_____	_____	_____	_____	_____

2   **Cambiar** Form a new sentence using the cue you hear as the subject. Repeat the correct answer after the speaker. (*8 items*)

> **modelo**
>
> Isabel es de los Estados Unidos. (yo)
> *Yo soy de los Estados Unidos.*

3   **Escoger** Listen to each question and choose the most logical response.

1. a. Soy Patricia.   b. Es la señora Gómez.
2. a. Es de California.   b. Él es conductor.
3. a. Es de Ecuador.   b. Es un diccionario.
4. a. Es de Patricia.   b. Soy estudiante.
5. a. Él es conductor.   b. Es de España.
6. a. Es un cuaderno.   b. Soy de los Estados Unidos.

4   **Preguntas** Answer each question you hear using the cue provided. Repeat the correct response after the speaker.

> **modelo**
>
> *You hear:* ¿De dónde es Pablo?
> *You see:* Estados Unidos
> *You say:* Él es de los Estados Unidos.

1. España   2. California   3. México   4. Ecuador   5. Puerto Rico   6. Colorado

5   **¿Quiénes son?** Listen to this conversation and write the answers to the questions.

1. ¿Cómo se llama la mujer? _____
2. ¿Cómo se llama el hombre? _____
3. ¿De dónde es él? _____
4. ¿De dónde es ella? _____
5. ¿Quién es estudiante? _____
6. ¿Quién es profesor(a)? _____

     Lección 1 Laboratory Activities   **5**

1.4 Telling time

1 **La hora** Look at the clock and listen to the statement. Indicate whether the statement is **cierto** or **falso**.

	Cierto	Falso		Cierto	Falso		Cierto	Falso
1.	○	○	2.	○	○	3.	○	○
4.	○	○	5.	○	○	6.	○	○

2 **Preguntas** Some people want to know what time it is. Answer their questions using the cues. Repeat the correct response after the speaker.

> **modelo**
>
> *You hear:* ¿Qué hora es, por favor?
> *You see:* 3:10 p.m.
> *You say:* Son las tres y diez de la tarde.

1. 1:30 p.m.   3. 2:05 p.m.   5. 4:54 p.m.

2. 9:06 a.m.   4. 7:15 a.m.   6. 10:23 p.m.

3 **¿A qué hora?** You are trying to plan your class schedule. Ask your counselor what time these classes meet and write the answer.

> **modelo**
>
> *You see:* la clase de economía
> *You say:* ¿A qué hora es la clase de economía?
> *You hear:* Es a las once y veinte de la mañana.
> *You write:* 11:20 a.m.

1. la clase de biología: _____   4. la clase de literatura: _____

2. la clase de arte: _____   5. la clase de historia: _____

3. la clase de matemáticas: _____   6. la clase de sociología: _____

Lab Manual

PREPARACIÓN

Lección 2

1 **Identificar** Look at each drawing and listen to the statement. Indicate whether the statement is **cierto** or **falso**.

	Cierto	Falso			Cierto	Falso			Cierto	Falso

1. ○ ○   2. ○ ○   3. ○ ○

4. ○ ○   5. ○ ○   6. ○ ○

2 **¿Qué día es?** Your friend Diego is never sure what day of the week it is. Respond to his questions saying that it is the day before the one he mentions. Then repeat the correct answer after the speaker. (*6 items*)

> **modelo**
> Hoy es domingo, ¿no?
> No, hoy es sábado.

3 **Preguntas** You will hear a series of questions. Look at Susana's schedule for today and answer each question. Then repeat the correct response after the speaker. (*6 items*)

---

martes 18

○

9:00 economía — Sr. Rivera

11:00 química — Sra. Hernández

12:15 cafetería — Carmen

1:30 prueba de contabilidad — Sr. Ramos

3:00 matemáticas — Srta. Torres

4:30 laboratorio de computación — Héctor

○

Lección 2 Laboratory Activities   **7**

Lab Manual

PRONUNCIACIÓN

Spanish vowels

Spanish vowels are never silent; they are always pronounced in a short, crisp way without the glide sounds used in English.

a   e   i   o   u

The letter **a** is pronounced like the *a* in *father*, but shorter.

Álex   cl**a**se   n**a**d**a**   enc**a**nt**a**da

The letter **e** is pronounced like the *e* in *they*, but shorter.

el   **e**n**e**   m**e**sa   **e**l**e**fante

The letter **i** sounds like the *ee* in *beet*, but shorter.

Inés   ch**i**ca   t**i**za   señor**i**ta

The letter **o** is pronounced like the *o* in *tone*, but shorter.

h**o**la   c**o**n   libr**o**   d**o**n Francisc**o**

The letter **u** sounds like the *oo* in *room*, but shorter.

uno   reg**u**lar   sal**u**dos   g**u**sto

---

1   **Práctica** Practice the vowels by repeating the names of these places in Spain after the speaker.

1. Madrid   5. Barcelona
2. Alicante   6. Granada
3. Tenerife   7. Burgos
4. Toledo   8. La Coruña

---

2   **Oraciones** Repeat each sentence after the speaker, focusing on the vowels.

1. Hola. Me llamo Ramiro Morgado.
2. Estudio arte en la Universidad de Salamanca.
3. Tomo también literatura y contabilidad.
4. Ay, tengo clase en cinco minutos. ¡Nos vemos!

---

3   **Refranes** Repeat each saying after the speaker to practice vowels.

1. Del dicho al hecho hay un gran trecho.
2. Cada loco con su tema.

---

4   **Dictado** You will hear a conversation. Listen carefully and write what you hear during the pauses. The entire conversation will then be repeated so you can check your work.

JUAN _____

_____

_____

ROSA _____

JUAN _____

ROSA _____

---

8   **Lección 2** Laboratory Activities

GRAMÁTICA

2.1 Present tense of regular –ar verbs

1 **Identificar** Listen to each sentence and mark the subject of the verb.

> **modelo**
>
> *You hear:* Trabajo en la cafetería.
> *You mark:* yo

	yo	tú	él/ella	nosotros/as	ellos/ellas
Modelo	X				
1.					
2.					
3.					
4.					
5.					
6.					
7.					
8.					

2 **Cambiar** Form a new sentence using the cue you hear as the subject. Repeat the correct answer after the speaker. (*6 items*)

> **modelo**
>
> María practica los verbos ahora (*now*). (José y María)
> *José y María practican los verbos ahora.*

3 **Preguntas** Answer each question you hear in the negative. Repeat the correct response after the speaker. (*8 items*)

> **modelo**
>
> ¿Estudias geografía?
> *No, yo no estudio geografía.*

4 **Completar** Listen to the following description and write the missing words.

Teresa y yo ——————1—————— en la Universidad Autónoma de España. Teresa

——————2—————— lenguas extranjeras. Ella ——————3—————— trabajar en las

Naciones Unidas (*United Nations*). Yo ——————4—————— clases de periodismo. También me

gusta ——————5—————— y ——————6——————. Los sábados

——————7—————— con (*with*) una tuna. Una tuna es una orquesta (*orchestra*) estudiantil. Los

jóvenes de la tuna ——————8—————— por las calles (*streets*) y ——————9——————

canciones (*songs*) tradicionales de España.

Lab Manual

2.2 Forming questions in Spanish

1   **Escoger**   Listen to each question and choose the most logical response.

1. a. Porque (*Because*) mañana es la prueba.   b. Porque no hay clase mañana.

2. a. Viaja en autobús.   b. Viaja a Toledo.

3. a. Llegamos a las cuatro y media.   b. Llegamos al estadio.

4. a. Isabel y Diego dibujan.   b. Dibujan en la clase de arte.

5. a. No, enseña física.   b. No, enseña en la Universidad Politécnica.

6. a. Escuchan la clase.   b. Escuchan música clásica.

7. a. Sí, me gusta mucho.   b. Miro la televisión en la residencia.

8. a. Hay diccionarios en la biblioteca.   b. Hay tres.

2   **Cambiar**   Change each sentence into a question using the cue provided. Repeat the correct response after the speaker.

> **modelo**
>
> *You hear:* Los turistas toman el autobús.
> *You see:* ¿Quiénes?
> *You say:* **¿Quiénes toman el autobús?**

1. ¿Dónde?   3. ¿Qué?   5. ¿Cuándo?   7. ¿Quiénes?

2. ¿Cuántos?   4. ¿Quién?   6. ¿Dónde?   8. ¿Qué?

3   **¿Lógico o ilógico?**   You will hear some questions and the responses. Decide if they are **lógico** (*logical*) or **ilógico** (*illogical*).

1. Lógico   Ilógico   3. Lógico   Ilógico   5. Lógico   Ilógico

2. Lógico   Ilógico   4. Lógico   Ilógico   6. Lógico   Ilógico

4   **Un anuncio**   Listen to this radio advertisement and answer the questions.

1. ¿Dónde está (*is*) la Escuela Cervantes? _____

_____

2. ¿Qué cursos ofrecen (*do they offer*) en la Escuela Cervantes? _____

_____

3. ¿Cuándo practican los estudiantes el español? _____

_____

4. ¿Adónde viajan los estudiantes de la Escuela Cervantes? _____

_____

Lab Manual

2.3 The present tense of estar

1 **Describir** Look at the drawing and listen to each statement. Indicate whether the statement is **cierto** or **falso**.

	Cierto	Falso			Cierto	Falso			Cierto	Falso			Cierto	Falso
1.	○	○		3.	○	○		5.	○	○		7.	○	○
2.	○	○		4.	○	○		6.	○	○		8.	○	○

2 **Cambiar** Form a new sentence using the cue you hear. Repeat the correct answer after the speaker. (*8 items*)

> *modelo*
>
> Irma está en la biblioteca. (Irma y Hugo)
> Irma y Hugo *están en la biblioteca.*

3 **Escoger** You will hear some sentences with a beep in place of the verb. Decide which form of **ser** or **estar** should complete each sentence and select it.

> *modelo*
>
> *You hear:* Javier *(beep)* estudiante.
> *You select:* es because the sentence is *Javier es estudiante.*

1. a. es	b. está		5. a. es	b. está
2. a. es	b. está		6. a. eres	b. estás
3. a. es	b. está		7. a. son	b. están
4. a. Somos	b. Estamos		8. a. Son	b. Están

Lección 2 Laboratory Activities   **11**

Lab Manual

2.4 Numbers 31–100

1 **Números de teléfono** You want to invite some classmates to a party, but you don't have their telephone numbers. Ask the person who sits beside you what their telephone numbers are and write the answer.

> **modelo**
>
> *You see:* Elián
> *You say:* ¿Cuál es el número de teléfono de Elián?
> *You hear:* Es el ocho, cuarenta y tres, cero ocho, treinta y cinco.
> *You write:* 843-0835

1. Arturo: _____   5. Simón: _____

2. Alicia: _____   6. Eva: _____

3. Roberto: _____   7. José Antonio: _____

4. Graciela: _____   8. Mariana: _____

2 **Preguntas** You and a coworker are taking inventory at the university bookstore. Answer your co-worker's questions using the cues. Repeat the correct response after the speaker.

> **modelo**
>
> *You hear:* ¿Cuántos diccionarios hay?
> *You see:* 45
> *You say:* Hay cuarenta y cinco diccionarios.

1. 56	3. 64	5. 95	7. 31
2. 32	4. 83	6. 48	8. 79

3 **Mensaje telefónico** Listen to this telephone conversation and complete the phone message with the correct information.

Mensaje telefónico

Para *(For)* _____

De parte de *(From)* _____

Teléfono _____

Mensaje _____

_____

_____

_____

Lab Manual

PREPARACIÓN

Lección 3

1 **Escoger** You will hear some questions. Look at the family tree and choose the correct answer to each question.

La familia
González

Juan Carlos   Sofía

Raquel   Eduardo   Ana María   Luis Miguel

Concha   José Antonio   Ramón   Pilar   Joaquín

1. a. Pilar   b. Concha   5. a. José Antonio y Ramón   b. Eduardo y Ana María
2. a. Luis Miguel   b. Eduardo   6. a. Joaquín   b. Eduardo
3. a. Sofía   b. Ana María   7. a. Ana María   b. Sofía
4. a. Raquel   b. Sofía   8. a. Luis Miguel   b. Juan Carlos

2 **La familia González** Héctor wants to verify the relationship between various members of the González family. Look at the drawing and answer his questions with the correct information. Repeat the correct response after the speaker. (*6 items*)

> **modelo**
> Juan Carlos es el abuelo de Eduardo, ¿verdad?
> No, Juan Carlos es el padre de Eduardo.

3 **Profesiones** Listen to each statement and write the number of the statement below the drawing it describes.

a. _____   b. _____   c. _____   d. _____

Lab Manual

PRONUNCIACIÓN

Diphthongs and linking

In Spanish, **a, e,** and **o** are considered strong vowels. The weak vowels are **i** and **u.**

    herm**a**n**o**   n**i**ñ**a**   c**u**ñ**a**d**o**

A diphthong is a combination of two weak vowels or of a strong vowel and a weak vowel. Diphthongs are pronounced as a single syllable.

    r**ui**do   parientes   per**io**dista

Two identical vowel sounds that appear together are pronounced like one long vowel.

    l**a a**buela   m**i hi**jo   una clas**e e**xcelente

Two identical consonants together sound like a single consonant.

    co**n N**atalia   su**s s**obrinos   la**s s**illas

A consonant at the end of a word is always linked with the vowel sound at the beginning of the next word.

    E**s i**ngeniera.   mi**s a**buelos   su**s hi**jos

A vowel at the end of a word is always linked with the vowel sound at the beginning of the next word.

    m**i h**ermano   s**u e**sposa   nuestr**o a**migo

1 **Práctica** Repeat each word after the speaker, focusing on the diphthongs.

1. historia	4. novia	7. puerta	10. estudiar
2. nieto	5. residencia	8. ciencias	11. izquierda
3. parientes	6. prueba	9. lenguas	12. ecuatoriano

2 **Oraciones** When you hear the number, read the corresponding sentence aloud. Then listen to the speaker and repeat the sentence.

1. Hola. Me llamo Anita Amaral. Soy del Ecuador.
2. Somos seis en mi familia.
3. Tengo dos hermanos y una hermana.
4. Mi papá es del Ecuador y mi mamá es de España.

3 **Refranes** Repeat each saying after the speaker to practice diphthongs and linking sounds.

1. Cuando una puerta se cierra, otra se abre.
2. Hablando del rey de Roma, por la puerta se asoma.

4 **Dictado** You will hear eight sentences. Each will be said twice. Listen carefully and write what you hear.

1. _____

2. _____

3. _____

4. _____

5. _____

6. _____

7. _____

8. _____

Lab Manual

GRAMÁTICA

3.1 Descriptive adjectives

1 **Transformar** Change each sentence from the masculine to the feminine. Repeat the correct answer after the speaker. (*6 items*)

> **modelo**
> El chico es mexicano.
> La chica es mexicana.

2 **Cambiar** Change each sentence from the singular to the plural. Repeat the correct answer after the speaker. (*6 items*)

> **modelo**
> El profesor es ecuatoriano.
> Los profesores son ecuatorianos.

3 **Mis compañeros de clase** Describe your classmates, using the cues provided. Repeat the correct response after the speaker.

> **modelo**
> *You hear:* María
> *You see:* alto
> *You say:* María es alta.

1. simpático
2. rubio
3. inteligente
4. pelirrojo y muy bonito
5. alto y moreno
6. delgado y trabajador
7. bajo y gordo
8. tonto

4 **Completar** Listen to the following description and write the missing words.

Mañana mis parientes llegan de Guayaquil. Son cinco personas: mi abuela Isabel, tío Carlos y tía Josefina y mis primos Susana y Tomás. Mi prima es _____ 1 _____ y _____ 2 _____. Baila muy bien. Tomás es un niño _____ 3 _____, pero es _____ 4 _____. Tío Carlos es _____ 5 _____ y _____ 6 _____. Tía Josefina es _____ 7 _____ y _____ 8 _____. Mi abuela es _____ 9 _____ y muy _____ 10 _____.

5 **La familia Rivas** Look at the photo of the Rivas family and listen to each statement. Indicate whether the statement is **cierto** or **falso**.

	Cierto	Falso		Cierto	Falso
1.	○	○	5.	○	○
2.	○	○	6.	○	○
3.	○	○	7.	○	○
4.	○	○			

Lab Manual

3.2 Possessive adjectives

1 **Identificar** Listen to each statement and mark the possessive adjective you hear.

You hear: Es mi diccionario de español.

You mark: my

	my	*your* (familiar)	*your* (formal)	*his/her*	*our*	*their*
Modelo	X					
1.						
2.						
3.						
4.						
5.						
6.						
7.						
8.						

2 **Escoger** Listen to each question and choose the most logical response.

1. a. No, su hijastro no está aquí.
   b. Sí, tu hijastro está aquí.
2. a. No, nuestros abuelos son canadienses.
   b. Sí, sus abuelos son norteamericanos.
3. a. Sí, tu hijo trabaja ahora (*now*).
   b. Sí, mi hijo trabaja en la librería Goya.
4. a. Sus padres regresan a las nueve.
   b. Mis padres regresan a las nueve.
5. a. Nuestra hermana se llama Margarita.
   b. Su hermana se llama Margarita.
6. a. Tus plumas están en el escritorio.
   b. Sus plumas están en el escritorio.
7. a. No, mi sobrino es ingeniero.
   b. Sí, nuestro sobrino es programador.
8. a. Su horario es muy bueno.
   b. Nuestro horario es muy bueno.

3 **Preguntas** Answer each question you hear in the affirmative using the appropriate possessive adjective. Repeat the correct response after the speaker. (*7 items*)

¿Es tu lápiz?

Sí, *es mi lápiz.*

Lab Manual

3.3 Present tense of regular –er and –ir verbs

1   **Identificar**   Listen to each statement and mark the subject of the verb.

> **modelo**
> *You hear:* Corro con (*with*) Dora mañana.
> *You mark:* yo

	yo	tú	él/ella	nosotros/as	ellos/ellas
Modelo	X				
1.	_____	_____	_____	_____	_____
2.	_____	_____	_____	_____	_____
3.	_____	_____	_____	_____	_____
4.	_____	_____	_____	_____	_____
5.	_____	_____	_____	_____	_____
6.	_____	_____	_____	_____	_____

2   **Cambiar**   Listen to the following statements. Using the cues you hear, say that these people do the same activities. Repeat the correct answer after the speaker. (*8 items*)

> **modelo**
> Julia aprende francés. (mi amigo)
> Mi amigo también (*also*) aprende francés.

3   **Preguntas**   Answer each question you hear in the negative. Repeat the correct response after the speaker. (*8 items*)

> **modelo**
> ¿Viven ellos en una residencia estudiantil?
> No, ellos no viven en una residencia estudiantil.

4   **Describir**   Listen to each statement and write the number of the statement below the drawing it describes.

a. _____   b. _____   c. _____   d. _____

    Lección 3 Laboratory Activities   **17**

Lab Manual

3.4 Present tense of **tener** and **venir**

1   Cambiar Form a new sentence using the cue you hear as the subject. Repeat the correct answer after the speaker. (6 *items*)

> **modelo**
> Alicia viene a las seis. (David y Rita)
> David y Rita vienen a las seis.

2   Consejos (*Advice*) Some people are not doing what they should. Say what they have to do. Repeat the correct response after the speaker. (6 *items*)

> **modelo**
> Elena no trabaja.
> Elena tiene que trabajar.

3   Preguntas Answer each question you hear using the cue. Repeat the correct answer after the speaker.

> **modelo**
> ¿Tienen sueño los niños? (no)
> No, los niños no tienen sueño.

1. sí   3. no   5. sí   7. el domingo
2. Roberto   4. dos   6. mis tíos

4   Situaciones Listen to each situation and choose the appropriate **tener** expression. Each situation will be repeated.

1. a. Tienes sueño.   b. Tienes prisa.
2. a. Tienen mucho cuidado.   b. Tienen hambre.
3. a. Tenemos mucho calor.   b. Tenemos mucho frío.
4. a. Tengo sed.   b. Tengo hambre.
5. a. Ella tiene razón.   b. Ella no tiene razón.
6. a. Tengo miedo.   b. Tengo sueño.

5   Mi familia Listen to the following description. Then read the statements and decide whether they are **cierto** or **falso**.

	Cierto	Falso		Cierto	Falso
1. Francisco tiene 20 años.	○	○	4. Su madre es inglesa.	○	○
2. Francisco desea ser periodista.	○	○	5. Francisco tiene un hermano.	○	○
3. Francisco vive con su familia.	○	○	6. Él tiene una familia pequeña.	○	○

Lab Manual

PREPARACIÓN

Lección 4

1 **Lugares** You will hear six people describe what they are doing. Choose the place that corresponds to the activity.

1. _____
2. _____
3. _____
4. _____
5. _____
6. _____

a. el museo
b. el café
c. la piscina
d. el cine

e. el estadio
f. las montañas
g. el parque
h. la biblioteca

2 **Describir** For each drawing, you will hear two statements. Choose the one that corresponds to the drawing.

1. a.   b.

2. a.   b.

3. a.   b.

4. a.   b.

3 **Completar** Listen to this description and write the missing words.

Chapultepec es un _____₁ muy grande en el _____₂ de la

_____₃ de México. Los _____₄ muchas

_____₅ llegan a Chapultepec a pasear, descansar y practicar

_____₆ como (*like*) el _____₇, el fútbol, el vóleibol y

el _____₈. Muchos turistas también (*also*) _____₉ por

Chapultepec. Visitan los _____₁₀ y el _____₁₁ a los

Niños Héroes.

Lab Manual

PRONUNCIACIÓN

Word stress and accent marks

Every Spanish syllable contains at least one vowel. When two vowels are joined in the same syllable, they form a diphthong. A monosyllable is a word formed by a single syllable.

| pe - **lí** - cu - la | e - di - fi - **cio** | ver | **yo** |

The syllable of a Spanish word that is pronounced most emphatically is the "stressed" syllable.

| bi - blio - **te** - ca | vi - si - **tar** | **par** - que | **fút** - bol |

Words that end in **n**, **s**, or a *vowel* are usually stressed on the next to last syllable.

| pe - **lo** - ta | pis - **ci** - na | **ra**- tos | **ha** - blan |

If words that end in **n**, **s**, or a *vowel* are stressed on the last syllable, they must carry an accent mark on the stressed syllable.

| na - ta - **ción** | pa - **pá** | in - **glés** | Jo - **sé** |

Words that do *not* end in **n**, **s**, or a *vowel* are usually stressed on the last syllable.

| bai - **lar** | es - pa - **ñol** | u - ni - ver - si - **dad** | tra - ba - ja - **dor** |

If words that do *not* end in **n**, **s**, or a *vowel* are stressed on the next to last syllable, they must carry an accent mark on the stressed syllable.

| **béis** - bol | **lá** - piz | **ár** - bol | **Gó** - mez |

1   **Práctica** Repeat each word after the speaker, stressing the correct syllable.

1. profesor	4. Mazatlán	7. niños	10. México
2. Puebla	5. examen	8. Guadalajara	11. están
3. ¿Cuántos?	6. ¿Cómo?	9. programador	12. geografía

2   **Conversación** Repeat the conversation after the speaker to practice word stress.

MARINA Hola, Carlos. ¿Qué tal?

CARLOS Bien. Oye, ¿a qué hora es el partido de fútbol?

MARINA Creo que es a las siete.

CARLOS ¿Quieres ir?

MARINA Lo siento, pero no puedo. Tengo que estudiar biología.

3   **Refranes** Repeat each saying after the speaker to practice word stress.

1. Quien ríe de último, ríe mejor.   2. En la unión está la fuerza.

4   **Dictado** You will hear six sentences. Each will be said twice. Listen carefully and write what you hear.

1. _____

2. _____

3. _____

4. _____

5. _____

6. _____

Lab Manual

GRAMÁTICA

4.1 The present tense of ir

1 **Identificar** Listen to each sentence and mark the subject of the verb you hear.

> **modelo**
>
> *You hear:* Van a ver una película.
> *You mark: ellos/ellas*

	yo	tú	él/ella	nosotros/as	ellos/ellas
Modelo	____	____	____	____	____X____
1.	____	____	____	____	____
2.	____	____	____	____	____
3.	____	____	____	____	____
4.	____	____	____	____	____
5.	____	____	____	____	____
6.	____	____	____	____	____

2 **Cambiar** Form a new sentence using the cue you hear as the subject. Repeat the correct answer after the speaker. (*8 items*)

> **modelo**
>
> Ustedes van al Museo Frida Kahlo. (yo)
> *Yo voy al Museo Frida Kahlo.*

3 **Preguntas** Answer each question you hear using the cue. Repeat the correct response after the speaker.

> **modelo**
>
> *You hear:* ¿Quiénes van a la piscina?
> *You see:* Gustavo y Elisa
> *You say: Gustavo y Elisa van a la piscina.*

1. mis amigos   3. al partido de baloncesto   5. sí
2. en el Café Tacuba   4. no   6. pasear en bicicleta

4 **¡Vamos!** Listen to this conversation. Then read the statements and decide whether they are **cierto** or **falso**.

	Cierto	Falso
1. Claudia va a ir al gimnasio.	○	○
2. Claudia necesita comprar una mochila.	○	○
3. Sergio va a visitar a su tía.	○	○
4. Sergio va al gimnasio a las ocho de la noche.	○	○
5. Sergio va a ir al cine a las seis.	○	○
6. Claudia y Sergio van a ver una película.	○	○

Lab Manual

4.2 Stem-changing verbs: e→ie, o→ue

1 **Identificar** Listen to each sentence and write the infinitive form of the verb you hear.

> **modelo**
> *You hear:* No entiendo el problema.
> *You write:* entender

1. _____   4. _____   7. _____

2. _____   5. _____   8. _____

3. _____   6. _____

2 **Preguntas** Answer each question you hear using the cue provided. Repeat the correct response after the speaker.

> **modelo**
> *You hear:* ¿A qué hora comienza el partido?
> *You see:* 2:15 p.m.
> *You say:* El partido comienza a las dos y cuarto de la tarde.

1. el jueves   3. sí   5. leer una revista   7. a las tres
2. no   4. sí   6. mirar la televisión   8. Samuel

3 **Diversiones** Look at these listings from the entertainment section in a newspaper. Then listen to the questions and write the answers.

23D

MÚSICA
Palacio de Bellas Artes
Ballet folklórico
Viernes 9, 8:30 p.m.

Bosque de Chapultepec
Concierto de música mexicana
Domingo 11, 1:00 p.m.

MUSEOS
Museo de Arte Moderno

Pinturas de José Clemente
Orozco
De martes a domingo,
de 10:00 a.m. a 6:00 p.m.
Entrada libre

DEPORTES
Copa Internacional de Fútbol
México vs. Guatemala
Estadio Martín
Viernes 9, 8:30 p.m.

Campeonato de baloncesto
Los Universitarios vs. Los Toros
Gimnasio Municipal
Sábado 10, 7:30 p.m.

Torneo de Golf
con Lee Treviño
Club de Golf Atlas
Domingo 11, 9:00 a.m.

1. _____

2. _____

3. _____

4. _____

5. _____

Lab Manual

4.3 Stem-changing verbs: e→i

1   **Completar**   Listen to this radio broadcast and fill in the missing words.

Este fin de semana los excursionistas _____ 1 más senderos (*trails*). Dicen que

ir de _____ 2 a las montañas es una _____ 3 muy popular y

_____ 4 que _____ 5 más senderos. Si lo

_____ 6, la gente va a _____ 7 muy feliz. Si no, ustedes

pueden _____ 8 la historia aquí, en Radio Montaña.

2   **Escoger**   Listen to each question and choose the most logical response.

1. a. Normalmente pido tacos.   b. Voy al restaurante los lunes.

2. a. Consigo novelas en la biblioteca.   b. Compro revistas en el centro.

3. a. Repiten la película el sábado.   b. No deseo verla.

4. a. Sigue un programa de baloncesto.   b. No, está buceando.

5. a. Nunca (*I never*) pido pizza.   b. Nunca pido perdón.

6. a. Prefiere visitar un monumento.   b. Prefiere buscarla en la biblioteca.

7. a. ¿Quién fue el primer presidente?   b. A las cuatro de la tarde.

8. a. ¡Sí, es muy interesante!   b. Sí, mi hermano juega.

3   **Conversación**   Listen to the conversation and answer the questions.

1. ¿Qué quiere Paola?

_____

2. ¿Por qué repite Paola las palabras?

_____

3. ¿Hace Miguel el favor que (*that*) pide Paola?

_____

4. ¿Dónde puede conseguir la revista?

_____

Lab Manual

4.4 Verbs with irregular yo forms

1 **Describir** For each drawing, you will hear two statements. Choose the one that corresponds to the drawing.

1. a. _____ b. _____

2. a. _____ b. _____

3. a. _____ b. _____

4. a. _____ b. _____

2 **Yo también** Listen to the following statements about Roberto and respond by saying that you do the same things. Repeat the correct answer after the speaker. (*5 items*)

> **modelo**
> Roberto siempre (*always*) hace ejercicio.
> *Yo también hago ejercicio.*

3 **Completar** Listen to this telephone conversation and complete the statements.

1. Cristina ve _____.

2. Manuel y Ricardo quieren ir al parque para _____.

3. Manuel y Ricardo _____ las pelotas.

4. Manuel _____ la hora porque (*because*) Cristina no _____.

5. Los chicos salen para el parque _____.

Lab Manual

PREPARACIÓN   # Lección 5

---

1 **Identificar** You will hear a series of words. Write the word that does not belong in each series.

1. _____   5. _____

2. _____   6. _____

3. _____   7. _____

4. _____   8. _____

---

2 **Describir** For each drawing, you will hear two statements. Choose the one that corresponds to the drawing.

1. a.   b.

2. a.   b.

3. a.   b.

4. a.   b.

---

3 **En la agencia de viajes** Listen to this conversation between Mr. Vega and a travel agent. Then read the statements and decide whether they are **cierto** or **falso**.

	Cierto	Falso
1. El señor Vega quiere esquiar, pescar y hacer turismo.	○	○
2. El señor Vega va a Puerto Rico.	○	○
3. El señor Vega quiere ir de vacaciones la primera semana de mayo.	○	○
4. Una habitación en Las Tres Palmas cuesta (*costs*) $85.00.	○	○
5. El hotel tiene restaurante, piscina y *jacuzzi*.	○	○

Lab Manual

PRONUNCIACIÓN

Spanish **b** and **v**

There is no difference in pronunciation between the Spanish letters **b** and **v**. However, each letter can be pronounced two different ways, depending on which letters appear next to them.

bueno	**v**ólei**b**ol	**b**i**b**lioteca	**v**ivir

B and **v** are pronounced like the English hard *b* when they appear either as the first letter of a word, at the beginning of a phrase, or after **m** or **n**.

bonito	**v**iajar	tam**b**ién	in**v**estigar

In all other positions, **b** and **v** have a softer pronunciation, which has no equivalent in English. Unlike the hard **b**, which is produced by tightly closing the lips and stopping the flow of air, the soft **b** is produced by keeping the lips slightly open.

de**b**er	no**v**io	a**b**ril	cer**v**eza

In both pronunciations, there is no difference in sound between **b** and **v**. The English *v* sound, produced by friction between the upper teeth and lower lip, does not exist in Spanish. Instead, the soft **b** comes from friction between the two lips.

bola	**v**ela	Cari**b**e	decli**v**e

When **b** or **v** begins a word, its pronunciation depends on the previous word. At the beginning of a phrase or after a word that ends in **m** or **n**, it is pronounced as a hard **b**.

Verónica y su esposo cantan ‿**b**oleros.

Words that begin with **b** or **v** are pronounced with a soft **b** if they appear immediately after a word that ends in a vowel or any consonant other than **m** or **n**.

Benito es de ‿**B**oquerón pero ‿**v**ive en ‿**V**ictoria.

1 Práctica Repeat these words after the speaker to practice the **b** and the **v**.

1. hablamos	4. van	7. doble	10. cabaña
2. trabajar	5. contabilidad	8. novia	11. llave
3. botones	6. bien	9. béisbol	12. invierno

2 Oraciones When you hear the number, read the corresponding sentence aloud, focusing on the **b** and **v** sounds. Then listen to the speaker and repeat the sentence.

1. Vamos a Guaynabo en autobús.
2. Voy de vacaciones a la isla Culebra.
3. Tengo una habitación individual en el octavo piso.
4. Víctor y Eva van por avión al Caribe.
5. La planta baja es bonita también.
6. ¿Qué vamos a ver en Bayamón?
7. Beatriz, la novia de Víctor, es de Arecibo, Puerto Rico.

3 Refranes Repeat each saying after the speaker to practice the **b** and the **v**.

1. No hay mal que por bien no venga.
2. Hombre prevenido vale por dos.

4 Dictado You will hear four sentences. Each will be said twice. Listen carefully and write what you hear.

1. _____
2. _____
3. _____
4. _____

Lab Manual

GRAMÁTICA

5.1 Estar with conditions and emotions

1   **Describir**   For each drawing, you will hear two statements. Choose the one that corresponds to the drawing.

1. a. _____   b. _____   2. a. _____   b. _____

3. a. _____   b. _____   4. a. _____   b. _____

2   **Cambiar**   Form a new sentence using the cue you hear as the subject. Repeat the correct answer after the speaker. (*5 items*)

> **modelo**
>
> Rubén está enojado con Patricia. (mamá)
> Mamá *está enojada con Patricia.*

3   **Preguntas**   Answer each question you hear using the cues provided. Repeat the correct response after the speaker.

> **modelo**
>
> *You hear:* ¿Está triste Tomás?
> *You see:* no / contento/a
> *You say:* No, Tomás *está contento.*

1. no / abierto/a   3. su hermano   5. no / sucio/a
2. sí   4. no / ordenado/a   6. estar de vacaciones

4   **Situaciones**   You will hear four brief conversations. Choose the statement that expresses how the people feel in each situation.

1. a. Ricardo está nervioso.   b. Ricardo está cansado.
2. a. La señora Fuentes está contenta.   b. La señora Fuentes está preocupada.
3. a. Eugenio está aburrido.   b. Eugenio está avergonzado.
4. a. Rosario y Alonso están equivocados. b. Rosario y Alonso están enojados.

Lab Manual

5.2 The present progressive

1 **Escoger** Listen to what these people are doing. Then read the statements provided and choose the appropriate description.

1. a. Es profesor.   b. Es estudiante.

2. a. Es botones.   b. Es inspector de aduanas.

3. a. Eres artista.   b. Eres huésped.

4. a. Son jugadoras de fútbol.   b. Son programadoras.

5. a. Es ingeniero.   b. Es botones.

6. a. Son turistas.   b. Son empleados.

2 **Transformar** Change each sentence from the present tense to the present progressive. Repeat the correct answer after the speaker. (*6 items*)

> **modelo**
> Adriana confirma su reservación.
> Adriana *está confirmando su reservación.*

3 **Preguntas** Answer each question you hear using the cue provided and the present progressive. Repeat the correct response after the speaker.

> **modelo**
> *You hear:* ¿Qué hacen ellos?
> *You see:* acampar
> *You say:* Ellos *están acampando.*

1. hacer las maletas   3. dormir   5. hablar con el botones

2. pescar en el mar   4. correr en el parque   6. comer en el café

4 **Describir** You will hear some questions. Look at the drawing and respond to each question. Repeat the correct answer after the speaker. (*6 items*)

Lab Manual

5.3 Comparing ser and estar

1 **Escoger** You will hear some questions with a beep in place of the verb. Decide which form of **ser** or **estar** should complete each question and select it.

> **modelo**
>
> *You hear:* ¿Cómo *(beep)?*
> *You select:* estás because the question is *¿Cómo estás?*

1. es	está	4. Es	Está
2. Son	Están	5. Es	Está
3. Es	Está	6. Es	Está

2 **¿Cómo es?** You just met Rosa Beltrán at a party. Describe her to a friend by using **ser** or **estar** with the cues you hear. Repeat the correct response after the speaker. (*6 items*)

> **modelo**
>
> muy amable
> *Rosa es muy amable.*

3 **¿Ser o estar?** You will hear the subject of a sentence. Complete the sentence using a form of **ser** or **estar** and the cue provided. Repeat the correct response after the speaker.

> **modelo**
>
> *You hear:* papá
> *You see:* en San Juan
> *You say:* Papá está en San Juan.

1. inspector de aduanas	3. a las diez	5. el 14 de febrero
2. la estación del tren	4. ocupados	6. corriendo a clase

4 **¿Lógico o no?** You will hear some statements. Decide if they are **lógico** or **ilógico**.

1. Lógico	Ilógico	4. Lógico	Ilógico
2. Lógico	Ilógico	5. Lógico	Ilógico
3. Lógico	Ilógico	6. Lógico	Ilógico

5 **Ponce** Listen to Carolina's description of her vacation and answer the questions.

1. ¿Dónde está Ponce?

_____

2. ¿Qué tiempo hace?

_____

3. ¿Qué es el Parque de Bombas?

_____

4. ¿Qué día es hoy?

_____

5. ¿Por qué no va al Parque de Bombas hoy?

_____

Lab Manual

5.4 Direct object nouns and pronouns

1 **Escoger** Listen to each question and choose the most logical response.

1. a. Sí, voy a comprarlo.
   b. No, no voy a comprarla.

2. a. Joaquín lo tiene.
   b. Joaquín la tiene.

3. a. Sí, los puedo llevar.
   b. No, no te puedo llevar.

4. a. Irene los tiene.
   b. Irene las tiene.

5. a. Sí, te llevamos al partido.
   b. Sí, nos llevas al partido.

6. a. No, vamos a hacerlo mañana.
   b. No, vamos a hacerla mañana.

7. a. Va a conseguirlos mañana.
   b. Va a conseguirlas mañana.

8. a. Pienso visitarla el fin de semana.
   b. Pienso visitarte el fin de semana.

2 **Cambiar** Restate each sentence you hear using a direct object pronoun. Repeat the correct answer after the speaker. (*6 items*)

> **modelo**
> Isabel está mirando la televisión.
> Isabel *está mirándola.*

Isabel está mirando la televisión... con Diego.

3 **No veo nada** You just broke your glasses and now you can't see anything. Respond to each statement using a direct object pronoun. Repeat the correct answer after the speaker. (*6 items*)

> **modelo**
> Allí (*There*) está el Museo de Arte e Historia.
> *¿Dónde? No lo veo.*

4 **Preguntas** Answer each question you hear in the negative. Repeat the correct response after the speaker. (*6 items*)

> **modelo**
> ¿Haces la excursión a El Yunque?
> *No, no la hago.*

PREPARACIÓN

Lección 6

1 **¿Lógico o ilógico?** Listen to each statement and indicate if it is **lógico** or **ilógico**.

1. Lógico   Ilógico   5. Lógico   Ilógico
2. Lógico   Ilógico   6. Lógico   Ilógico
3. Lógico   Ilógico   7. Lógico   Ilógico
4. Lógico   Ilógico   8. Lógico   Ilógico

2 **Escoger** Listen as each person talks about the clothing he or she needs to buy. Then choose the activity for which the clothing would be appropriate.

1. a. ir a la playa   b. ir al cine
2. a. jugar al golf   b. buscar trabajo (*work*)
3. a. salir a bailar   b. ir a la montaña
4. a. montar a caballo   b. bucear
5. a. jugar al vóleibol   b. comer en un restaurante elegante
6. a. hacer un viaje   b. patinar en línea

3 **Preguntas** Respond to each question saying that the opposite is true. Repeat the correct answer after the speaker. (*6 items*)

> **modelo**
> Las sandalias cuestan mucho, ¿no?
> No, las sandalias *cuestan poco.*

4 **Describir** You will hear some questions. Look at the drawing and write the answer to each question.

Diana   Carmen

1. _____
2. _____
3. _____
4. _____

Lab Manual

PRONUNCIACIÓN

The consonants d and t

Like **b** and **v**, the Spanish **d** can have a hard sound or a soft sound, depending on which letters appear next to it.

      ¿**D**ón**d**e?   ven**d**er   na**d**ar   ver**d**a**d**

At the beginning of a phrase and after **n** or **l**, the letter **d** is pronounced with a hard sound. This sound is similar to the English *d* in *dog*, but a little softer and duller. The tongue should touch the back of the upper teeth, not the roof of the mouth.

      Don   **d**inero   tien**d**a   fal**d**a

In all other positions, **d** has a soft sound. It is similar to the English *th* in *there*, but a little softer.

      me**d**ias   ver**d**e   vesti**d**o   huéspe**d**

When **d** begins a word, its pronunciation depends on the previous word. At the beginning of a phrase or after a word that ends in **n** or **l**, it is pronounced as a hard **d**.

      Don **D**iego no tiene el **d**iccionario.

Words that begin with **d** are pronounced with a soft **d** if they appear immediately after a word that ends in a vowel or any consonant other than **n** or **l**.

      Doña **D**olores es **d**e la capital.

When pronouncing the Spanish **t**, the tongue should touch the back of the upper teeth, not the roof of the mouth. In contrast to the English *t*, no air is expelled from the mouth.

      traje   pan**t**alones   **t**arje**t**a   **t**ienda

1   **Práctica**   Repeat each phrase after the speaker to practice the **d** and the **t**.

1. Hasta pronto.
2. De nada.
3. Mucho gusto.
4. Lo siento.
5. No hay de qué.
6. ¿De dónde es usted?
7. ¡Todos a bordo!
8. No puedo.
9. Es estupendo.
10. No tengo computadora.
11. ¿Cuándo vienen?
12. Son las tres y media.

2   **Oraciones**   When you hear the number, read the corresponding sentence aloud, focusing on the **d** and **t** sounds. Then listen to the speaker and repeat the sentence.

1. Don Teodoro tiene una tienda en un almacén en La Habana.
2. Don Teodoro vende muchos trajes, vestidos y zapatos todos los días.
3. Un día un turista, Federico Machado, entra en la tienda para comprar un par de botas.
4. Federico regatea con don Teodoro y compra las botas y también un par de sandalias.

3   **Refranes**   Repeat each saying after the speaker to practice the **d** and the **t**.

1. En la variedad está el gusto.   2. Aunque la mona se vista de seda, mona se queda.

4   **Dictado**   You will hear four sentences. Each will be said twice. Listen carefully and write what you hear.

1. _____
2. _____
3. _____
4. _____

GRAMÁTICA

6.1 Numbers 101 and higher

1 **¿Cierto o falso?** Your friend Ana won the lottery and with that money she is buying presents for her friends and family. Look at the figures in the chart and listen to each statement. Then indicate whether each statement is **cierto** or **falso**.

Nombre	Comprar	Precio (en bolívares*)
mamá y papá	casa	3.351.250
hermano	auto	27.850
tía Tere	abrigo	13.405
abuelos	barco	56.749
José Luis	10 trajes	12.622
Cecilia	viaje al Caribe	8.967
Sergio	motocicleta	9.831
Laura	caballo	14.294
niños pobres del barrio	ropa y zapatos	39.997
	TOTAL	**3.534.965**

bolívar = Venezuelan currency

Cierto   Falso
1. ○   ○
2. ○   ○
3. ○   ○
4. ○   ○
5. ○   ○
6. ○   ○

2 **Dictado** Listen carefully and write each number as numerals rather than words.

1. _____   4. _____   7. _____

2. _____   5. _____   8. _____

3. _____   6. _____   9. _____

3 **Preguntas** Answer each question you hear using the cue. Repeat the correct response after the speaker.

> **modelo**
> *You hear:* ¿Cuántas personas hay en Bolivia?
> *You see:* 10.290.000
> *You say:* Hay diez millones, doscientos noventa mil personas en Bolivia.

1. 800   3. 1.284   5. 172
2. 356   4. 711   6. unos 43.000

4 **Un anuncio** Listen to this radio advertisement and write the prices for each item listed. Then figure out what the total cost for the trip would be.

Pasaje de avión: _____

Barco: _____

Excursiones: _____

TOTAL: _____

Lab Manual

6.2 The preterite tense of regular verbs

1 **Identificar** Listen to each sentence and decide whether the verb is in the present or the preterite tense. Mark the appropriate column.

> **modelo**
> *You hear:* Alejandro llevó un suéter marrón (*brown*).
> *You mark:* Preterite

	Present	*Preterite*
Modelo	_____	**X**
1.	_____	_____
2.	_____	_____
3.	_____	_____
4.	_____	_____
5.	_____	_____
6.	_____	_____
7.	_____	_____
8.	_____	_____

2 **Cambiar** Change each sentence from the present to the preterite. Repeat the correct answer after the speaker. (*8 items*)

> **modelo**
> Compro unas sandalias baratas.
> *Compré unas sandalias baratas.*

3 **Preguntas** Answer each question you hear using the cue provided. Repeat the correct response after the speaker.

> **modelo**
> *You hear:* ¿Dónde conseguiste tus botas?
> *You see:* en la tienda Lacayo
> *You say:* Conseguí mis botas en la tienda Lacayo.

1. $26,00   2. ayer   3. Marta   4. no   5. no   6. no

4 **¿Estás listo?** Listen to this conversation between Matilde and Hernán. Make a list of the tasks Hernán has already done in preparation for his trip and a list of the tasks he still needs to do.

Tareas completadas   **Tareas que necesita hacer**

_____   _____

_____   _____

_____   _____

_____   _____

6.3 Indirect object pronouns

1 **Escoger** Listen to each question and choose the most logical response.

1. a. Sí, le mostré el abrigo.

   b. Sí, me mostró el abrigo.

2. a. No, no le presté el suéter azul.

   b. No, no te prestó el suéter azul.

3. a. Voy a comprarles ropa interior.

   b. Vamos a comprarle ropa interior.

4. a. Sí, está preguntándoles el precio.

   b. Sí, está preguntándole el precio.

5. a. Nos costaron veinte dólares.

   b. Les costaron veinte dólares.

6. a. Sí, nos puede traer un sombrero.

   b. Sí, te puedo traer un sombrero.

2 **Identificar** Listen to each sentence and mark the column for the subject of the verb.

> **modelo**
> *You hear:* ¿Me das dinero para ir de compras?
> *You mark:* **tú**

	yo	tú	él/ella	nosotros/as	ellos/ellas
Modelo	_____	**X**	_____	_____	_____
1.	_____	_____	_____	_____	_____
2.	_____	_____	_____	_____	_____
3.	_____	_____	_____	_____	_____
4.	_____	_____	_____	_____	_____
5.	_____	_____	_____	_____	_____
6.	_____	_____	_____	_____	_____

3 **En el centro comercial** Listen to this conversation and answer the questions.

1. ¿Cuánto le costó a Norma su vestido?

_____

2. ¿A quién le quiere dar un vestido Patricia?

_____

3. ¿Le da Norma muchos regalos a su hermana?

_____

4. ¿Dónde compró el vestido Norma?

_____

5. ¿Qué le dice la dependienta a Norma?

_____

Lab Manual

6.4 Demonstrative adjectives and pronouns

1   **En el mercado**   A group of tourists is shopping at an open-air market. Listen to what they say, and mark the demonstrative adjective you hear.

> **modelo**
>
> *You hear:* Me gusta mucho esa bolsa.
> *You mark:* **that**

	this	that	these	those
Modelo	_____	**X**	_____	_____
1.	_____	_____	_____	_____
2.	_____	_____	_____	_____
3.	_____	_____	_____	_____
4.	_____	_____	_____	_____

2   **Cambiar**   Form a new sentence using the cue you hear. Repeat the correct answer after the speaker. (*6 items*)

> **modelo**
>
> Quiero este suéter. (chaqueta)
> *Quiero esta chaqueta.*

3   **Transformar**   Form a new sentence using the cue you hear. Repeat the correct answer after the speaker. (*6 items*)

> **modelo**
>
> Aquel abrigo es muy hermoso. (corbatas)
> *Aquellas corbatas son muy hermosas.*

4   **Preguntas**   Answer each question you hear in the negative using a form of the demonstrative pronoun **ése**. Repeat the correct response after the speaker. (*8 items*)

> **modelo**
>
> ¿Quieres esta blusa?
> *No, no quiero ésa.*

5   **De compras**   Listen to this conversation. Then read the statements and decide whether they are **cierto** or **falso**.

	Cierto	Falso
1. Flor quiere ir al almacén Don Guapo.	O	O
2. Enrique trabaja en el almacén Don Guapo.	O	O
3. Enrique no trabaja en el centro comercial.	O	O
4. Van al almacén que está al lado del Hotel Plaza.	O	O

Lab Manual

PREPARACIÓN   # Lección 7

---

1 **Describir** For each drawing, you will hear two statements. Choose the one that corresponds to the drawing.

1. a. _____   b. _____   2. a. _____   b. _____

3. a. _____   b. _____   4. a. _____   b. _____

---

2 **Preguntas** Clara is going to baby-sit your nephew. Answer her questions about your nephew's daily routine using the cues provided. Repeat the correct response after the speaker.

> **modelo**
>
> *You hear:* ¿A qué hora va a la escuela?
> *You see:* 8:30 a.m.
> *You say:* Va a la escuela a las *ocho* y *media de* la mañana.

1. 7:00 a.m.   4. champú para niños
2. se lava la cara   5. 9:00 p.m.
3. por la noche   6. después de comer

---

3 **Entrevista** Listen to this interview. Then read the statements and decide whether they are **cierto** or **falso**.

	Cierto	Falso
1. Sergio Santos es jugador de fútbol.	○	○
2. Sergio se levanta a las 5:00 a.m.	○	○
3. Sergio se ducha por la mañana y por la noche.	○	○
4. Sergio se acuesta a las 11:00 p.m.	○	○

Lab Manual

Lección 7 Laboratory Activities   **37**

PRONUNCIACIÓN

The consonant r

In Spanish, **r** has a strong trilled sound at the beginning of a word. No English words have a trill, but English speakers often produce a trill when they imitate the sound of a motor.

    ropa   **r**utina   **r**ico   **R**amón

In any other position, **r** has a weak sound similar to the English *tt* in *better* or the English *dd* in *ladder*. In contrast to English, the tongue touches the roof of the mouth behind the teeth.

    gusta**r**   du**r**ante   p**r**ime**r**o   c**r**ema

The letter combination **rr**, which only appears between vowels, always has a strong trilled sound.

    piza**rr**a   co**rr**o   ma**rr**ón   abu**rr**ido

Between vowels, the difference between the strong trilled **rr** and the weak **r** is very important, as a mispronunciation could lead to confusion between two different words.

    caro   carro   pero   perro

1   **Práctica** Repeat each word after the speaker to practice the **r** and the **rr**.

1. Perú
2. Rosa
3. borrador
4. madre
5. comprar
6. favor
7. rubio
8. reloj
9. Arequipa
10. tarde
11. cerrar
12. despertador

2   **Oraciones** When you hear the number, read the corresponding sentence aloud, focusing on the **r** and **rr** sounds. Then listen to the speaker and repeat the sentence.

1. Ramón Robles Ruiz es programador. Su esposa Rosaura es artista.
2. A Rosaura Robles le encanta regatear en el mercado.
3. Ramón nunca regatea… le aburre regatear.
4. Rosaura siempre compra cosas baratas.
5. Ramón no es rico pero prefiere comprar cosas muy caras.
6. ¡El martes Ramón compró un carro nuevo!

3   **Refranes** Repeat each saying after the speaker to practice the **r** and the **rr**.

1. Perro que ladra no muerde.
2. No se ganó Zamora en una hora.

4   **Dictado** You will hear seven sentences. Each will be said twice. Listen carefully and write what you hear.

1. _____
2. _____
3. _____
4. _____
5. _____
6. _____
7. _____

Lab Manual

GRAMÁTICA

7.1 Reflexive verbs

1   **Describir**   For each drawing, you will hear two statements. Choose the one that corresponds to the drawing.

1. a.   b.   2. a.   b.

3. a.   b.   4. a.   b.

2   **Preguntas**   Answer each question you hear in the affirmative. Repeat the correct response after the speaker. (*7 items*)

> **modelo**
>
> ¿Se levantó temprano Rosa?
> Sí, Rosa se levantó temprano.

3   **¡Esto fue el colmo** (*the last straw*)**!**   Listen as Julia describes what happened in her dorm yesterday. Then choose the correct ending for each statement.

1. Julia se ducha en cinco minutos porque (*because*)...
   a. siempre se levanta tarde.   b. las chicas de su piso comparten un baño.
2. Ayer la chica nueva...
   a. se quedó dos horas en el baño.   b. se preocupó por Julia.
3. Cuando salió, la chica nueva...
   a. se enojó mucho.   b. se sintió (*felt*) avergonzada.

7.2 Indefinite and negative words

1 **¿Lógico o ilógico?** You will hear some questions and the responses. Decide if they are **lógico** or **ilógico**.

	Lógico	Ilógico			Lógico	Ilógico
1.	○	○		5.	○	○
2.	○	○		6.	○	○
3.	○	○		7.	○	○
4.	○	○		8.	○	○

2 **¿Pero o sino?** You will hear some sentences with a beep in place of a word. Decide if **pero** or **sino** should complete each sentence.

> **modelo**
>
> *You hear:* Ellos no viven en Lima *(beep)* en Arequipa.
> *You select:* sino because the sentence is Ellos *no viven en Lima sino en Arequipa.*

1.	pero	sino		5.	pero	sino
2.	pero	sino		6.	pero	sino
3.	pero	sino		7.	pero	sino
4.	pero	sino		8.	pero	sino

3 **Transformar** Change each sentence you hear to say the opposite is true. Repeat the correct answer after the speaker. (*6 items*)

> **modelo**
>
> Nadie se ducha ahora.
> *Alguien se ducha ahora.*

4 **Preguntas** Answer each question you hear in the negative. Repeat the correct response after the speaker. (*6 items*)

> **modelo**
>
> ¿Qué estás haciendo?
> *No estoy haciendo nada.*

5 **Entre amigos** Listen to this conversation between Felipe and Mercedes. Then decide whether the statements are **cierto** or **falso**.

	Cierto	Falso
1. No hay nadie en la residencia.	○	○
2. Mercedes quiere ir al Centro Estudiantil.	○	○
3. Felipe tiene un amigo peruano.	○	○
4. Mercedes no visitó ni Machu Picchu ni Cuzco.	○	○
5. Felipe nunca visitó el Perú.	○	○
6. Mercedes no quiere volver jamás al Perú.	○	○

Lab Manual (side tab)

7.3 Preterite of **ser** and **ir**

1   **Escoger**   Listen to each sentence and indicate whether the verb is a form of **ser** or **ir**.

1.	ser ir		5.	ser ir
2.	ser ir		6.	ser ir
3.	ser ir		7.	ser ir
4.	ser ir		8.	ser ir

2   **Cambiar**   Change each sentence from the present to the preterite. Repeat the correct answer after the speaker. (*8 items*)

> **modelo**
> Ustedes van en avión.
> *Ustedes fueron en avión.*

3   **Preguntas**   Answer each question you hear using the cue provided. Repeat the correct response after the speaker.

> **modelo**
> *You hear:* ¿Quién fue tu profesor de química?
> *You see:* el señor Ortega
> *You say:* El señor Ortega fue mi profesor de química.

1. al mercado al aire libre   4. fabulosa
2. muy buenas   5. al parque
3. no   6. difícil

4   **¿Qué hicieron** (*did they do*) **anoche?**   Listen to this telephone conversation and answer the questions.

1. ¿Adónde fue Carlos anoche?

_____

2. ¿Fue un buen partido? ¿Por qué?

_____

3. ¿Adónde fueron Katarina y Esteban anoche?

_____

4. Y Esteban, ¿qué hizo (*did he do*) durante la película?

_____

Lab Manual

7.4 Gustar and verbs like gustar

1   **Escoger**   Listen to each question and choose the most logical response.

1. a. Sí, me gusta.   b. Sí, te gusta.
2. a. No, no le interesa.   b. No, no le interesan.
3. a. Sí, les molestan mucho.   b. No, no les molesta mucho.
4. a. No, no nos importa.   b. No, no les importa.
5. a. Sí, le falta.   b. Sí, me falta.
6. a. Sí, les fascina.   b. No, no les fascinan.

2   **Cambiar**   Form a new sentence using the cue you hear. Repeat the correct answer after the speaker. (6 *items*)

> **modelo**
>
> A ellos les interesan los deportes. (a Ricardo)
> A Ricardo le interesan los deportes.

3   **Preguntas**   Answer each question you hear using the cue. Repeat the correct response after the speaker.

> **modelo**
>
> *You hear:* ¿Qué te encanta hacer?
> *You see:* patinar en línea
> *You say:* Me encanta patinar en línea.

1. la familia y los amigos   5. el baloncesto y el béisbol
2. sí   6. no
3. las computadoras   7. no / nada
4. $2,00   8. sí

4   **Preferencias**   Listen to this conversation. Then fill in the chart with Eduardo's preferences and answer the question.

Le gusta	No le gusta

¿Qué van a hacer los chicos esta tarde? _____

Lab Manual

PREPARACIÓN

Lección 8

1   **Identificar**   Listen to each question and mark the appropriate category.

> **modelo**
> *You hear:* ¿Qué es la piña?
> *You mark:* fruta

	carne	pescado	verdura	fruta	bebida
Modelo	_____	_____	_____	**X**	_____
1.	_____	_____	_____	_____	_____
2.	_____	_____	_____	_____	_____
3.	_____	_____	_____	_____	_____
4.	_____	_____	_____	_____	_____
5.	_____	_____	_____	_____	_____
6.	_____	_____	_____	_____	_____
7.	_____	_____	_____	_____	_____
8.	_____	_____	_____	_____	_____

2   **Describir**   Listen to each sentence and write the number of the sentence below the drawing of the food or drink mentioned.

a. _____

b. _____

c. _____

d. _____

e. _____

f. _____

g. _____

h. _____

i. _____

3   **En el restaurante**   You will hear a couple ordering a meal in a restaurant. Write the items they order in the appropriate categories.

	SEÑORA	SEÑOR
Primer plato		
Plato principal		
Verdura		
Bebida		

Lab Manual

   Lección 8 Laboratory Activities   **43**

PRONUNCIACIÓN

ll, ñ, c, and z

Most Spanish speakers pronounce the letter **ll** like the *y* in *yes*.

po**ll**o   **ll**ave   e**ll**a   cebo**ll**a

The letter **ñ** is pronounced much like the *ny* in *canyon*.

ma**ñ**ana   se**ñ**or   ba**ñ**o   ni**ñ**a

Before **a, o,** or **u,** the Spanish **c** is pronounced like the *c* in *car*.

café   **c**olombiano   **c**uando   ri**c**o

Before **e** or **i,** the Spanish **c** is pronounced like the *s* in *sit*. In parts of Spain, **c** before **e** or **i** is pronounced like the *th* in *think*.

cereales   deli**c**ioso   condu**c**ir   cono**c**er

The Spanish **z** is pronounced like the *s* in *sit*. In parts of Spain, **z** before a vowel is pronounced like the *th* in *think*.

zeta   **z**anahoria   almuer**z**o   cerve**z**a

---

1   **Práctica** Repeat each word after the speaker to practice pronouncing **ll, ñ, c,** and **z.**

1. mantequilla	5. español	9. quince
2. cuñado	6. cepillo	10. compañera
3. aceite	7. zapato	11. almorzar
4. manzana	8. azúcar	12. calle

---

2   **Oraciones** When the speaker pauses, repeat the corresponding sentence or phrase, focusing on **ll, ñ, c,** and **z.**

1. Mi compañero de cuarto se llama Toño Núñez. Su familia es de la Ciudad de Guatemala y de Quetzaltenango.

2. Dice que la comida de su mamá es deliciosa, especialmente su pollo al champiñón y sus tortillas de maíz.

3. Creo que Toño tiene razón porque hoy cené en su casa y quiero volver mañana para cenar allí otra vez.

---

3   **Refranes** Repeat each saying after the speaker to practice pronouncing **ll, ñ, c,** and **z.**

1. Las aparencias engañan.

2. Panza llena, corazón contento.

---

4   **Dictado** You will hear five sentences. Each will be said twice. Listen carefully and write what you hear.

1. _____

2. _____

3. _____

4. _____

5. _____

Lab Manual

GRAMÁTICA

8.1 Preterite of stem-changing verbs

1 Identificar Listen to each sentence and decide whether the verb is in the present or the preterite tense. Mark the appropriate column.

> **modelo**
> *You hear:* Pido bistec con (*with*) papas fritas.
> *You mark:* Present

	Present	Preterite
Modelo	X	
1.		
2.		
3.		
4.		
5.		
6.		
7.		
8.		

2 Cambiar Change each sentence you hear substituting the new subject given. Repeat the correct response after the speaker. (*6 items*)

> **modelo**
> Tú no dormiste bien anoche. (los niños)
> *Los niños no durmieron bien anoche.*

3 Preguntas Answer each question you hear using the cue provided. Repeat the correct response after the speaker.

> **modelo**
> *You hear:* ¿Qué pediste?
> *You see:* pavo asado con papas y arvejas
> *You say:* *Pedí pavo asado con papas y arvejas.*

1. sí   3. leche   5. no
2. no   4. sí   6. la semana pasada

4 Un día largo Listen as Ernesto describes what he did yesterday. Then read the statements and decide whether they are **cierto** or **falso**.

	Cierto	Falso
1. Ernesto se levantó a las seis y media de la mañana.	○	○
2. Se bañó y se vistió.	○	○
3. Los clientes empezaron a llegar a la una.	○	○
4. Almorzó temprano.	○	○
5. Pidió pollo asado con papas.	○	○
6. Después de almorzar, Ernesto y su primo siguieron trabajando.	○	○

8.2 Double object pronouns

1 **Escoger** The manager of **El Gran Pavo** Restaurant wants to know what items the chef is going to serve to the customers today. Listen to each question and choose the correct response.

1. a. Sí, se las voy a servir.   b. No, no se los voy a servir.

2. a. Sí, se la voy a servir.   b. No, no se lo voy a servir.

3. a. Sí, se los voy a servir.   b. No, no se las voy a servir.

4. a. Sí, se la voy a servir.   b. No, no se las voy a servir.

5. a. Sí, se la voy a servir.   b. No, no se lo voy a servir.

6. a. Sí, se lo voy a servir.   b. No, no se los voy a servir.

2 **Cambiar** Repeat each statement, replacing the direct object noun with a pronoun. (*6 items*)

> **modelo**
> María te hace ensalada.
> María te la hace.

3 **Preguntas** Answer each question using the cue you hear and object pronouns. Repeat the correct response after the speaker. (*5 items*)

> **modelo**
> ¿Me recomienda usted los mariscos? (sí)
> Sí, se los recomiendo.

4 **Una fiesta** Listen to this conversation between Eva and Marcela. Then read the statements and decide whether they are **cierto** or **falso**.

	Cierto	Falso
1. Le van a hacer una fiesta a Sebastián.	○	○
2. Le van a preparar langosta.	○	○
3. Le van a preparar una ensalada de mariscos.	○	○
4. Van a tener vino tinto, cerveza, agua mineral y té helado.	○	○
5. Clara va a comprar cerveza.	○	○
6. Le compraron un cinturón.	○	○

Lab Manual

8.3 Saber and conocer

1 **¿Saber o conocer?** You will hear some sentences with a beep in place of the verb. Decide which form of **saber** or **conocer** should complete each sentence and select it.

> **modelo**
> You hear: (Beep) cantar.
> You select: Sé because the sentence is Sé cantar.

1. Sé	Conozco	3. Sabemos	Conocemos	5. Sé	Conozco
2. Saben	Conocen	4. Sé	Conozco	6. Sabes	Conoces

2 **Cambiar** Listen to the following statements and say that you do the same activities. Repeat the correct answer after the speaker. (*5 items*)

> **modelo**
> Julia sabe nadar.
> Yo también sé nadar.

3 **Preguntas** Answer each question using the cue you hear. Repeat the correct response after the speaker. (*6 items*)

> **modelo**
> ¿Conocen tus padres Antigua? (sí)
> Sí, mis padres conocen Antigua.

4 **Mi compañera de cuarto** Listen as Jennifer describes her roommate. Then read the statements and decide whether they are **cierto** or **falso**.

	Cierto	Falso
1. Jennifer conoció a Laura en la escuela primaria.	O	O
2. Laura sabe hacer muchas cosas.	O	O
3. Laura sabe hablar alemán.	O	O
4. Laura sabe preparar comida mexicana.	O	O
5. Laura sabe patinar en línea.	O	O
6. Laura conoce a algunos muchachos simpáticos.	O	O

5 **La mejor comida** Listen to this conversation between Jorge and Rosalía. Then choose the correct answers to the questions.

1. ¿Por qué conoce Jorge muchos restaurantes?
   a. Es aficionado a los restaurantes.
   b. Él es camarero.

2. ¿Qué piensa Rosalía de la buena comida?
   a. Piensa que la gente no necesita ir a un restaurante para comer bien.
   b. Piensa que la gente encuentra la mejor comida en un restaurante.

3. ¿Dónde están Jorge y Rosalía?
   a. Están en la universidad.
   b. Están trabajando.

4. ¿Sabe Rosalía dónde está el restaurante?
   a. Sí, lo sabe.
   b. No lo conoce.

Lab Manual

8.4 Comparatives and superlatives

1 **Escoger** You will hear a series of descriptions. Choose the statement that expresses the correct comparison.

1. a. Yo tengo más dinero que Rafael.

   b. Yo tengo menos dinero que Rafael.

2. a. Elena es mayor que Juan.

   b. Elena es menor que Juan.

3. a. Enrique come más hamburguesas que José.

   b. Enrique come tantas hamburguesas como José.

4. a. La comida de La Fonda es mejor que la comida del Café Condesa.

   b. La comida de La Fonda es peor que la comida del Café Condesa.

5. a. Las langostas cuestan tanto como los camarones.

   b. Los camarones cuestan menos que las langostas.

6. a. El pavo es más caro que la salchicha.

   b. La salchicha cuesta más que el pavo.

2 **Comparar** Look at each drawing and answer the question you hear with a comparative statement. Repeat the correct response after the speaker.

1.

Ricardo   Sara

2.

Héctor   Alejandro

3.

Leonor   Melisa

3 **Cambiar** You are babysitting Anita, a small child, who starts boasting about herself and her family. Respond to each statement using a comparative of equality. Then repeat the correct answer after the speaker. (6 *items*)

> *modelo*
> Mi mamá es más bonita que tu mamá.
> Mi mamá es tan bonita como tu mamá.

4 **Preguntas** Answer each question you hear using the absolute superlative. Repeat the correct response after the speaker. (6 *items*)

> *modelo*
> La comida de la cafetería es mala, ¿no?
> Sí, es malísima.

PREPARACIÓN

Lección 9

1 **¿Lógico o ilógico?** You will hear some statements. Decide if they are **lógico** or **ilógico**.

1. Lógico   Ilógico   5. Lógico   Ilógico
2. Lógico   Ilógico   6. Lógico   Ilógico
3. Lógico   Ilógico   7. Lógico   Ilógico
4. Lógico   Ilógico   8. Lógico   Ilógico

2 **Escoger** For each drawing, you will hear three statements. Choose the one that corresponds to the drawing.

1. a.   b.   c.

2. a.   b.   c.

3. a.   b.   c.

4. a.   b.   c.

3 **Una celebración** Listen as señora Jiménez talks about a party she has planned. Then answer the questions.

1. ¿Para quién es la fiesta?

_____

2. ¿Cuándo es la fiesta?

_____

3. ¿Por qué hacen la fiesta?

_____

4. ¿Quiénes van a la fiesta?

_____

5. ¿Qué van a hacer los invitados en la fiesta?

_____

Lab Manual

PRONUNCIACIÓN

The letters h, j, and g

The Spanish **h** is always silent.

| **h**elado | **h**ombre | **h**ola | **h**ermosa |

The letter **j** is pronounced much like the English *h* in *his*.

| **J**osé | **j**ubilarse | de**j**ar | pare**j**a |

The letter **g** can be pronounced three different ways. Before **e** or **i**, the letter **g** is pronounced much like the English *h*.

| a**g**encia | **g**eneral | **G**il | **G**isela |

At the beginning of a phrase or after the letter **n**, the Spanish **g** is pronounced like the English *g* in *girl*.

Gustavo, **g**racias por llamar el domin**g**o.

In any other position, the Spanish **g** has a somewhat softer sound.

Me **g**radué en a**g**osto.

In the combinations **gue** and **gui**, the **g** has a hard sound and the **u** is silent. In the combination **gua**, the **g** has a hard sound and the **u** is pronounced like the English *w*.

| **gue**rra | conse**gui**r | **gua**ntes | a**gua** |

1   **Práctica** Repeat each word after the speaker to practice pronouncing **h, j,** and **g.**

1. hamburguesa	4. guapa	7. espejo	10. gracias	13. Jorge
2. jugar	5. geografía	8. hago	11. hijo	14. tengo
3. oreja	6. magnífico	9. seguir	12. galleta	15. ahora

2   **Oraciones** When you hear the number, read the corresponding sentence aloud. Then listen to the speaker and repeat the sentence.

1. Hola. Me llamo Gustavo Hinojosa Lugones y vivo en Santiago de Chile.
2. Tengo una familia grande; somos tres hermanos y tres hermanas.
3. Voy a graduarme en mayo.
4. Para celebrar mi graduación mis padres van a regalarme un viaje a Egipto.
5. ¡Qué generosos son!

3   **Refranes** Repeat each saying after the speaker to practice pronouncing **h, j,** and **g.**

1. A la larga, lo más dulce amarga.   2. El hábito no hace al monje.

4   **Dictado** Victoria is talking to her friend Mirta on the phone. Listen carefully and during the pauses write what she says. The entire passage will then be repeated so that you can check your work.

_____

_____

_____

_____

Lab Manual

GRAMÁTICA

9.1 Irregular preterites

1 **Escoger** Listen to each question and choose the most logical response.

1. a. No, no conduje hoy.
   b. No, no condujo hoy.
2. a. Te dije que tengo una cita con Gabriela esta noche.
   b. Me dijo que tiene una cita con Gabriela esta noche.
3. a. Estuvimos en la casa de Marta.
   b. Estuvieron en la casa de Marta.
4. a. Porque tuvo que estudiar.
   b. Porque tiene que estudiar.
5. a. Lo supe la semana pasada.
   b. Lo supimos la semana pasada.
6. a. Los pusimos en la mesa.
   b. Los pusieron en la mesa.
7. a. No, sólo tradujimos un poco.
   b. No, sólo traduje un poco.
8. a. Sí, le di $20,00.
   b. Sí, le dio $20,00.

2 **Cambiar** Change each sentence from the present to the preterite. Repeat the correct answer after the speaker. (*8 items*)

> **modelo**
> Él pone el flan sobre la mesa.
> Él *puso el flan sobre la mesa.*

3 **Preguntas** Answer each question you hear using the cue. Substitute object pronouns for the direct object when possible. Repeat the correct answer after the speaker.

> **modelo**
> *You hear:* ¿Quién condujo el auto?
> *You see:* yo
> *You say:* Yo lo conduje.

1. Gerardo
2. Mateo y Yolanda
3. nosotros
4. muy buena
5. ¡Felicitaciones!
6. mi papá

4 **Completar** Listen to the dialogue and write the missing words.

_____(1)_____ por un amigo que los Márquez _____(2)_____ a visitar a su hija. Me _____(3)_____ que _____(4)_____ desde Antofagasta y que se _____(5)_____ en el Hotel Carrera. Les _____(6)_____ una llamada (*call*) anoche pero no _____(7)_____ el teléfono. Sólo _____(8)_____ dejarles un mensaje. Hoy ellos me _____(9)_____ y me _____(10)_____ si mi esposa y yo teníamos tiempo para almorzar con ellos. Claro que les _____(11)_____ que sí.

Lab Manual

9.2 Verbs that change meaning in the preterite

1 **Identificar** Listen to each sentence and mark the subject of the verb.

> **modelo**
>
> *You hear:* ¿Cuándo lo supiste?
> *You mark:* tú

	yo	tú	él/ella	nosotros/as	ellos/ellas
Modelo	____	**X**	____	____	____
1.	____	____	____	____	____
2.	____	____	____	____	____
3.	____	____	____	____	____
4.	____	____	____	____	____
5.	____	____	____	____	____
6.	____	____	____	____	____
7.	____	____	____	____	____
8.	____	____	____	____	____

2 **Preguntas** Answer each question you hear using the cue. Substitute object pronouns for the direct object when possible. Repeat the correct response after the speaker.

> **modelo**
>
> *You hear:* ¿Conocieron ellos a Sandra?
> *You see:* sí
> *You say:* Sí, la conocieron.

1. sí   2. en la casa de Ángela   3. el viernes   4. no   5. no   6. anoche

3 **¡Qué lástima!** (*What a shame!*) Listen as José talks about some news he recently received. Then read the statements and decide whether they are **cierto** or **falso**.

	Cierto	Falso
1. Supieron de la muerte ayer.	○	○
2. Se sonrieron cuando oyeron las noticias (*news*).	○	○
3. Carolina no se pudo comunicar con la familia.	○	○
4. Francisco era (*was*) joven.	○	○
5. Mañana piensan llamar a la familia de Francisco.	○	○

4 **Relaciones amorosas** Listen as Susana describes what happened between her and Pedro. Then answer the questions.

1. ¿Por qué no pudo salir Susana con Pedro? _____

2. ¿Qué supo por su amiga? _____

3. ¿Cómo se puso ella cuando Pedro llamó? _____

4. ¿Qué le dijo Susana a Pedro? _____

9.3 Relative pronouns

1 **Escoger** You will hear some sentences with a beep in place of the relative pronoun. Decide whether **que**, **quien**, or **lo que** should complete each sentence.

> **modelo**
>
> You hear: (*Beep*) me gusta de las bodas es la comida.
> You select: *Lo que* because the sentence is *Lo que me gusta de las bodas es la comida.*

1. que   quien   lo que   6. que   quien   lo que
2. que   quien   lo que   7. Que   Quien   Lo que
3. que   quien   lo que   8. que   quien   lo que
4. que   quien   lo que   9. que   quien   lo que
5. que   quien   lo que   10. que   quien   lo que

2 **Completar** Listen to this description and fill in the missing words.

Sandra y Enrique, _____ se casan hoy, celebran su matrimonio en el Hotel Plaza. Invitan a
                1
Andrés, a _____ conocen desde hace quince años. Andrés sabe _____ esperan
        2   3
unas palabras suyas. Practica _____ dice toda la semana: "Todos sabemos
                                    4
_____ esta pareja se ama. Y _____ es más importante, son personas queridas.
     5   6
Sólo hay paz y amor en su futuro". El momento de brindar llega. Adela, _____ está
                                                                     7
enamorada de Andrés, lo mira mucho. Cuando termina de hablar, Andrés va a bailar porque supone
_____ así Adela no lo pone nervioso.
    8

3 **Preguntas** Answer each question you hear using a relative pronoun and the cues provided. Repeat the correct response after the speaker.

> **modelo**
>
> You hear: ¿Quiénes son esos chicos?
> You see: los invitados / vienen a la fiesta
> You say: Son los invitados que vienen a la fiesta.

1. chica / conocí en la boda   4. vecino / celebra su cumpleaños
2. mis amigos / festejan su graduación   5. la pareja / nos regaló un pastel
3. chico / se casa Patricia   6. quinceañera / tuvo su fiesta ayer

4 **La fiesta sorpresa** Sandra's birthday is coming soon. Someone wants to throw her a party. It is supposed to be a surprise, but Sandra discovered a few things. Listen to her conclusions. Then complete the list of clues and answer the question.

Pistas

1. La agenda que _____

2. La tía Ramona, que _____

3. Manuel, quien _____

4. Mi prima Rita, quien _____

Pregunta

¿Quién está planeando hacer una fiesta sorpresa para Sandra? _____

Lección 9 Laboratory Activities   **53**

Lab Manual

9.4 ¿Qué? and ¿cuál?

1 **¿Lógico o ilógico?** You will hear some questions and the responses. Decide if they are **lógico** or **ilógico**.

1. Lógico   Ilógico   5. Lógico   Ilógico
2. Lógico   Ilógico   6. Lógico   Ilógico
3. Lógico   Ilógico   7. Lógico   Ilógico
4. Lógico   Ilógico   8. Lógico   Ilógico

2 **Preguntas** You will hear a series of responses to questions. Using **¿qué?** or **¿cuál?**, form the question that prompted each response. Repeat the correct answer after the speaker. (*8 items*)

> **modelo**
>
> Santiago de Chile es la capital de Chile.
> *¿Cuál es la capital de Chile?*

3 **De compras** Look at Marcela's shopping list for Christmas and answer each question you hear. Repeat the correct response after the speaker. (*6 items*)

Raúl	2 camisas, talla 17
Cristina	blusa, color azul
Pepe	bluejeans y tres pares de calcetines blancos
Abuelo	cinturón
Abuela	suéter blanco

4 **Escoger** Listen to this radio commercial and choose the most logical response to each question.

1. ¿Qué hace Fiestas Mar?
a. Organiza fiestas.   b. Es una tienda que vende cosas para fiestas.   c. Es un club en el mar.

2. ¿Para qué tipo de fiesta no usaría (*would not use*) Fiestas Mar?
a. Para una boda.   b. Para una fiesta sorpresa.   c. Para una cena con los suegros.

3. ¿Cuál de estos servicios no ofrece Fiestas Mar?
a. Poner las decoraciones.   b. Proveer (*provide*) el lugar.   c. Proveer los regalos.

4. ¿Qué tiene que hacer el cliente si usa Fiestas Mar?
a. Tiene que preocuparse por la lista de invitados.   b. Tiene que preocuparse por la música.
c. Tiene que preparar la comida.

5. Si uno quiere contactar Fiestas Mar, ¿qué debe hacer?
a. Debe escribirles un mensaje electrónico.   b. Debe llamarlos.   c. Debe ir a Casa Mar.

Lab Manual

PREPARACIÓN   # Lección 10

1   **Identificar** You will hear a series of words. Write each one in the appropriate category.

> **modelo**
> *You hear:* el hospital
> *You write:* el hospital under **Lugares**

Lugares	Medicinas	Condiciones y síntomas médicos
el hospital		

2   **Describir** For each drawing, you will hear two statements. Choose the one that corresponds to the drawing.

1. a.   b.   2. a.   b.

3. a.   b.   4. a.   b.

Lab Manual

PRONUNCIACIÓN

c (before a consonant) and q

In Lesson 8, you learned that, in Spanish, the letter **c** before the vowels **a, o,** and **u** is pronounced like the *c* in the English word *car*. When the letter **c** appears before any consonant except **h,** it is also pronounced like the *c* in *car*.

| **cl**ínica | bici**cl**eta | **cr**ema | do**ct**ora | o**ct**ubre |

In Spanish, the letter **q** is always followed by a **u,** which is silent. The combination **qu** is pronounced like the *k* sound in the English word *kitten*. Remember that the sounds **kwa, kwe, kwi, kwo,** and **koo** are always spelled with the combination **cu** in Spanish, never with **qu.**

| **qu**erer | par**qu**e | **qu**eso | **qu**ímica | mante**qu**illa |

1 Práctica Repeat each word after the speaker, focusing on the **c** and **q** sounds.

1. quince	5. conductor	9. aquí
2. querer	6. escribir	10. ciclismo
3. pequeño	7. contacto	11. electrónico
4 equipo	8. increíble	12. quitarse

2 Oraciones When you hear the number, read the corresponding sentence aloud. Then listen to the speaker and repeat the sentence.

1. El doctor Cruz quiso sacarle la muela.
2. Clara siempre se maquilla antes de salir de casa.
3. ¿Quién perdió su equipaje?
4. Pienso comprar aquella camisa porque me queda bien.
5. La chaqueta cuesta quinientos cuarenta dólares, ¿no?
6. Esa clienta quiere pagar con tarjeta de crédito.

3 Refranes Repeat each saying after the speaker to practice the **c** and **q** sounds.

1. Ver es creer.[1]
2. Quien mal anda, mal acaba.[2]

4 Dictado You will hear five sentences. Each will be said twice. Listen carefully and write what you hear.

1. _____
2. _____
3. _____
4. _____
5. _____

[1]*Seeing is believing.*
[2]*He who lives badly, ends badly.*

GRAMÁTICA

10.1 The imperfect tense

1 **Identificar** Listen to each sentence and circle the verb tense you hear.

1. a. present   b. preterite   c. imperfect   6. a. present   b. preterite   c. imperfect
2. a. present   b. preterite   c. imperfect   7. a. present   b. preterite   c. imperfect
3. a. present   b. preterite   c. imperfect   8. a. present   b. preterite   c. imperfect
4. a. present   b. preterite   c. imperfect   9. a. present   b. preterite   c. imperfect
5. a. present   b. preterite   c. imperfect   10. a. present   b. preterite   c. imperfect

2 **Cambiar** Form a new sentence using the cue you hear. Repeat the correct answer after the speaker. (6 *items*)

> **modelo**
> Iban a casa. (Eva)
> Eva *iba a casa.*

3 **Preguntas** A reporter is writing an article about funny things people used to do when they were children. Answer her questions using the cues provided. Then repeat the correct response after the speaker.

> **modelo**
> *You hear:* ¿Qué hacía Miguel de niño?
> *You see:* ponerse pajitas (*straws*) en la nariz
> *You say:* Miguel se ponía pajitas en la nariz.

1. quitarse los zapatos en el restaurante   4. jugar con un amigo invisible
2. vestirnos con la ropa de mamá   5. usar las botas de su papá
3. sólo querer comer dulces   6. comer con las manos

4 **Completar** Listen to this description of Ángela's medical problem and write the missing words.

Ángela _____ 1 día y noche. _____ 2 que _____ 3 un resfriado, pero se _____ 4 bastante saludable. Se _____ 5 de la biblioteca después de poco tiempo porque les _____ 6 a los otros estudiantes. Sus amigas, Laura y Petra, siempre le _____ 7 que _____ 8 alguna alergia. Por fin, decidió hacerse un examen médico. La doctora le dijo que ella _____ 9 alérgica y que _____ 10 muchas medicinas para las alergias. Finalmente, le recetó unas pastillas. Al día siguiente (*following*), Ángela se _____ 11 mejor porque _____ 12 cuál era el problema y ella dejó de estornudar después de tomar las pastillas.

Lab Manual

10.2 Constructions with se

1 **Escoger** Listen to each question and choose the most logical response.

1. a. Ay, se te quedó en casa.
   b. Ay, se me quedó en casa.
2. a. No, se le olvidó llamarlo.
   b. No, se me olvidó llamarlo.
3. a. Se le rompieron jugando al fútbol.
   b. Se les rompieron jugando al fútbol.

4. a. Ay, se les olvidó.
   b. Ay, se nos olvidó.
5. a. No, se me perdió.
   b. No, se le perdió.
6. a. Se nos rompió.
   b. Se le rompieron.

2 **Preguntas** Answer each question you hear using the cue provided and the impersonal **se**. Repeat the correct response after the speaker.

> **modelo**
> *You hear:* ¿Qué lengua se habla en Costa Rica?
> *You see:* español
> *You say:* Se habla español.

1. a las seis
2. gripe
3. en la farmacia

4. en la caja
5. en la Oficina de Turismo
6. tomar el autobús #3

3 **Letreros** (*Signs*) Some or all of the type is missing on the signs. Listen to the speaker and write the appropriate text below each sign. The text for each sign will be repeated.

10.3 Adverbs

1 **Completar** Listen to each statement and choose the word or phrase that best completes it.

1. a. casi   b. mal   c. ayer
2. a. con frecuencia   b. además   c. ayer
3. a. poco   b. tarde   c. bien
4. a. a menudo   b. muy   c. menos
5. a. así   b. apenas   c. tranquilamente
6. a. bastante   b. a tiempo   c. normalmente

2 **Cambiar** Form a new sentence by changing the adjective to an adverb. Repeat the correct answer after the speaker.

> **modelo**
> *You hear:* Juan dibuja.
> *You see:* fabuloso
> *You say:* Juan dibuja fabulosamente.

1. regular   3. feliz   5. general
2. rápido   4. constante   6. fácil

3 **Preguntas** Answer each question you hear in the negative, using the cue provided. Repeat the correct response after the speaker.

> **modelo**
> *You hear:* ¿Salió bien la operación?
> *You see:* mal
> *You say:* No, la operación salió mal.

1. lentamente   3. muy   5. tristemente
2. tarde   4. nunca   6. poco

4 **Situaciones** You will hear four brief conversations. Choose the phrase that best completes each sentence.

1. Mónica…
   a. llegó tarde al aeropuerto.
   b. casi perdió el avión a San José.
   c. decidió no ir a San José.

2. Pilar…
   a. se preocupa por la salud de Tomás.
   b. habla con su médico.
   c. habla con Tomás sobre un
      problema médico.

3. La señora Blanco…
   a. se rompió la pierna hoy.
   b. quiere saber si puede correr mañana.
   c. se lastimó el tobillo hoy.

4. María está enojada porque Vicente…
   a. no va a recoger (*to pick up*) su medicina.
   b. no recogió su medicina ayer.
   c. no debe tomar antibióticos.

Lab Manual

Lección 10 Laboratory Activities   **59**

PREPARACIÓN

Lección 11

1 **Asociaciones** Circle the word or words that are not logically associated with each word you hear.

1. la impresora	el semáforo	el fax
2. guardar	imprimir	chocar
3. el carro	el motor	el sitio web
4. los frenos	el ratón	el aceite
5. el parabrisas	el camino	el mecánico
6. el kilómetro	el centímetro	el disco
7. el archivo	la televisión	la llanta
8. la conexión inalámbrica	la policía	la velocidad

2 **¿Lógico o ilógico?** You will hear some statements. Decide if they are **lógico** or **ilógico**.

	Lógico	Ilógico			Lógico	Ilógico
1.	○	○		5.	○	○
2.	○	○		6.	○	○
3.	○	○		7.	○	○
4.	○	○		8.	○	○

3 **Identificar** For each drawing, you will hear two statements. Choose the statement that best corresponds to the drawing.

1. a.   b.   2. a.   b.

3. a.   b.   4. a.   b.

PRONUNCIACIÓN

c (before e or i), s, and z

In Latin America, **c** before **e** or **i** sounds much like the *s* in *sit*.

medi**c**ina	**c**elular	cono**c**er	pa**c**iente

In parts of Spain, **c** before **e** or **i** is pronounced like the *th* in *think*.

condu**c**ir	poli**c**ía	**c**elebrar	velo**c**idad

The letter **s** is pronounced like the *s* in *sit*.

subir	be**s**ar	**s**onar	impre**s**ora

In Latin America, the Spanish **z** is pronounced like the **s**.

cabe**z**a	nari**z**	abra**z**ar	embara**z**ada

The **z** is pronounced like the *th* in *think* in parts of Spain.

zapatos	**z**ona	pla**z**a	bra**z**o

1 **Práctica** Repeat each word after the speaker to practice pronouncing **s**, **z**, and **c** before **i** and **e**.

1. funcionar	4. sitio	7. zanahoria	10. perezoso
2. policía	5. disco	8. marzo	11. quizás
3. receta	6. zapatos	9. comenzar	12. operación

2 **Oraciones** When you hear each number, read the corresponding sentence aloud. Then listen to the speaker and repeat the sentence.

1. Vivió en Buenos Aires en su niñez pero siempre quería pasar su vejez en Santiago.

2. Cecilia y Zulaima fueron al centro a cenar al restaurante Las Delicias.

3. Sonó el despertador a las seis y diez pero estaba cansado y no quiso oírlo.

4. Zacarías jugaba al baloncesto todas las tardes después de cenar.

3 **Refranes** Repeat each saying after the speaker to practice pronouncing **s**, **z**, and **c** before **i** and **e**.

1. Zapatero, a tus zapatos.[1]

2. Primero es la obligación que la devoción.[2]

4 **Dictado** You will hear a friend describing Azucena's weekend experiences. Listen carefully and write what you hear during the pauses. The entire passage will be repeated so that you can check your work.

_____

_____

_____

_____

_____

_____

[1]*Mind your P's and Q's. (lit. Shoemaker, to your shoes.)*

[2]*Business before pleasure.*

Lab Manual

GRAMÁTICA

11.1 The preterite and the imperfect

1   **Identificar**   Listen to each statement and identify the verbs in the preterite and imperfect. Write them in the appropriate column.

> **modelo**
>
> *You hear:* Cuando arrancó el carro, llovía fuertemente.
> *You write:* arrancó under *Preterite,* and llovía under *Imperfect.*

	Preterite	Imperfect
Modelo	arrancó	llovía
1.		
2.		
3.		
4.		
5.		
6.		
7.		
8.		

2   **Responder**   Answer the questions using the cues. Substitute direct object pronouns for the direct object nouns when appropriate. Repeat the correct response after the speaker.

> **modelo**
>
> *You hear:* ¿Por qué no llamaste a Soledad la semana pasada?
> *You see:* teléfono estar descompuesto
> *You say:* Porque el teléfono estaba descompuesto.

1. ir al cine
2. no tener las llaves
3. ya tenerla
4. sábado

5. no haber mucho tráfico
6. haber aceite en la calle
7. en la calle
8. no, llevarla conmigo

3   **¡Qué día!**   Listen as Mercedes tells a friend about her day. Then read the statements and decide whether they are **cierto** or **falso**.

	Cierto	Falso
1. Mercedes tenía mucha experiencia con la computadora.	○	○
2. Mercedes no encontró nada interesante en Internet.	○	○
3. A Mercedes le dolía la cabeza porque tenía gripe.	○	○
4. Mercedes decidió escuchar un disco compacto.	○	○
5. Mercedes necesita tomar una clase de computación.	○	○
6. Mercedes imprimió unas páginas de un sitio web.	○	○

Lab Manual

11.2 Por and para

1 **Escoger** You will hear some sentences with a beep in place of a preposition. Decide if **por** or **para** should complete each sentence.

> **modelo**
>
> *You hear:* El teclado es (*beep*) la computadora de Nuria.
> *You mark:* para

	por	para
Modelo	_____	X _____
1.	_____	_____
2.	_____	_____
3.	_____	_____
4.	_____	_____
5.	_____	_____
6.	_____	_____
7.	_____	_____
8.	_____	_____

2 **La aventura** (*adventure*) Complete each phrase about Jaime with **por** or **para** and the cue provided. Repeat each correct response after the speaker.

> **modelo**
>
> *You hear:* Jaime estudió.
> *You see:* médico
> *You say:* Jaime estudió para médico.

1. unos meses
2. hacer sus planes
3. mil dólares
4. hacer turismo
5. la ciudad
6. su mamá
7. pesos
8. las montañas

3 **Los planes** Listen to the telephone conversation between Antonio and Sonia and then select the best response for the questions.

1. ¿Por dónde quiere ir Sonia para ir a Bariloche?
   a. Quiere ir por Santiago de Chile.
   b. Va a ir por avión.
2. ¿Para qué va Sonia a Bariloche?
   a. Va para esquiar.
   b. Va para comprar esquíes.
3. ¿Por qué tiene que ir de compras Sonia?
   a. Para comprar una bolsa.
   b. Necesita un abrigo por el frío.
4. ¿Por qué quiere ir Antonio con ella hoy?
   a. Quiere ir para estar con ella.
   b. Quiere ir para comprar un regalo.

11.3 Stressed possessive adjectives and pronouns

1 **Identificar** Listen to each statement and mark the possessive pronoun you hear.

> **modelo**
>
> You hear: Ya arreglaron todos los coches pero el tuyo no.
> You write: yours

	mine	yours	his/hers	ours	theirs
Modelo	_____	**X**	_____	_____	_____
1.	_____	_____	_____	_____	_____
2.	_____	_____	_____	_____	_____
3.	_____	_____	_____	_____	_____
4.	_____	_____	_____	_____	_____
5.	_____	_____	_____	_____	_____
6.	_____	_____	_____	_____	_____
7.	_____	_____	_____	_____	_____
8.	_____	_____	_____	_____	_____

2 **Transformar** Restate each sentence you hear, using the cues. Repeat the correct answer after the speaker.

> **modelo**
>
> You hear: ¿De qué año es el carro suyo?
> You see: mine
> You say: ¿De qué año es el carro mío?

1. his
2. ours
3. yours (fam.)
4. theirs
5. mine
6. hers

3 **Cierto o falso** You will hear two brief conversations. Listen carefully and then indicate whether the statements are **cierto** or **falso**.

	Cierto	Falso
1. Los de la primera conversación comparten sus cosas mejor que los de la segunda.	○	○
2. Está claro que los de la primera conversación van a ir a la universidad.	○	○
3. Los de la primera conversación van a vivir juntos.	○	○
4. Las personas que hablan o se mencionan en la segunda conversación no saben compartir sus cosas.	○	○
5. En la segunda conversación, Adela y su prima hacen planes para sus estudios.	○	○
6. En la segunda conversación, Julián necesita la calculadora para sus estudios.	○	○

Lab Manual

PREPARACIÓN   # Lección 12

1 **Describir** Listen to each sentence and write the number of the sentence below the drawing of the household item mentioned.

a. _____   b. _____   c. _____

d. _____   e. _____   f. _____

g. _____   h. _____

2 **Identificar** You will hear a series of words. Write the word that does not belong in each series.

1. _____   4. _____   7. _____

2. _____   5. _____   8. _____

3. _____   6. _____

3 **Quehaceres domésticos** Your children are complaining about the state of things in your house. Respond to their complaints by telling them what household chores they should do to correct the situation. Repeat the correct response after the speaker. (6 *items*)

> **modelo**
> La ropa está arrugada (*wrinkled*).
> Debes planchar la ropa.

4 **En la oficina de la agente inmobiliaria** Listen to this conversation between Mr. Fuentes and a real estate agent. Then read the statements and decide whether they are **cierto** or **falso**.

	Cierto	Falso
1. El señor Fuentes quiere alquilar una casa.	O	O
2. El señor Fuentes quiere vivir en las afueras.	O	O
3. Él no quiere pagar más de 900 balboas al mes.	O	O
4. Él vive solo (*alone*).	O	O
5. La casa de apartamentos tiene ascensor.	O	O
6. El apartamento tiene lavadora.	O	O

Lab Manual

PRONUNCIACIÓN

The letter x

In Spanish, the letter **x** has several sounds. When the letter **x** appears between two vowels, it is usually pronounced like the *ks* sound in *eccentric* or the *gs* sound in *egg salad*.

con**exi**ón   **exa**men   **saxo**fón

If the letter **x** is followed by a consonant, it is pronounced like *s* or *ks*.

e**xp**licar   se**xt**o   e**xc**ursión

In Old Spanish, the letter **x** had the same sound as the Spanish **j**. Some proper names and some words from native languages like Náhuatl and Maya have retained this pronunciation.

Don Qui**x**ote   Oa**x**aca   Te**x**as

---

1 **Práctica** Repeat each word after the speaker, focusing on the **x** sound.

1. éxito   5. expedición   9. excepto
2. reflexivo   6. mexicano   10. exagerar
3. exterior   7. expresión   11. contexto
4. excelente   8. examinar   12. Maximiliano

---

2 **Oraciones** When you hear the number, read the corresponding sentence aloud. Then listen to the speaker and repeat the sentence.

1. Xavier Ximénez va de excursión a Ixtapa.
2. Xavier es una persona excéntrica y se viste de trajes extravagantes.
3. Él es un experto en lenguas extranjeras.
4. Hoy va a una exposición de comidas exóticas.
5. Prueba algunos platos exquisitos y extraordinarios.

---

3 **Refranes** Repeat each saying after the speaker to practice the **x** sound.

1. Ir por extremos no es de discretos.[1]
2. El que de la ira se deja vencer, se expone a perder.[2]

---

4 **Dictado** You will hear five sentences. Each will be said twice. Listen carefully and write what you hear.

1. _____

2. _____

3. _____

4. _____

5. _____

---

[1] *Prudent people don't go to extremes.*
[2] *He who allows anger to overcome him, risks losing.*

Lab Manual

GRAMÁTICA

12.1 Usted and ustedes commands

1   Identificar   You will hear some sentences. If the verb is a formal command, select **Sí**. If the verb is not a command, select **No**.

> **modelo**
>
> *You hear:* Saque la basura.
> *You select:* Sí because *Saque* is a formal command.

1. Sí   No   6. Sí   No
2. Sí   No   7. Sí   No
3. Sí   No   8. Sí   No
4. Sí   No   9. Sí   No
5. Sí   No   10. Sí   No

2   Cambiar   A physician is giving a patient advice. Change each sentence you hear from an indirect command to a formal command. Repeat the correct answer after the speaker. (*6 items*)

> **modelo**
>
> Usted tiene que dormir ocho horas cada noche.
> *Duerma ocho horas cada noche.*

3   Preguntas   Answer each question you hear in the affirmative using a formal command and a direct object pronoun. Repeat the correct response after the speaker. (*8 items*)

> **modelo**
>
> ¿Cerramos las ventanas?
> *Sí, ciérrenlas.*

4   Más preguntas   Answer each question you hear using a formal command and the cue provided. Repeat the correct response after the speaker.

> **modelo**
>
> *You hear:* ¿Debo llamar al señor Rodríguez?
> *You see:* no / ahora
> *You say:* No, no lo llame ahora.

1. no   3. sí / aquí   5. el primer día del mes
2. a las cinco   4. no   6. que estamos ocupados

5   ¿Cómo llegar?   Julia is going to explain how to get to her home. Listen to her instructions, then number the instructions in the correct order. Two items will not be used.

_____ a. entrar al edificio que está al lado del Banco Popular

_____ b. tomar el ascensor al cuarto piso

_____ c. buscar la llave debajo de la alfombra

_____ d. ir detrás del edificio

_____ e. bajarse del metro en la estación Santa Rosa

_____ f. subir las escaleras al tercer piso

_____ g. caminar hasta el final del pasillo

Lab Manual

12.2 The present subjunctive

1 **Escoger** You will hear some sentences with a beep in place of a verb. Decide which verb should complete each sentence.

> **modelo**
>
> *You hear:* Es urgente que (*beep*) al médico.
> *You see:* vas   vayas
> *You select:* vayas because the sentence is **Es urgente que vayas al médico.**

1. tomamos   tomemos
2. conduzcan   conducen
3. aprenda   aprende
4. arreglas   arregles

5. se acuestan   se acuesten
6. sabes   sepas
7. almorcemos   almorzamos
8. se mude   se muda

2 **Cambiar** You are a Spanish instructor, and it's the first day of class. Tell your students what is important for them to do using the cues you hear. (*8 items*)

> **modelo**
>
> hablar español en la clase
> **Es importante que ustedes hablen español en la clase.**

3 **Transformar** Change each sentence you hear to the subjunctive mood using the expression provided. Repeat the correct answer after the speaker.

> **modelo**
>
> *You hear:* Pones tu ropa en el armario.
> *You see:* Es necesario
> *You say:* **Es necesario que pongas tu ropa en el armario.**

1. Es mejor   4. Es importante
2. Es urgente   5. Es bueno
3. Es malo   6. Es necesario

4 **¿Qué pasa aquí?** Listen to this conversation. Then choose the phrase that best completes each sentence.

1. Esta conversación es entre…
   a. un empleado y una clienta.
   b. un hijo y su madre.
   c. un camarero y la dueña de un restaurante.

2. Es necesario que Mario…
   a. llegue temprano.
   b. se lave las manos.
   c. use la lavadora.

3. Es urgente que Mario…
   a. ponga las mesas.
   b. quite las mesas.
   c. sea listo.

12.3 Subjunctive with verbs of will and influence

1 **Identificar** Listen to each sentence. If you hear a verb in the subjunctive, select **Sí**. If you don't hear the subjunctive, select **No**.

1. Sí No   4. Sí No
2. Sí No   5. Sí No
3. Sí No   6. Sí No

2 **Transformar** Some people are discussing what they or their friends want to do. Say that you don't want them to do those things. Repeat the correct response after the speaker. (*6 items*)

> **modelo**
>
> Esteban quiere invitar a tu hermana a una fiesta.
> No quiero que Esteban invite a mi hermana a una fiesta.

3 **Situaciones** Listen to each situation and make a recommendation using the cues.

> **modelo**
>
> *You hear:* Sacamos una "F" en el examen de química.
> *You see:* estudiar más
> *You say:* Les recomiendo que estudien más.

1. ponerte un suéter   4. no hacerlo
2. quedarse en la cama   5. comprarlas en la Casa Bonita
3. regalarles una lámpara   6. ir a La Cascada

4 **¿Qué hacemos?** Listen to this conversation and answer the questions.

1. ¿Qué quiere el señor Barriga que hagan los chicos?

_____

2. ¿Qué le pide el chico?

_____

3. ¿Qué les sugiere el señor a los chicos?

_____

4. ¿Qué tienen que hacer los chicos si no consiguen el dinero?

_____

5. Al final, ¿en qué insiste el señor Barriga?

_____

Lab Manual

PREPARACIÓN

Lección 13

1 **¿Lógico o ilógico?** You will hear some questions and the responses. Decide if they are **lógico** or **ilógico**.

1. Lógico   Ilógico   4. Lógico   Ilógico
2. Lógico   Ilógico   5. Lógico   Ilógico
3. Lógico   Ilógico   6. Lógico   Ilógico

2 **Eslóganes** You will hear some slogans created by environmentalists. Write the number of each slogan next to the ecological problem it addresses.

_____ a. la contaminación del aire   _____ d. la contaminación del agua
_____ b. la deforestación   _____ e. el calentamiento global
_____ c. la extinción de animales   _____ f. la basura en las calles

3 **Preguntas** Look at the drawings and answer each question you hear. Repeat the correct response after the speaker.

1.

2.

3.

4.

4 **Completar** Listen to this radio advertisement and write the missing words.

Para los que gustan del _____, la agencia Eco-Guías los invita a viajar a la
                                    1

_____ amazónica. Estar en el Amazonas es convivir (*to coexist*) con la
          2

_____. Venga y _____ los misterios del
          3   4

_____ tropical. Admire de cerca las diferentes _____ y
          5   6

_____ mientras navega por un _____ que parece mar.
          7   8

Duerma bajo un _____ lleno de _____. Piérdase en un
                          9   10

_____ de encanto (*enchantment*).
          11

Lab Manual

PRONUNCIACIÓN

l, ll, and y

In Spanish, the letter **l** is pronounced much like the *l* sound in the English word *lemon*.

cie**l**o	**l**ago	**l**ata	**l**una

In Lesson 8, you learned that most Spanish speakers pronounce the letter **ll** like the *y* in the English word *yes*. The letter **y** is often pronounced in the same manner.

estre**ll**a	va**ll**e	ma**y**o	pla**y**a

When the letter **y** occurs at the end of a syllable or by itself, it is pronounced like the Spanish letter **i**.

le**y**	mu**y**	vo**y**	**y**

1 **Práctica** Repeat each word after the speaker focusing on the **l**, **ll**, and **y** sounds.

1. lluvia	6. pasillo	11. yogur
2. desarrollar	7. limón	12. estoy
3. animal	8. raya	13. taller
4. reciclar	9. resolver	14. hay
5. llegar	10. pantalla	15. mayor

2 **Oraciones** When you hear the number, read the corresponding sentence aloud. Then listen to the speaker and repeat the sentence.

1. Ayer por la mañana Leonor se lavó el pelo y se maquilló.
2. Ella tomó café con leche y desayunó pan con mantequilla.
3. Después su yerno vino a su casa para ayudarla.
4. Pero él se cayó en las escaleras del altillo y se lastimó la rodilla.
5. Leonor lo llevó al hospital.
6. Allí le dieron unas pastillas para el dolor.

3 **Refranes** Repeat each saying after the speaker to practice the **l**, **ll**, and **y** sounds.

1. Quien no oye consejo, no llega a viejo.[1]
2. A caballo regalado, no le mires el diente.[2]

4 **Dictado** You will hear five sentences. Each will be said twice. Listen carefully and write what you hear.

1. _____

2. _____

3. _____

4. _____

5. _____

[1]*He who doesn't listen to advice, doesn't reach old age.*
[2]*Don't look a gift horse in the mouth.*

GRAMÁTICA

13.1 The subjunctive with verbs of emotion

1 **Escoger** Listen to each statement and choose the most logical response.

1. a. Ojalá que se mejore pronto.
   b. Me alegro de que esté bien.
2. a. Espero que podamos ir a nadar mañana.
   b. Es una lástima que ya no lo podamos usar.
3. a. Me sorprende que venga temprano.
   b. Siento que se pierda la película.
4. a. Temo que el río esté contaminado.
   b. Me alegro de que vea bien.

5. a. Es ridículo que el gobierno controle cuando nos bañemos.
   b. Me gusta cepillarme los dientes.
6. a. Es triste que la gente cuide la selva.
   b. Me molesta que no hagamos nada para mejorar la situación.

2 **Transformar** Change each sentence you hear to the subjunctive mood using the expression provided. Repeat the correct answer after the speaker.

> **modelo**
> *You hear:* Cada año hay menos árboles en el mundo.
> *You see:* Es una lástima
> *You say:* Es una lástima que cada año haya menos árboles en el mundo.

1. Es triste
2. Es extraño
3. Es terrible
4. Es ridículo
5. Es una lástima
6. Me molesta

3 **Preguntas** Answer each question you hear using the cues. Repeat the correct response after the speaker.

> **modelo**
> *You hear:* ¿De qué tienes miedo?
> *You see:* nosotros / no resolver la crisis de energía
> *You say:* Tengo miedo de que nosotros no resolvamos la crisis de energía.

1. Ricardo / estudiar ecología
2. muchas personas / no preocuparse por el medio ambiente
3. tú / hacer un viaje a la selva
4. el gobierno / controlar el uso de la energía nuclear
5. los turistas / recoger las flores
6. haber / tantas plantas en el desierto

4 **El Club de Ecología** Listen to this conversation. Then read the statements in your lab manual and decide whether they are **cierto** or **falso**.

	Cierto	Falso
1. Carmen se alegra de que la presidenta del club empiece un programa de reciclaje.	○	○
2. Héctor espera que Carmen se enoje con la presidenta.	○	○
3. Carmen teme que los otros miembros (*members*) quieran limpiar las playas.	○	○
4. A Carmen le gusta ir a la playa.	○	○
5. A Héctor le sorprende que Carmen abandone (*resigns from*) el club.	○	○
6. Carmen cree que la presidenta va a cambiar de idea.	○	○

Lab Manual

13.2 The subjunctive with doubt, disbelief, and denial

1   **Identificar**   Listen to each sentence and decide whether you hear a verb in the indicative or the subjunctive in the subordinate clause. Mark the appropriate column.

> **modelo**
>
> *You hear:* Creo que Nicolás va de excursión.
> *You mark:* indicative because you heard va.

	Indicative	Subjunctive
Modelo	X	
1.		
2.		
3.		
4.		
5.		
6.		
7.		

2   **Cambiar**   Change each sentence you hear to the negative. Repeat the correct answer after the speaker. (*7 items*)

> **modelo**
>
> Dudo que haga frío en Bogotá.
> *No dudo que hace frío en Bogotá.*

3   **Te ruego**   Listen to this conversation between a father and daughter. Then choose the word or phrase that best completes each sentence.

1. Juanita quiere ir a la selva amazónica para _____.
   a. vivir con los indios   b. estudiar las plantas tropicales   c. estudiar los animales

2. Ella _____ que quiere ir.
   a. está segura de   b. no está segura de   c. niega

3. Su papá _____ que se enferme con malaria.
   a. está seguro   b. teme   c. niega

4. Juanita _____ que se enferme.
   a. duda   b. no duda   c. cree

5. _____ que el papá no quiera que ella vaya.
   a. Es cierto   b. No es cierto   c. No hay duda de

6. El papá dice que _____ que la selva amazónica es un lugar fantástico.
   a. es improbable   b. es imposible   c. no cabe duda de

7. _____ Juanita va a la selva amazónica.
   a. Es seguro que   b. Tal vez   c. No es probable que

8. Juanita _____ que su papá es el mejor papá del mundo.
   a. duda   b. no cree   c. cree

13.3 The subjunctive with conjunctions

1 **¿Lógico o ilógico?** You will hear some sentences. Decide if they are **lógico** or **ilógico**.

1. Lógico   Ilógico   4. Lógico   Ilógico
2. Lógico   Ilógico   5. Lógico   Ilógico
3. Lógico   Ilógico   6. Lógico   Ilógico

2 **A la entrada del parque** Listen to the park ranger's instructions. Then number the drawings in the correct order.

a. _____

b. _____

c. _____

d. _____

3 **Identificar** Listen to each sentence and mark the appropiate column to indicate whether the subordinate clause expresses a future action, a habitual action, or a past action.

> **modelo**
>
> *You hear:* Voy a ir a caminar por el sendero tan pronto como llegues a la casa.
> *You mark:* future action

	future action	habitual action	past action
Modelo	X	_____	_____
1.	_____	_____	_____
2.	_____	_____	_____
3.	_____	_____	_____
4.	_____	_____	_____
5.	_____	_____	_____
6.	_____	_____	_____

Lab Manual

PREPARACIÓN   **Lección 14**

1 **¿Lógico o ilógico?** You will hear some questions and the responses. Decide if they are **lógico** or **ilógico**.

1. Lógico   Ilógico   4. Lógico   Ilógico   7. Lógico   Ilógico
2. Lógico   Ilógico   5. Lógico   Ilógico   8. Lógico   Ilógico
3. Lógico   Ilógico   6. Lógico   Ilógico

2 **Hacer diligencias** Look at the drawing and listen to Sofía's description of her day. During each pause, write the name of the place she went. The first one has been done for you.

1. _____ Lavandería Rosa _____   5. _____
2. _____   6. _____
3. _____   7. _____
4. _____   8. _____

3 **Preguntas** Look once again at the drawing in activity 2 and answer each question you hear with the correct information. Repeat the correct response after the speaker. (*5 items*)

> modelo
> La joyería está al norte de la plaza, ¿verdad?
> No, la joyería *está* al *este* de la plaza.

4 **Perdidos en el centro** Listen to Carlos and Victoria's conversation and answer the questions.

1. ¿Qué buscan Carlos y Victoria? _____

2. ¿Quién les da la dirección? _____

3. ¿Qué deben hacer en el semáforo? _____

4. ¿A cuántas cuadras está del semáforo? _____

PRONUNCIACIÓN

m and n

The letter **m** is pronounced like the *m* in the English word *made*.

    mamá   **m**arzo   **m**andar   **m**esa

The letter **n** is pronounced like the *n* in the English word *none*.

    norte   **n**adie   **n**unca   **n**ieto

When **n** is followed by the letter **v**, the **n** is pronounced like the Spanish **m**.

    e**nv**iar   i**nv**ierno   i**nv**itado   con **V**íctor

1   **Práctica** Repeat each word or phrase after the speaker to practice pronouncing **m** and **n**.

1. imposible	5. número	9. enamorado	13. matrimonio
2. mañana	6. invitar	10. monumento	14. confirmar
3. mano	7. moreno	11. empleado	15. con Víctor
4. manejar	8. envase	12. encima	16. ningún

2   **Oraciones** When you hear each number, read the corresponding sentence aloud. Then listen to the speaker and repeat the sentence.

1. A mí no me gustan nada los mariscos.
2. En el mercado compro naranjas, melocotones y manzanas.
3. Mañana invito a Mario Martín a cenar conmigo.
4. Mario es el mejor mecánico de motocicletas del mundo.
5. También le importa mucho la conservación del medio ambiente.
6. Siempre envía los envases de aluminio al centro de reciclaje en Valencia.

3   **Refranes** Repeat each saying after the speaker to practice pronouncing **m** and **n**.

1. Más vale poco y bueno que mucho y malo.[1]
2. Mala hierba nunca muere.[2]

4   **Dictado** You will hear a paragraph. Listen carefully and write what you hear during the pauses. The entire paragraph will then be repeated so that you can check your work.

_____

_____

_____

_____

_____

_____

[1]*Quality is more important than quantity.*

[2]*Like a bad penny, it just keeps turning up. (lit. Bad grass never dies.)*

Lab Manual

GRAMÁTICA

14.1 The subjunctive in adjective clauses

1   **Identificar**   Listen to each statement or question. If it refers to a person, place, or thing that clearly exists or is known, mark the **Sí** row. If it refers to a person, place, or thing that either does not exist or whose existence is uncertain, mark the **No** row.

> **modelo**
>
> *You hear:* Buscamos un hotel que tenga piscina.
> *You mark:* the No row because the existence of the hotel is uncertain.

	Modelo	1.	2.	3.	4.	5.	6.
Sí	_____	_____	_____	_____	_____	_____	_____
No	X	_____	_____	_____	_____	_____	_____

2   **Escoger**   You will hear some sentences with a beep in place of the verb. Select the verb that best completes each sentence.

> **modelo**
>
> *You hear:* Tengo una cuenta corriente que *(beep)* gratis.
> *You select:* es because the existence of the *cuenta corriente* is not in doubt.

1. tiene   tenga   2. vende   venda   3. vende   venda   4. hacen   hagan

3   **Cambiar**   Change each sentence you hear into the negative. Repeat the correct answer after the speaker. (*6 items*)

> **modelo**
>
> Hay un restaurante aquí que sirve comida venezolana.
> No hay ningún restaurante aquí que sirva comida venezolana.

4   **Buscando amistad**   Read the ads for pen pals. Then listen to the four recorded personal ads. Write the name of the person whose written ad best suits each recorded personal ad.

Nombre: Gustavo Carrasquillo
Dirección: Casilla 204, La Paz, Bolivia
Edad: 20 años
Pasatiempos: Ver películas en inglés, leer revistas de política, escalar montañas, esquiar y hacer amistad con jóvenes de todo el mundo. Me pueden escribir en inglés o alemán.

Nombre: Claudia Morales
Dirección: Calle 4–14, Guatemala, Guatemala
Edad: 18 años
Pasatiempos: Ir a conciertos de rock, escuchar la radio, ver películas extranjeras, mandar y recibir correo electrónico.

Nombre: Alicia Duque
Dirección: Avenida Gran Capitán 26, Córdoba, España
Edad: 18 años
Pasatiempos: Ir al cine, a fiestas, bailar, hablar por teléfono y escribir canciones de amor. Pueden escribirme en francés.

Nombre: Antonio Ávila
Dirección: Apartado Postal 3007, Panamá, Panamá

Edad: 21 años
Pasatiempos: Entre mis pasatiempos están escribir cartas a amigos por todas partes del mundo, escuchar la radio, practicar deportes y leer revistas.

Nombre: Rosalinda Guerrero
Dirección: Calle 408 #3, Hatillo, Puerto Rico
Edad: 19 años
Pasatiempos: Navegar por Internet, leer sobre política, ir a conciertos y visitar museos de arte.

1. _____   3. _____

2. _____   4. _____

Lab Manual

14.2 Familiar (tú) commands

1 **Identificar** You will hear some sentences. If the verb is a **tú** command, select **Sí**. If the verb is not a **tú** command, select **No**.

> **modelo**
> *You hear:* Camina en el parque.
> *You select:* Sí because *Camina* is a **tú** command.

1. Sí   No   6. Sí   No
2. Sí   No   7. Sí   No
3. Sí   No   8. Sí   No
4. Sí   No   9. Sí   No
5. Sí   No   10. Sí   No

2 **¿Dónde están?** Eduardo's wife has asked him to do some errands for her. Using the map and her directions, write down the places she mentions.

1. _____
2. _____
3. _____
4. _____
5. _____
6. _____
7. _____
8. _____

3 **Consejos prácticos** You will hear a conversation between a man who is visiting Panamá and his travel agent. Using **tú** commands and the ideas presented, write six pieces of advice that someone can follow when visiting Panamá.

1. _____
2. _____
3. _____
4. _____
5. _____
6. _____

Lab Manual

14.3 Nosotros/as commands

1 **Identificar** Listen to each statement. Mark the **Sí** row if it is a command. Mark the **No** row if it is not.

> **modelo**
> *You hear:* Abramos la tienda.
> *You mark:* Sí

	Modelo	1.	2.	3.	4.	5.	6.
Sí	X						
No							

2 **Cambiar** Change each sentence you hear to a **nosotros/as** command. Repeat the correct answer after the speaker. (*8 items*)

> **modelo**
> Vamos a visitar la Plaza Bolívar.
> Visitemos la Plaza Bolívar.

3 **Preguntas** Answer each question you hear negatively. Then make another suggestion using the cue provided and a **nosotros/as** command.

> **modelo**
> *You hear:* ¿Cocinamos esta noche?
> *You see:* Restaurante Cambur
> *You say:* No, no cocinemos esta noche. Comamos en el Restaurante Cambur.

1. jugar a las cartas   3. ir a la biblioteca

2. esquiarla   4. limpiar el sótano

4 **¿Cierto o falso?** Listen to Manuel and Elisa's conversation. Then read the statements and decide whether they are **cierto** or **falso**.

	Cierto	Falso
1. Manuel está muy ocupado.	○	○
2. Manuel va a acompañar a Elisa a hacer diligencias.	○	○
3. Primero van a ir al correo para comprar sellos.	○	○
4. Elisa quiere primero depositar el cheque.	○	○
5. Manuel y Elisa van a comprar el postre antes de que vayan al banco.	○	○
6. Elisa sugiere cortarse el pelo de último.	○	○

Lab Manual

PREPARACIÓN   # Lección 15

1 Identificar You will hear a series of words or phrases. Write the word or phrase that does not belong in each group.

1. _____   3. _____   5. _____

2. _____   4. _____   6. _____

2 Describir For each drawing, you will hear a brief description. Indicate whether it is **cierto** or **falso** according to what you see.

1.   Cierto   Falso   2.   Cierto   Falso

3.   Cierto   Falso   4.   Cierto   Falso

3 A entrenarse Listen as Marisela describes her new fitness program. Then list the activities she plans to do each day.

lunes: _____

martes: _____

miércoles: _____

jueves: _____

viernes: _____

sábado: _____

domingo: _____

Lab Manual

PRONUNCIACIÓN

ch and p

In Spanish, the **ch** is pronounced like the *ch* sound in *church* and *chair*.

Coch**abamba   no**ch**e   mo**ch**ila   mu**ch**a**ch**o   que**ch**ua

In English, the letter *p* at the beginning of a word is pronounced with a puff of air. In contrast, the Spanish **p** is pronounced without the puff of air. It is somewhat like the *p* sound in *spin*. To check your pronunciation, hold the palm of your hand in front of your mouth as you say the following words. If you are making the **p** sound correctly, you should not feel a puff of air.

La **P**az   **p**eso   **p**iscina   a**p**urarse   **p**roteína

1   Práctica Repeat each word after the speaker, focusing on the **ch** and **p** sounds.

1. archivo
2. derecha
3. chau
4. lechuga
5. preocupado
6. operación
7. pie
8. cuerpo
9. computadora
10. chuleta
11. champiñón
12. leche

2   Oraciones When you hear the number, read the corresponding sentence aloud. Then listen to the speaker and repeat the sentence.

1. A muchos chicos les gusta el chocolate.
2. Te prohibieron comer chuletas por el colesterol.
3. ¿Has comprado el champán para la fiesta?
4. Chela perdió el cheque antes de depositarlo.
5. Levanto pesas para perder peso.
6. ¿Me prestas el champú?

3   Refranes Repeat each saying after the speaker to practice the **ch** and **p** sounds.

1. Del dicho al hecho, hay mucho trecho.[1]
2. A perro flaco todo son pulgas.[2]

4   Dictado You will hear eight sentences. Each will be said twice. Listen carefully and write what you hear.

1. _____
2. _____
3. _____
4. _____
5. _____
6. _____
7. _____
8. _____

[1]*It's easier said than done.*
[2]*It never rains, but it pours.*

Lab Manual

GRAMÁTICA

15.1 Past participles used as adjectives

1 **Identificar** Listen to each sentence and write the past participle that is being used as an adjective.

> **modelo**
> *You hear:* Estoy interesada en estar en buena forma.
> *You write:* interesada

1. _____   5. _____

2. _____   6. _____

3. _____   7. _____

4. _____   8. _____

2 **Preguntas** Pablo wants to go to the gym with his friend Manuel, but everything is going wrong. Answer each question using the cue provided.

> **modelo**
> *You hear:* ¿Y mi amigo Manuel?
> *You see:* dormir
> *You say:* Tu amigo Manuel está dormido.

1. congelar   3. perder   5. dañar   7. cerrar

2. romper   4. abrir   6. vender   8. morir

3 **¿Cierto o falso?** Look at the drawing and listen to each statement. Indicate whether each statement is **cierto** or **falso**.

	Cierto	Falso
1.	○	○
2.	○	○
3.	○	○
4.	○	○
5.	○	○
6.	○	○
7.	○	○
8.	○	○

Lab Manual

15.2 The present perfect

1   **Identificar** Listen to each statement and mark the column for the subject of the verb.

> **modelo**
> *You hear:* Nunca han hecho ejercicios aeróbicos.
> *You mark:* ellos/ellas

	yo	tú	él/ella	nosotros/as	ellos/ellas
Modelo	_____	_____	_____	_____	X _____
1.	_____	_____	_____	_____	_____
2.	_____	_____	_____	_____	_____
3.	_____	_____	_____	_____	_____
4.	_____	_____	_____	_____	_____
5.	_____	_____	_____	_____	_____
6.	_____	_____	_____	_____	_____

2   **Transformar** Change each sentence you hear from the present indicative to the present perfect indicative. Repeat the correct answer after the speaker. (*8 items*)

> **modelo**
> Pedro y Ernesto salen del gimnasio.
> *Pedro y Ernesto han salido del gimnasio.*

3   **Preguntas** Answer each question you hear using the cue. Repeat the correct response after the speaker.

> **modelo**
> *You hear:* ¿Ha adelgazado Miguel?
> *You see:* sí / un poco
> *You say:* Sí, Miguel ha adelgazado un poco.

1. sí   3. no   5. no

2. sí   4. sí   6. no / todavía

4   **Consejos de una amiga** Listen to this conversation between Eva and Manuel. Then choose the correct ending for each statement.

1. Ellos están hablando de…
     a. que fumar es malo.   b. la salud de Manuel.   c. los problemas con sus clases.

2. Manuel dice que sufre presiones cuando…
     a. tiene exámenes.   b. hace gimnasia.   c. no puede dormir y fuma mucho.

3. Eva dice que ella…
     a. estudia durante el día.   b. ha estudiado poco.   c. también está nerviosa.

4. Eva le dice a Manuel que…
     a. deje de fumar.   b. estudie más.   c. ellos pueden estudiar juntos.

15.3 The past perfect

1 **¿Lógico o ilógico?** You will hear some brief conversations. Indicate if they are **lógico** or **ilógico**.

1. Lógico   Ilógico
2. Lógico   Ilógico
3. Lógico   Ilógico
4. Lógico   Ilógico
5. Lógico   Ilógico
6. Lógico   Ilógico

2 **Describir** Using the cues provided, describe what you and your friends had already done before your parents arrived for a visit. Repeat the correct answer after the speaker.

> **modelo**
> You see: preparar la cena
> You hear: mis amigas
> You say: Mis amigas ya habían preparado la cena.

1. limpiar el baño y la sala
2. sacar la basura
3. sacudir los muebles
4. poner la mesa
5. hacer las camas
6. darle de comer al gato

3 **Completar** Listen to this conversation and write the missing words. Then answer the questions.

JORGE ¡Hola, chico! Ayer vi a Carmen y no me lo podía creer, me dijo que te _____(1)_____ en el gimnasio. ¡Tú, que siempre _____(2)_____ tan sedentario! ¿Es cierto?

RUBÉN Pues, sí. _____(3)_____ mucho de peso y me dolían las rodillas. Hacía dos años que el médico me _____(4)_____ que tenía que mantenerme en forma. Y finalmente, hace cuatro meses (*four months ago*), decidí hacer gimnasia casi todos los días.

JORGE Te felicito (*I congratulate*), amigo. Yo también _____(5)_____ hace un año a hacer gimnasia. ¿Qué días vas? Quizás nos podemos encontrar allí.

RUBÉN _____(6)_____ todos los días al salir del trabajo. ¿Y tú? ¿Vas con Carmen?

JORGE Siempre _____(7)_____ juntos hasta que compré mi propio carro. Ahora voy cuando quiero. Pero la semana que viene voy a tratar de ir después del trabajo para verte por allí.

1. ¿Por qué es extraño que Rubén esté en el gimnasio?

2. ¿Qué le había dicho el médico a Rubén?

3. ¿Por qué no va Jorge con Carmen al gimnasio?

PREPARACIÓN   **Lección 16**

1 **Identificar** Listen to each description and then complete the sentence by identifying the person's occupation.

> **modelo**
> *You hear:* La señora Ortiz enseña a los estudiantes. Ella es...
> *You write:* maestra

1. _____   3. _____   5. _____

2. _____   4. _____   6. _____

2 **Anuncios clasificados** Look at the ads and listen to each statement. Then decide if the statement is **cierto** or **falso**.

```
┌──────────────────────────────┐
│         EMPRESA              │
│     INTERNACIONAL           │
│           busca              │
│        CONTADOR             │
│  Requisitos:                 │
│  •Tenga estudios de          │
│   administración de empresas │
│  • Hable español e inglés    │
│                              │
│  Se ofrece:                  │
│  • Horario flexible          │
│  • Salario semanal de 700    │
│    córdobas                  │
│  • Posibilidades de ascenso  │
│                              │
│     Contacto: Sr. Flores     │
│       Tel: 492 2043          │
└──────────────────────────────┘
```

```
SE BUSCA DISEÑADOR

• Se ofrece un salario anual de 250.000
  córdobas.
• Excelentes beneficios
• Debe tener cinco años de experiencia.

Si está interesado, envíe currículum a
        EMPRESA LÓPEZ
         Fax 342 2396
```

	Cierto	Falso			Cierto	Falso			Cierto	Falso
1.	○	○		3.	○	○		5.	○	○
2.	○	○		4.	○	○		6.	○	○

3 **Publicidad** Listen to this radio advertisement and answer the questions.

1. ¿Qué tipo de empresa es Mano a Obra?

_____

2. ¿Qué hace esta empresa?

_____

3. ¿Cuál es la ocupación del señor Mendoza?

_____

4. ¿Qué le va a dar la empresa al señor Mendoza en un año?

_____

5. ¿En qué profesiones se especializa (*specializes*) Mano a Obra?

_____

Lab Manual

PRONUNCIACIÓN

Intonation

Intonation refers to the rise and fall in the pitch of a person's voice when speaking. Intonation patterns in Spanish are not the same as those in English, and they vary according to the type of sentence.

In normal statements, the pitch usually rises on the first stressed syllable.

A **mí** me ofrecieron un ascenso.   **Ca**da aspirante debe entregar una solicitud.

In exclamations, the pitch goes up on the first stressed syllable.

¡Oja**lá** venga!   ¡**Cla**ro que sí!

In questions with yes or no answers, the pitch rises to the highest level on the last stressed syllable.

¿Trajiste el cu**rrí**culum?   ¿Es usted arqui**tec**to?

In questions that request information, the pitch is highest on the stressed syllable of the interrogative word.

¿**Cuán**do renunciaste al trabajo?   ¿**Cuál** es su número de teléfono?

---

1 **Práctica** Repeat each sentence after the speaker, imitating the intonation.

1. ¿Vas a venir a la reunión?   4. Estoy buscando un nuevo trabajo.
2. ¿Dónde trabajaba anteriormente?   5. Quiero cambiar de profesión.
3. ¡Qué difícil!   6. ¿Te interesa el puesto?

---

2 **Oraciones** When you hear the number, say the speaker's lines in this dialogue aloud. Then listen to the speaker and repeat the sentences.

1. **REPARTIDOR** (*DELIVERYMAN*) Trabajo para la Compañía de Transportes Alba. ¿Es usted el nuevo jefe?
2. **JEFE** Sí. ¿Qué desea?
3. **REPARTIDOR** Aquí le traigo los muebles de oficina. ¿Dónde quiere que ponga el escritorio?
4. **JEFE** Allí delante, debajo de la ventana. ¡Tenga cuidado! ¿Quiere romper la computadora?
5. **REPARTIDOR** ¡Perdón! Ya es tarde y estoy muy cansado.
6. **JEFE** Perdone usted, yo estoy muy nervioso. Hoy es mi primer día en el trabajo.

---

3 **Dictado** You will hear a phone conversation. Listen carefully and write what you hear during the pauses. The entire conversation will then be repeated so that you can check your work.

PACO _____

_____

ISABEL _____

_____

PACO _____

_____

ISABEL _____

_____

PACO _____

Lab Manual

GRAMÁTICA

16.1 The future tense

1 **Identificar** Listen to each sentence and mark the column for the subject of the verb.

> **modelo**
>
> *You hear:* Iré a la reunión.
> *You mark:* yo

	yo	tú	él/ella	nosotros/as	ustedes
Modelo	X	_____	_____	_____	_____
1.	_____	_____	_____	_____	_____
2.	_____	_____	_____	_____	_____
3.	_____	_____	_____	_____	_____
4.	_____	_____	_____	_____	_____
5.	_____	_____	_____	_____	_____
6.	_____	_____	_____	_____	_____
7.	_____	_____	_____	_____	_____
8.	_____	_____	_____	_____	_____

2 **Cambiar** Change each sentence you hear to the future tense. Repeat the correct answer after the speaker. (*8 items*)

> **modelo**
>
> Ellos van a salir pronto.
> Ellos saldrán pronto.

3 **Preguntas** Answer each question you hear using the cues. Repeat the correct response after the speaker.

> **modelo**
>
> *You hear:* ¿Con quién saldrás esta noche?
> *You see:* Javier
> *You say:* Yo saldré con Javier.

1. no / nada
2. el lunes por la mañana

3. Santo Domingo
4. esta noche
5. 2:00 p.m.

6. sí
7. de periodista
8. la próxima (*next*) semana

4 **Nos mudamos** Listen to this conversation between Fernando and Marisol. Then read the statements and decide whether they are **cierto** or **falso**.

	Cierto	Falso
1. Marisol y Emilio se mudarán a Granada.	○	○
2. Ellos saben cuándo se mudan.	○	○
3. Marisol y Emilio harán una excursión a la selva y las playas antes de que él empiece su nuevo trabajo.	○	○
4. Fernando no podrá visitarlos en Nicaragua en un futuro próximo (*near*).	○	○

Lab Manual

16.2 The conditional tense

1   Identificar Listen to each sentence and decide whether you hear a verb in the future, the conditional, or the imperfect tense.

  1. a. future   b. conditional   c. imperfect

  2. a. future   b. conditional   c. imperfect

  3. a. future   b. conditional   c. imperfect

  4. a. future   b. conditional   c. imperfect

  5. a. future   b. conditional   c. imperfect

  6. a. future   b. conditional   c. imperfect

  7. a. future   b. conditional   c. imperfect

  8. a. future   b. conditional   c. imperfect

  9. a. future   b. conditional   c. imperfect

10. a. future   b. conditional   c. imperfect

2   Cambiar Form a new sentence replacing **iba a** + [*infinitive*] construction with the corresponding verb in the conditional. Repeat the correct answer after the speaker. (*6 items*)

> *modelo*
>
> Andrea dijo que iba a cambiar de trabajo.
> Andrea dijo que *cambiaría de trabajo.*

3   Entrevista You are a good cook and you are considering opening a Salvadorian restaurant. The investor wants to know what it will be like. Answer his questions using the cues provided. Then repeat the correct response after the speaker.

> *modelo*
>
> *You hear:* ¿Cómo se llamaría el restaurante?
> *You see:* Rincón Salvadoreño
> *You say:* El restaurante se llamaría Rincón Salvadoreño.

1. 10   4. $60.000

2. sí / periódico   5. seguro médico

3. yo   6. sí / un año

4   La conferencia de negocios Cristina is planning a business conference. Listen to her ideas and then indicate whether the statements are **cierto** or **falso**.

	Cierto	Falso
1. La conferencia sería en la compañía.	○	○
2. Hablaría un hombre de negocios de mucho éxito.	○	○
3. El mejor cocinero de la ciudad haría la cena.	○	○
4. Los reporteros entrevistarían a Cristina.	○	○
5. Cristina podría obtener un aumento de sueldo.	○	○
6. Cristina no debería pensar en otra idea.	○	○

Lab Manual

16.3 The past subjunctive

1 **Identificar** Listen to the following verbs. Select **Sí** if the verb is in the past subjunctive and **No** if it is in another tense.

1.	Sí	No	7.	Sí	No
2.	Sí	No	8.	Sí	No
3.	Sí	No	9.	Sí	No
4.	Sí	No	10.	Sí	No
5.	Sí	No	11.	Sí	No
6.	Sí	No	12.	Sí	No

2 **Cambiar** Form a new sentence using the cue you hear. Repeat the correct answer after the speaker. (*8 items*)

> **modelo**
> Marisa quería que yo dejara el trabajo. (mi hermana)
> **Marisa quería que mi hermana dejara el trabajo.**

3 **Completar** Complete each phrase you hear using the cue provided and the past subjunctive. Repeat the correct response after the speaker.

> **modelo**
> *You hear:* Esperábamos que tú...
> *You see:* seguir otra carrera
> *You say:* **Esperábamos que tú siguieras otra carrera.**

1. ir a renunciar al puesto
2. darte el aumento
3. invertir en su empresa
4. saber la verdad
5. poner un anuncio en los periódicos
6. llegar temprano al trabajo
7. ofrecerles mejores beneficios
8. gastar menos dinero

4 **El mundo de los negocios** Listen to this conversation between two coworkers and answer the questions.

1. ¿Qué le pidió el jefe a Elisa cuando la llamó por teléfono?

_____

2. ¿Qué le pidió el jefe a la empleada cuando entró (*entered*) en su oficina?

_____

3. ¿Qué le preguntó el jefe a Elisa?

_____

4. ¿Qué le contestó Elisa?

_____

Lab Manual

Bienvenida, Marissa

Lección 1

Antes de ver el video

1 **¡Mucho gusto!** In this episode, Marissa will be meeting the **familia Díaz** for the first time. Look at the image and write down what you think Marissa, Mrs. Díaz, and Mr. Díaz are saying.

_____
_____
_____
_____
_____
_____
_____

Mientras ves el video

2 **Completar** Watch **Bienvenida, Marissa** and fill in the blanks.

SRA. DÍAZ ¿(1) _____ hora es?

MARISSA (2) _____ las cuatro menos diez.

DON DIEGO Buenas tardes, (3) _____. Señorita, bienvenida a la Ciudad de México.

MARISSA ¡Muchas gracias! Me (4) _____ Marissa.

¿(5) _____ se llama usted?

DON DIEGO Yo soy Diego, mucho (6) _____.

MARISSA El gusto es (7) _____, don Diego.

DON DIEGO ¿Cómo (8) _____ usted hoy, señora Carolina?

SRA. DÍAZ Muy bien, gracias, ¿y (9) _____?

DON DIEGO Bien, (10) _____.

SRA. DÍAZ Ahí hay (11) _____ maletas. Son de Marissa.

DON DIEGO Con (12) _____.

3 **¿Cierto o falso?** Indicate whether each statement is **cierto** or **falso**.

	Cierto	Falso
1. Marissa es de Wisconsin.	○	○
2. Jimena es profesora.	○	○
3. La señora Díaz es de Cuba.	○	○
4. Felipe es estudiante.	○	○
5. El señor Díaz es de la Ciudad de México.	○	○
6. Marissa no tiene (*doesn't have*) diccionario.	○	○

Después de ver el video

4 **¿Quién?** Write the name of the person who said each of the following sentences.

1. Ellos son estudiantes. _____

2. Son las cuatro y veinticinco. _____

3. Hasta luego, señor Díaz. _____

4. La chica de Wisconsin. _____

5. Bienvenida, Marissa. _____

6. Nosotros somos tu diccionario. _____

7. Hay... tres cuadernos... un mapa... un libro de español... _____

8. Marissa, te presento a Roberto, mi esposo. _____

9. De nada. _____

10. Lo siento, Marissa. _____

11. Hola. _____

12. No hay de qué. _____

13. ¿Qué hay en esta cosa? _____

14. ¿Quiénes son los dos chicos de las fotos? ¿Jimena y Felipe? _____

15. Gracias, don Diego. _____

5 **Ho, ho, hola...** Imagine that you have just met the man or woman of your dreams, and that person speaks only Spanish! Don't be shy! Write what the two of you would say in your first conversation.

_____

_____

_____

_____

_____

_____

_____

_____

6 **En la clase** Imagine that you are in Mexico studying Spanish. Write your conversation with your Spanish professor on the first day.

_____

_____

_____

_____

_____

_____

¿Qué estudias?   Lección 2

Antes de ver el video

1 **Impresiones** Based on your impressions of Marissa, Felipe, and Jimena in **Lección 1**, write the names of the classes you think each person is taking or is most interested in. Circle the name of the person you believe is the most studious, and underline the name of the character you believe is the most talkative.

MARISSA	FELIPE	JIMENA
_____	_____	_____
_____	_____	_____
_____	_____	_____

Mientras ves el video

2 **¿Quién y a quién?** Watch **¿Qué estudias?** and say who asks these questions and to whom.

Preguntas	¿Quién?	¿A quién?
1. ¿A quién buscas?	_____	_____
2. ¿Cuántas clases tomas?	_____	_____
3. ¿Qué estudias?	_____	_____
4. ¿Dónde está tu diccionario?	_____	_____
5. ¿Hablas con tu mamá?	_____	_____

3 **¿Qué cosas hay?** Make a check mark beside the actions, items and places shown in **¿Qué estudias?**

_____ 1. libros   _____ 5. comprar   _____ 9. pizarra

_____ 2. laboratorio _____ 6. tiza   _____ 10. dibujar

_____ 3. caminar   _____ 7. hablar   _____ 11. reloj

_____ 4. castillo   _____ 8. horario   _____ 12. mochila

4 **Completar** Fill in the blanks.

1. Marissa está en México para _____.
2. Marissa toma cuatro _____.
3. La _____ de Marissa es arqueología.
4. La especialización de Miguel es _____.
5. A Miguel le gusta _____.
6. Marissa _____ muy bien el español.
7. Juan Carlos toma química con el _____ Morales.
8. El profesor Morales enseña en un laboratorio sin _____.
9. A Felipe le gusta estar _____ el reloj y la puerta.
10. Maru _____ con su mamá.

Video Manual: *Escenas*

Después de ver el video

5 **Corregir** The underlined words in the following statements are incorrect. Fill in the blanks with the correct ones.

1. <u>Maru</u> es de los Estados Unidos. _____

2. <u>Miguel</u> toma una clase de computación. _____

3. <u>Felipe</u> necesita comprar libros. _____

4. En clase, a Marissa le gusta estar cerca <u>del reloj</u>. _____

5. <u>Felipe</u> es de Argentina. _____

6. Marissa toma español, <u>periodismo</u>, literatura y geografía. _____

7. Felipe busca a Juan Carlos y a <u>Maru</u>. _____

8. Felipe necesita practicar <u>español</u>. _____

6 **Asociar** Write the words or phrases in the box next to the names.

¿A la biblioteca?	cuatro clases	¿Por qué tomo química
arqueología	Ésta es la Ciudad de México.	y computación?
Buenos Aires	Hola, mamá, ¿cómo estás?	Te gusta la tarea.
ciencias ambientales	Me gusta mucho la cultura mexicana.	Y sin diccionario.

1. Marissa _____ _____

   _____

2. Felipe _____ _____

   _____

3. Juan Carlos _____ _____

   _____

4. Maru _____ _____

   _____

7 **¿Y tú?** Write a paragraph saying who you are, where you are from, where you study (city and name of university), and what classes you are taking this semester.

_____

_____

_____

_____

_____

_____

_____

_____

Un domingo en familia   **Lección 3**

Antes de ver el video

1

Examinar el título Look at the title of the episode. Based on the title and the image below, imagine what you think you will see.

_____
_____
_____
_____
_____
_____
_____

Mientras ves el video

2

Completar Fill in the blanks for each sentence from column A with a word from column B, according to **Un domingo en familia**.

A	B
1. Marta _____ ocho años.	trabajadora
2. Las hijas de Nayeli son simpáticas y _____.	tiene
3. La _____ de Ramón y Roberto se llama Ana María.	vive
4. Jimena dice que Felipe es _____ y feo.	gordo
5. Jimena es muy _____.	bonitas
6. Ana María _____ en Mérida.	hermana

3

En Xochimilco Check off each person or thing that appears in this episode.

____ 1. a Biology book   ____ 5. Felipe's uncle   ____ 9. people eating

____ 2. Marissa's grandparents   ____ 6. a soccer ball   ____ 10. Felipe's girlfriend

____ 3. Jimena's cousins   ____ 7. trajineras   ____ 11. Jimena's dad

____ 4. a desk   ____ 8. mariachis   ____ 12. Ana María's son-in-law

4

¿Cierto o falso? Indicate whether each statement is **cierto** or **falso**.

	Cierto	Falso
1. Felipe tiene mucha hambre.	○	○
2. El ex novio de Marissa es alemán.	○	○
3. Ana María tiene tres hijos.	○	○
4. Marissa tiene una sobrina que se llama Olivia.	○	○
5. La señora Díaz dice que su cuñada es muy simpática.	○	○

Video Manual: Escenas

Después de ver el video

5 **Seleccionar** Select the letter of the word or phrase that goes in each sentence.

1. Roberto es el _____ de Felipe y Jimena.

   a. tío   b. primo   c. padre   d. sobrino

2. Los abuelos de Marissa son _____.

   a. ecuatorianos   b. españoles   c. mexicanos   d. alemanes

3. Adam es el _____ de Marissa.

   a. hermano menor   b. tío   c. primo   d. cuñado

4. Carolina tiene una _____ que se llama Ana María.

   a. tía   b. cuñada   c. hermana   d. prima

5. Las _____ de Nayeli son _____.

   a. primas; altas   b. hermanas; trabajadoras   c. hijas; simpáticas   d. sobrinas; guapas

6. La _____ de Nayeli es muy _____.

   a. sobrina; trabajadora   b. abuela; vieja   c. mamá; simpática   d. tía; alta

7. La _____ de Carolina tiene _____.

   a. tía; hambre   b. hija; sed   c. sobrina; frío   d. familia; sueño

8. Marissa decide ir a _____.

   a. la librería   b. la cafetería   c. Mérida   d. el estadio

6 **Preguntas** Answer the questions, using complete sentences.

1. ¿Quién tiene tres hermanos?

   _____

2. ¿Cuántos años tiene Valentina, la hija de Nayeli?

   _____

3. ¿Quién es hija única?

   _____

4. ¿Cómo se llama el hermano de Jimena?

   _____

5. ¿Cómo se llama el padre de Felipe?

   _____

7 **Preguntas personales** Answer the questions about your family.

1. ¿Cuántas personas hay en tu familia? ¿Cuál es más grande (*bigger*), tu familia o la familia

   de Jimena? _____

   _____

2. ¿Tienes hermanos/as? ¿Cómo se llaman? _____

   _____

3. ¿Tienes un(a) primo/a favorito/a? ¿Cómo es? _____

   _____

4. ¿Cómo es tu tío/a favorito/a? ¿Dónde vive? _____

   _____

Video Manual: *Escenas*

Fútbol, cenotes y mole   Lección 4

Antes de ver el video

1 **El cenote** In this episode, Miguel, Maru, Marissa, and Jimena are going to a cenote to swim. What do you think they will see? What will they talk about?

_____
_____
_____
_____
_____
_____
_____

Mientras ves el video

2 **Verbos** These sentences are taken from **Fútbol, cenotes y mole**. As you watch this segment, fill in the blanks with the missing verbs.

1. ¿No vamos a _____? ¿Qué es un cenote?

2. Ella nada y _____ al tenis y al golf.

3. Bueno, chicos, ya es hora, ¡_____!

4. Si _____, compramos el almuerzo.

3 **¿Qué ves?** Check what you see.

_____ 1. una pelota de fútbol   _____ 5. una revista

_____ 2. un mensaje de correo electrónico   _____ 6. un restaurante

_____ 3. una iglesia   _____ 7. una plaza

_____ 4. un mapa   _____ 8. un cine

4 **Completar** Fill in the blanks in Column A with words from Column B.

A	B
1. Miguel dice (*says*) que un cenote es una _____ natural.	montañas
2. Marissa dice que donde ella vive no hay _____.	pasatiempos
3. La tía Ana María tiene muchos _____ y actividades.	comer
4. La tía Ana María va al cine y a los _____.	museos
5. Eduardo y Pablo dicen que hay un partido de fútbol en el _____.	nadan
6. Don Guillermo dice que hay muchos _____ buenos en Mérida.	piscina
7. Felipe desea _____ mole.	restaurantes
8. Marissa y sus amigos _____ en el cenote.	parque

Después de ver el video

5 **¿Qué hacen?** For numbers 1–11, fill in the missing letters in each word. For number 12, put the letters in the boxes in the right order.

1. Pablo dice que si no consigue más jugadores, su equipo va a ☐ _ _ d _ _.

2. Miguel dice que en México sólo hay _ _ n _ _ _ ☐ en la península de Yucatán.

3. Felipe dice que el restaurante del mole está en el _ _ _ ☐ _ o.

4. La tía Ana María sale mucho los _ _ n _ ☐ de semana.

5. Don Guillermo dice que hay un buen restaurante en la ☐ _ a _ _.

6. El mole de la tía Ana María es el _ _ v _ _ ☐ _ _ de Jimena.

7. Juan Carlos y Felipe van a _ _ _ ☐ r al fútbol con Eduardo y Pablo.

8. Eduardo juega con la p ☐ _ _ _ _ después del partido.

9. Eduardo y Pablo van a pagar lo que Felipe y Juan Carlos van a ☐ _ m _ _ _ _ _.

10. Marissa no escala ☐ _ _ t _ _ _ _.

11. Los chicos hablan con don Guillermo después de jugar al _ _ _ b ☐ _.

12. La tía Ana María tiene muchos _____.

6 **Me gusta** Fill in the chart with the activities, hobbies, or sports that you enjoy. Also say when and where you do each activity.

Mis pasatiempos favoritos	¿Cuándo?	¿Dónde?

7 **Preguntas** Answer these questions in Spanish.

1. ¿Son aficionados/as a los deportes tus amigos/as? ¿Cuáles son sus deportes favoritos?

_____

_____

_____

2. ¿Qué hacen tú y tus amigos/as cuando tienen ratos libres?

_____

_____

_____

3. ¿Qué vas a hacer esta noche? ¿Vas a estudiar? ¿Descansar? ¿Mirar televisión? ¿Ver una película?
¿Por qué? _____

_____

_____

_____

¡Vamos a la playa!

Lección 5

Antes de ver el video

1 **¿Qué hacen?** The six friends have just arrived at the beach. Based on the image, what do you think Maru and Jimena are doing? What do you think they will do next?

_____

_____

_____

_____

_____

_____

_____

Mientras ves el video

2 **¿Quién?** Watch the episode and write the name of the person that goes with each expression.

Expresión	Nombre
1. En Yucatán hace mucho calor.	_____
2. ¿Están listos para su viaje a la playa?	_____
3. No podemos perder el autobús.	_____
4. Bienvenidas. ¿En qué puedo servirles?	_____
5. No está nada mal el hotel, ¿verdad? Limpio, cómodo.	_____

3 **¿Qué ves?** Check what is shown.

_____ 1. un inspector de aduanas   _____ 5. unas maletas   _____ 9. la planta baja del hotel

_____ 2. el mar   _____ 6. una pelota   _____ 10. unas llaves

_____ 3. un aeropuerto   _____ 7. una agencia de viajes   _____ 11. un libro

_____ 4. un botones   _____ 8. el campo   _____ 12. personas en la playa

4 **Completar** Fill in the blanks.

1. **TÍA ANA MARÍA**   Excelente, entonces… ¡A la _____!

2. **MARU**   Tenemos una _____ para seis personas para esta noche.

3. **EMPLEADO**   Dos _____ en el primer piso para seis huéspedes.

4. **MIGUEL**   Ellos son mis amigos. Ellos sí son _____ conmigo.

5. **MARISSA**   Yo estoy un poco _____. ¿Y tú? ¿Por qué no estás nadando?

Video Manual: *Escenas*

Después de ver el video

5 **¿Cierto o falso?** Say whether each statement is **cierto** or **falso**. Correct the false statements.

1. Miguel está enojado con Felipe.

_____

2. Felipe y Marissa hablan con un empleado del hotel.

_____

3. Los ascensores del hotel están a la izquierda.

_____

4. Maru y su novio quieren hacer windsurf, pero no tienen tablas.

_____

5. Felipe dice que el hotel es feo y desagradable.

_____

6. Jimena dice que estudiar en la playa es muy divertido.

_____

6 **Resumir** Write a summary of this episode in Spanish. Try not to leave out any important information.

_____

_____

_____

_____

_____

_____

_____

_____

7 **Preguntas** Answer these questions in Spanish.

1. ¿Te gusta ir de vacaciones? ¿Por qué? _____

_____

_____

2. ¿Adónde te gusta ir de vacaciones? ¿Por qué? _____

_____

_____

3. ¿Con quién(es) vas de vacaciones? _____

_____

En el mercado

Antes de ver el video

1 **Describir** Look at the image and describe what you see, answering these questions: Where are Maru, Jimena, and Marissa? Who are they talking to? What is the purpose of their conversation?

_____

_____

_____

_____

_____

_____

Mientras ves el video

2 **Ordenar** Watch **En el mercado** and indicate the order in which you hear the following.

_____ a. Acabamos de comprar tres bolsas por 480 pesos.

_____ b. ¿Encontraron el restaurante?

_____ c. Esta falda azul es muy elegante.

_____ d. Le doy un muy buen precio.

_____ e. Mira, son cuatro. Roja, amarilla, blanca, azul.

_____ f. Acabo de ver una bolsa igual a ésta que cuesta 30 pesos menos.

3 **Mérida** Check each thing you see.

_____ 1. una tarjeta de crédito   _____ 4. un impermeable

_____ 2. una blusa   _____ 5. unos aretes

_____ 3. un mercado   _____ 6. un vendedor

4 **¿Quién lo dijo?** Indicate whether Marissa, Miguel, or don Guillermo said each sentence.

_____ 1. Quiero comprarle un regalo a Maru.

_____ 2. ¿Me das aquella blusa rosada? Me parece que hace juego con esta falda.

_____ 3. ¿Puedo ver ésos, por favor?

_____ 4. Hasta más tarde. Y ¡buena suerte!

_____ 5. Me contaron que los vendedores son muy simpáticos.

Video Manual: *Escenas*

Después de ver el video

5 **Completar** Complete the following sentences with words from the box.

azul	hermana	novia
camisetas	mercado	regatear
en efectivo	negro	vender

1. Juan Carlos, Felipe y Miguel creen que las chicas no saben (*know*) _____.

2. Los seis amigos van de compras a un _____.

3. Marissa dice que el color _____ está de moda.

4. Miguel quiere comprarle un regalo a su _____ Maru.

5. Las _____ de Juan Carlos y Felipe costaron 200 pesos.

6. Las chicas pagan 480 pesos _____ por las bolsas.

6 **Corregir** All these statements are false. Rewrite them so they are true.

1. Jimena dice que la ropa del mercado es muy fea.

_____

2. Marissa usa la talla 6.

_____

3. Maru compró una blusa.

_____

4. Miguel compró un abrigo para Maru.

_____

7 **Preguntas** Answer these questions in Spanish.

1. ¿Te gusta ir de compras? ¿Por qué? _____

_____

2. ¿Adónde vas de compras? ¿Por qué? _____

_____

3. ¿Con quién(es) vas de compras? ¿Por qué? _____

_____

4. Imagina que estás en un centro comercial y que tienes mil dólares. ¿Qué vas a comprar? ¿Por qué?

_____

_____

5. Cuando compras un auto, ¿regateas con el/la vendedor(a)? _____

Video Manual: *Escenas*

¡Necesito arreglarme!   Lección 7

Antes de ver el video

1 **En el baño** In this episode, Marissa, Felipe, and Jimena want to get ready at the same time. What do you think they might say?

_____

_____

_____

_____

_____

_____

_____

Mientras ves el video

2 **¿Marissa o Felipe?** Watch **¡Necesito arreglarme!** and put a check mark in a column to show whether the plans are Marissa's or Felipe's.

Actividad	Marissa	Felipe
1. ir al cine	_____	_____
2. afeitarse	_____	_____
3. ir al café a molestar a su amigo	_____	_____
4. arreglarse el pelo	_____	_____
5. ir al café con Juan Carlos	_____	_____

3 **Ordenar** Number the following events from one to six, in the order they occurred.

____ a. Jimena termina de maquillarse.

____ b. Todos quieren usar el espejo al mismo tiempo.

____ c. Marissa quiere entrar al baño y la puerta está cerrada.

____ d. Las chicas comparten el espejo.

____ e. Marissa busca una toalla.

____ f. Felipe entra al baño.

4 **Completar** Fill in the blanks.

1. **FELIPE**   Cada vez que quiero usar el _____, una de ustedes está aquí.

2. **JIMENA**   Me estoy _____ la cara.

3. **MARISSA**   ¡_____ debe estudiar los viernes!

4. **JIMENA**   ¿Por qué no te _____ por la mañana?

5. **FELIPE**   Siempre hay _____ en vivo.

Lección 7 Escenas Video Activities   **13**

Después de ver el video

5 **Preguntas** Answer these questions in Spanish.

1. ¿Qué está haciendo Jimena cuando Marissa quiere entrar al baño?

_____

2. ¿Por qué Jimena quiere maquillarse primero?

_____

3. ¿Por qué se quiere afeitar Felipe?

_____

4. ¿Cómo es el café donde van a ir Felipe y Juan Carlos?

_____

5. ¿Por qué Marissa quiere arreglarse?

_____

6. ¿Cuándo fue la última vez que Jimena vio a Juan Carlos?

_____

6 **Preguntas personales** Answer these questions in Spanish.

1. ¿A qué hora te levantas durante la semana? ¿Y los fines de semana?

_____

_____

2. ¿Te gusta más (*more*) bañarte o ducharte? ¿Por qué?

_____

_____

3. ¿Cuántas veces por día (*How many times a day*) te cepillas los dientes?

_____

_____

4. ¿Te lavas el pelo todos los días (*every day*)? ¿Por qué?

_____

_____

5. ¿Cómo cambia (*changes*) tu rutina los días que vas a la universidad y los días que sales con tus amigos?

_____

_____

7 **Escribir** Describe in Spanish what happens from the point of view of Jimena, Marissa, or Felipe.

_____

_____

_____

_____

_____

14 **Lección 7 Escenas** Video Activities

Una cena... romántica

Lección 8

Antes de ver el video

1 **En un restaurante** What do you do and say when you have dinner at a restaurant?

_____

_____

_____

_____

_____

_____

_____

_____

Mientras ves el video

2 **¿Quién?** Watch **Una cena... romántica** and write the name of the person who says each sentence.

Oración	Nombre
1. La ensalada viene con aceite y vinagre.	_____
2. Vino blanco para mí.	_____
3. Mejor pido la ensalada de pera con queso.	_____
4. Los espárragos están sabrosísimos esta noche.	_____
5. Señor, él es más responsable que yo.	_____

3 **Ordenar** Show the order in which the following took place.

____ a. Felipe les pone pimienta a los platillos.

____ b. Miguel pide una cerveza.

____ c. El camarero recomienda la sopa de frijoles.

____ d. El gerente llega a la mesa de Maru y Miguel.

4 **Completar** Fill in the missing words.

1. **MARU** No sé qué pedir. ¿Qué me _____?

2. **CAMARERO** ¿Ya decidieron qué _____ quieren?

3. **MARU** Tienes razón, Felipe. Los espárragos están _____.

4. **FELIPE** ¿Quién _____ jamón?

5. **JUAN CARLOS** ¿Aquí vienen _____ mexicanos _____ extranjeros?

Video Manual: *Escenas*

Después de ver el video

5 **Opiniones** Say who expressed the following opinions, either verbally or through body language.

_____ 1. Los mariscos parecen tan ricos como el jamón.

_____ 2. Este joven me está molestando con sus preguntas.

_____ 3. Los champiñones están deliciosos.

_____ 4. Felipe tiene la culpa (*is guilty*) de lo que pasó.

_____ 5. Vamos a la cocina para que paguen lo que hicieron (*did*).

6 **Corregir** Correct these statements.

1. Miguel le dice a Maru que la langosta se ve muy buena.

_____

2. De beber, Maru y Miguel piden té.

_____

3. El plato principal es ceviche de camarones con cilantro y limón.

_____

4. Maru pide el jamón con arvejas.

_____

5. Felipe dice que los champiñones saben a vinagre.

_____

6. Felipe dice que es el mejor camarero del mundo.

_____

7 **Preguntas personales** Answer these questions in Spanish.

1. ¿Almuerzas en la cafetería de tu universidad? ¿Por qué? _____

_____

2. ¿Cuál es tu plato favorito? ¿Por qué? _____

_____

3. ¿Cuál es el mejor restaurante de tu comunidad? Explica (*Explain*) tu opinión. _____

_____

4. ¿Cuál es tu restaurante favorito? ¿Cuál es la especialidad de ese restaurante? _____

_____

5. ¿Sales mucho a cenar con tus amigos/as? ¿Adónde van a cenar? _____

El Día de Muertos

Antes de ver el video

1 **La celebración** In this episode, the Díaz family celebrates the Day of the Dead. What kinds of things do you expect to see?

_____

_____

_____

_____

_____

_____

_____

Mientras ves el video

2 **Ordenar** Put the following events in order.

____ a. La tía Ana María le dice a Marissa cómo se enamoraron sus papás.

____ b. El señor Díaz brinda por los abuelos de la familia.

____ c. Marissa prueba el mole que prepara la tía Ana María.

____ d. Maite Fuentes habla del Día de Muertos en la televisión.

____ e. Jimena pregunta dónde puso las galletas y el pastel.

3 **¿Qué ves?** Place a check mark beside each thing you see.

____ 1. una botella   ____ 5. calaveras de azúcar   ____ 9. un regalo de Navidad

____ 2. una foto de boda   ____ 6. una quinceañera   ____ 10. helados

____ 3. una graduación   ____ 7. galletas   ____ 11. un altar

____ 4. flores   ____ 8. bolsas   ____ 12. un flan

4 **¿Quién lo dijo?** Write a name next to each sentence to indicate who says it.

_____ 1. Su familia es muy interesante.

_____ 2. El Día de Muertos se celebra en México el primero y el dos de noviembre.

_____ 3. ¡Estoy seguro que se lo van a pasar bien!

_____ 4. Al principio, mi abuela no quiso aceptar el matrimonio.

Después de ver el video

5 **Corregir** Rewrite these sentences to reflect what took place.

1. El Día de Muertos se celebra con flores, calaveras de azúcar, música y champán.

_____

2. El mole siempre fue el plato favorito de la mamá de la tía Ana María.

_____

3. Jimena intentó preparar mole para la fiesta de aniversario de sus tíos.

_____

4. La tía Ana María se casó con un ingeniero que trabaja muchísimo.

_____

5. Felipe y su papá prepararon pastel de chocolate para la familia.

_____

6. A Valentina le gusta el helado.

_____

6 **Eventos importantes** Describe in Spanish the three most important events in this episode, and explain your choices.

_____

_____

_____

_____

_____

_____

_____

7 **Preguntas personales** Answer these questions in Spanish.

1. ¿Qué días de fiesta celebras con tu familia? _____

_____

2. De los días de fiesta, ¿cuál es tu favorito? ¿Por qué? _____

_____

3. ¿Qué haces el Día de Acción de Gracias? _____

_____

4. ¿Cómo celebras tu cumpleaños? ¿Te gusta recibir regalos? _____

_____

¡Qué dolor!

Lección 10

Antes de ver el video

1 **Una cita** Look at the image. Where do you think Jimena is? What is happening?

_____

_____

_____

_____

_____

_____

_____

_____

Mientras ves el video

2 **¿Quién?** Watch **¡Qué dolor!** and use check marks to show who said what.

Expresión	Jimena	Elena	Dr. Meléndez
1. ¿Cuáles son tus síntomas?	_____	_____	_____
2. Tengo un dolor de cabeza terrible.	_____	_____	_____
3. Empecé a toser esta mañana.	_____	_____	_____
4. Te voy a mandar algo para la garganta.	_____	_____	_____
5. ¡Es tan sólo un resfriado!	_____	_____	_____

3 **¿Qué ves?** Place a check mark beside the things you see in the video.

____ 1. un letrero (*sign*) que dice: "Se prohíbe fumar"   ____ 6. una sala de emergencias

____ 2. un termómetro   ____ 7. una receta

____ 3. pastillas para el resfriado   ____ 8. un antibiótico

____ 4. una radiografía   ____ 9. un doctor

____ 5. un consultorio   ____ 10. una bolsa de la farmacia

4 **Completar** Write the name of the person who said each sentence and fill in the missing words.

_____ 1. A mi hermanito le dolía (*hurt*) la _____ con frecuencia.

_____ 2. ¿Cuánto tiempo hace que tienes estos _____?

_____ 3. Tengo _____ y estoy congestionada.

_____ 4. Nunca tenía (*had*) resfriados, pero me _____ el brazo dos veces.

_____ 5. No tienes _____. ¿Te pusiste un suéter anoche?

Video Manual: *Escenas*

Después de ver el video

5 Seleccionar Write the letter of the word or words that match each sentence.

1. ____ hizo cita con el Dr. Meléndez para llevar a Jimena.

   a. Don Diego   b. La señora Díaz   c. Elena   d. Miguel

2. Jimena puede ir inmediatamente a la ____ por los medicamentos.

   a. sala de emergencias   b. clínica   c. dentista   d. farmacia

3. Elena toma ____ para ____.

   a. aspirina; el dolor de cabeza   b. antibióticos; la gripe   c. pastillas; el resfriado

   d. medicamentos; el dolor de estómago

4. Elena dice que el té de jengibre es bueno para el dolor de ____.

   a. estómago   b. garganta   c. cabeza   d. brazos

5. La señora Díaz dice que a Jimena le dio ____ porque olvidó ponerse un suéter.

   a. fiebre   b. un resfriado   c. dolor de estómago   d. gripe

6. Cuando era niña, Jimena casi no ____.

   a. tomaba antibióticos   b. tomaba aspirinas   c. se rompía huesos   d. se enfermaba

6 Preguntas Answer the following questions in Spanish.

1. ¿Tiene fiebre Jimena? ¿Está mareada?

2. ¿Cuánto tiempo hace que a Jimena le duele la garganta? ¿Cuándo empezó a toser?

3. Según (*According to*) don Diego, ¿qué es lo mejor para los dolores de cabeza?

4. ¿Cuantas veces se rompió el brazo Elena?

5. ¿Qué le daban (*gave*) al hermanito de don Diego cuando le dolía la garganta?

7 Preguntas personales Answer these questions in Spanish.

1. ¿Te gusta ir al/a la médico/a? ¿Por qué? _____

2. ¿Tienes muchas alergias? ¿Eres alérgico/a a algún medicamento? _____

3. ¿Cuándo es importante ir a la sala de emergencias? _____

4. ¿Qué haces cuando tienes fiebre y te duele la garganta? _____

En el taller

Lección 11

Antes de ver el video

1 **¿Qué pasa?** In this image, where do you think Miguel is? What do you think he is doing, and why?

_____
_____
_____
_____
_____
_____
_____
_____

Mientras ves el video

2 **¿Qué oíste?** Watch **En el taller** and place a check mark beside what you hear.

_____ 1. ¿Cuál es tu dirección electrónica?

_____ 2. ¿Está descompuesta tu computadora?

_____ 3. ¿Y revisaste el aceite?

_____ 4. El navegador GPS también está descompuesto.

_____ 5. Mal día para la tecnología, ¿no?

_____ 6. ¡Te están llamando!

_____ 7. Se me acabó la pila.

_____ 8. Me gusta mucho la televisión por cable.

_____ 9. ¿Me pasas la llave?

_____ 10. No manejes con el cofre abierto.

3 **¿Qué viste?** Place a check mark beside what you see.

_____ 1. un teléfono celular

_____ 2. una llave

_____ 3. el capó de un coche

_____ 4. un reproductor de CD

_____ 5. un mecánico

_____ 6. la pantalla de un televisor

_____ 7. una arroba (@ *symbol*)

_____ 8. una cámara de video

_____ 9. un taller mecánico

_____ 10. un archivo

4 **¿Quién dice?** Write the name of the person who said each sentence.

_____ 1. ¿Quién es el mecánico?

_____ 2. Está descargando el programa antivirus ahora.

_____ 3. Acaba de enviarme un mensaje de texto.

_____ 4. Este coche tiene más de 150.000 kilómetros.

_____ 5. Por favor, ¡arréglalo (*fix it*)!

Video Manual: *Escenas*

Después de ver el video

5 **Corregir** Rewrite these statements so they are true.

1. Miguel le llevó su coche a Felipe, el mecánico.

_____

2. La computadora de Maru funciona muy bien.

_____

3. Jorge no tiene problemas para arreglar el coche de Miguel.

_____

4. Se le acabó la pila al teléfono celular de Miguel.

_____

5. Maru necesita una cámara digital nueva y Miguel necesita un reproductor de MP3 nuevo.

_____

6. Jorge le dice a Miguel que revise el aceite cada mil kilómetros.

_____

6 **Un mensaje** Imagine that Maru is writing a short message to a friend about today's events. Write in Spanish what you think she would say.

_____

_____

_____

_____

_____

_____

_____

_____

7 **Preguntas personales** Answer these questions in Spanish.

1. Cuando tu carro está descompuesto, ¿lo llevas a un(a) mecánico/a o lo arreglas tú mismo/a? ¿Por qué? _____

_____

_____

2. ¿Conoces a un(a) buen(a) mecánico/a? ¿Cómo se llama? _____

_____

_____

3. ¿Tienes un teléfono celular? ¿Para qué lo usas? _____

_____

_____

Los quehaceres

Antes de ver el video

1 **En la casa** In this episode, Jimena and Felipe need to clean the house if they want to travel with Marissa to the Yucatan Peninsula. Look at the image and describe what you think is going on.

_____

_____

_____

_____

_____

_____

_____

Mientras ves el video

2 **¿Cierto o falso?** Watch **Los quehaceres** and indicate whether each statement is **cierto** or **falso**.

	Cierto	Falso
1. A Jimena le gusta sacar la basura.	○	○
2. Felipe y Jimena deben limpiar la casa porque sus papás les pagaron el viaje.	○	○
3. Marissa sabe cómo cambiar la bolsa de la aspiradora.	○	○
4. Las servilletas estaban sobre la lavadora.	○	○
5. Don Diego y los chicos prepararon quesadillas para cenar.	○	○

3 **¿Qué cosas ves?** Place a check mark beside what you see.

_____ 1. un lavaplatos   _____ 4. vasos   _____ 7. platos

_____ 2. un garaje   _____ 5. un sofá   _____ 8. un sótano

_____ 3. un jardín   _____ 6. un balcón   _____ 9. tenedores

4 **Ordenar** Number the events from one to five, in the order they occur.

_____ a. Don Diego sugiere a las chicas que se organicen en equipos para limpiar.

_____ b. Juan Carlos pone la mesa.

_____ c. Marissa quiere quitar la bolsa de la aspiradora.

_____ d. La señora Díaz entra a la cocina y saluda a sus hijos.

_____ e. Jimena le dice a Felipe que limpie el baño.

Video Manual: Escenas

Después de ver el video

5 **Seleccionar** Write the letter of the words that go in each sentence.

1. La señora Díaz les pide a sus hijos que quiten ____ de la mesa.

    a. los vasos   b. las tazas   c. los platos

2. La señora Díaz les ____ a sus hijos que limpien ____ si quieren viajar.

    a. ruega; el patio   b. sugiere; el apartamento   c. recomienda; el altillo

3. Jimena va a limpiar ____ y ____.

    a. el refrigerador; la estufa   b. el armario; la pared   c. el sillón; la lámpara

4. Don Diego le aconseja a Felipe que sacuda el ____.

    a. sótano   b. garaje   c. estante

5. Juan Carlos no sabe dónde están ____.

    a. las copas   b. los vasos   c. los tenedores

6 **Preguntas** Answer the following questions in Spanish.

1. Según el señor Díaz, ¿para qué hora deben preparar la cena Jimena y Felipe?

_____

_____

2. ¿Qué les piden sus padres a Marissa y a sus hermanos?

_____

_____

3. ¿Quiénes se sientan en el sofá para ver el partido de fútbol?

_____

_____

4. ¿Quién cambia la bolsa de la aspiradora?

_____

_____

5. ¿Qué dice la señora Díaz cuando ve el apartamento limpio?

_____

_____

7 **Escribir** Imagine that you are one of the characters. Write a paragraph from that person's point of view, summarizing what happened in the episode.

_____

_____

_____

_____

_____

_____

Aventuras en la naturaleza   Lección 13

Antes de ver el video

1 **En Tulum** Marissa and Jimena visit a turtle sanctuary while Felipe and Juan Carlos take a tour through the jungle. What do you think the four friends will talk about when they are back together?

_____

_____

_____

_____

_____

_____

_____

Mientras ves el video

2 **Opiniones** Watch **Aventuras en la naturaleza** and place a check mark beside each opinion that is expressed.

_____ 1. Necesitamos aprobar leyes para proteger a las tortugas.

_____ 2. A menos que protejamos a los animales, muchos van a estar en peligro de extinción.

_____ 3. No es posible hacer mucho para proteger el medio ambiente.

_____ 4. Hoy estamos en Tulum, ¡y el paisaje es espectacular!

_____ 5. El mar está muy contaminado.

3 **La aventura en la selva** As you watch Felipe and Juan Carlos' flashback about their adventure in the jungle, place a check mark beside what you see.

_____ 1. un volcán   _____ 4. un desierto

_____ 2. unos árboles   _____ 5. un teléfono celular

_____ 3. unas plantas   _____ 6. una cámara

4 **¿Quién lo dijo?** Say who makes each statement, and fill in the blanks.

_____ 1. Espero que Felipe y Juan Carlos no estén perdidos en la _____...

_____ 2. No lo van a _____.

_____ 3. Estábamos muy emocionados porque íbamos a aprender sobre los

_____.

_____ 4. Por favor, síganme y eviten pisar las _____.

_____ 5. Decidí seguir un _____ que estaba cerca.

Video Manual: Escenas

Después de ver el video

5 **¿Cierto o falso?** Indicate whether each sentence is **cierto** or **falso**. If an item is false, rewrite it so it is correct.

1. Marissa dice que el paisaje de Tulum es espectacular.

_____

2. A Jimena le gustaría viajar a Wisconsin para visitar a Marissa.

_____

3. Según la guía, hay compañías que cuidaron la selva.

_____

4. Felipe y Juan Carlos estaban muy aburridos porque iban a conocer la selva.

_____

5. Marissa y Jimena aprendieron las normas que existen para cazar tortugas.

_____

_____

6 **Preguntas** Answer the following questions in Spanish.

1. ¿Por qué cree Jimena que ése es el último viaje del año que todos hacen juntos?

_____

_____

2. ¿Por qué estaban emocionados Juan Carlos y Felipe antes de visitar la selva?

_____

_____

3. ¿Por qué se separaron del grupo Juan Carlos y Felipe?

_____

_____

4. ¿Marissa cree la historia de Felipe?

_____

_____

5. Según Jimena, ¿qué pasa ahora con la población de tortugas?

_____

_____

7 **Describir** List a few things that people can do to protect your community's environment.

_____

_____

_____

_____

_____

_____

Corriendo por la ciudad

Lección 14

Antes de ver el video

1 **En la calle** In this episode, Maru needs to deliver a package but she experiences some problems. What do you think they might be?

_____

_____

_____

_____

_____

_____

_____

Mientras ves el video

2 **Ordenar** Watch **Corriendo por la ciudad** and number the following events from one to five, in the order they occurred.

_____ a. Maru le dice a Mónica que hay una joyería en el centro.

_____ b. Mónica dice que el correo está cerca.

_____ c. Maru busca el coche de Miguel.

_____ d. Maru habla por teléfono con su mamá.

_____ e. Maru cree que perdió el paquete.

3 **Completar** Fill in the blanks in the following sentences.

1. Voy a pasar al _____ porque necesito dinero.

2. ¿Puedes _____ por correo?

3. Estoy haciendo _____ y me gasté casi todo el efectivo.

4. Mi coche está en el _____ de la calle Constitución.

5. En esta esquina _____ a la derecha.

4 **¿Quién lo dijo?** Write the names of the people who said the following sentences.

_____ 1. Dobla en la avenida Hidalgo. Luego cruza la calle Independencia y dobla a la derecha.

_____ 2. Lo siento, tengo que ir a entregar un paquete.

_____ 3. Necesito ir a una joyería, pero la que está aquí al lado está cerrada.

_____ 4. Tengo que llegar al Museo de Antropología antes de que lo cierren.

_____ 5. Hay demasiado tráfico.

Video Manual: *Escenas*

Nombre _____ Fecha _____

Después de ver el video

5 **Seleccionar** Write the letter of the word or words that complete each sentence.

1. Maru le dice a Miguel que está enfrente ____.
   a. del salón de belleza   b. de la panadería   c. de la joyería

2. Maru decide irse en taxi al ____.
   a. banco   b. correo   c. museo

3. Maru le ____ a Mónica porque no tiene efectivo (*cash*).
   a. paga a plazos   b. pide dinero prestado   c. paga al contado

4. Mónica gastó el dinero en la carnicería, la frutería y ____.
   a. al supermercado   b. el salón de belleza   c. la panadería

5. ____ de Maru estaba en el coche de Miguel.
   a. El paquete   b. El dinero   c. La bolsa

6. Mónica ____ a la izquierda en el semáforo.
   a. hizo cola   b. dobló   c. cruzó

6 **Escribir** Write a summary of today's events from Maru's point of view.

_____
_____
_____
_____
_____
_____
_____
_____

7 **Las diligencias** Write a paragraph describing some of the errands you ran last week. What did they involve, and what places in your community did you visit?

_____
_____
_____
_____
_____
_____
_____
_____

Video Manual: Escenas

Chichén Itzá

Antes de ver el video

1 **Una excursión** List what you would probably do and say during a trip to an archaeological site.

_____
_____
_____
_____
_____
_____
_____

Mientras ves el video

2 **¿Quién?** As you watch this episode of the **Aventuras** video, indicate who said each sentence.

_____ 1. Chichén Itzá es impresionante.

_____ 2. Nuestros papás nos trajeron cuando éramos niños.

_____ 3. Hay que estar en buena forma para recorrer las ruinas.

_____ 4. Pues, a mí me gustan las gorditas.

_____ 5. Qué lástima que no dejen subir hasta la cima.

3 **Completar** Fill in the blanks in these sentences.

1. _____ bajo mucha presión.

2. La universidad hace que seamos _____.

3. ¿Y Juan Carlos todavía no te _____ a salir?

4. Ofrecemos varios servicios para _____.

5. Su _____ es muy importante para nosotros.

4 **Ordenar** Number the events from one to four, putting them in order.

_____ a. Felipe y Juan Carlos corren.

_____ b. Marissa y Felipe sacan fotos del lugar.

_____ c. Jimena y Juan Carlos se toman de las manos.

_____ d. Una empleada les explica a los chicos qué ofrecen en el spa.

Video Manual: *Escenas*

Después de ver el video

5 **¿Cierto o falso?** Indicate whether each sentence is **cierto** or **falso**. If an item is false, rewrite it so that it is true.

1. Felipe quería regresar al D.F. desde (*since*) que leyó el *Chilam Balam*.

_____

2. Marissa lee en la guía que el Castillo fue construido entre el año 1000 y el 1200 d. C. y es una de las siete maravillas del mundo moderno.

_____

3. Según Felipe, algunos dicen que los mayas inventaron la gimnasia.

_____

4. Jimena dice que se ha relajado mucho en la universidad últimamente.

_____

5. Jimena ya había estudiado mucho antes de salir del D.F.

_____

6 **Preguntas personales** Answer the following questions in Spanish.

1. ¿Haces ejercicio todos los días? ¿Por qué? _____

_____

2. ¿Sacas muchas fotos cuando estás de vacaciones? ¿Por qué? _____

_____

3. ¿Te gusta ir a un spa para aliviar la tensión? Explica por qué. _____

_____

4. ¿Has visitado una zona arqueológica tan impresionante como la que visitaron Marissa, Felipe, Jimena y Juan Carlos? ¿Dónde? _____

_____

5. ¿Quieres hacer una excursión como la que hicieron los cuatro estudiantes? Explica tu respuesta.

_____

_____

7 **Describir** Write a description of what you do or would like to do to reduce stress in your life.

_____

_____

_____

_____

_____

_____

_____

Nombre _____ Fecha _____

Antes de ver el video

1 **Planes para el futuro** Marissa, Jimena, Felipe, and Juan Carlos discuss their future plans in this episode. What do you think they will say?

_____
_____
_____
_____
_____
_____
_____

Mientras ves el video

2 **Planes y profesiones** Watch **La entrevista de trabajo**. Then indicate who makes each statement, and fill in the blanks with the missing words.

_____ 1. Cuando yo termine la carrera, a ti ya te habrán despedido (*they will have fired you*) de tu segundo _____.

_____ 2. Con el título de administrador de empresas seré _____.

_____ 3. Estoy muy feliz de poder ayudarte con _____.

_____ 4. Quiero trabajar en un museo y ser un _____ famoso.

_____ 5. Él será un excelente _____.

3 **Las profesiones** Place a check mark beside the professions mentioned.

____ 1. arqueóloga ____ 4. hombre de negocios

____ 2. política ____ 5. reportero

____ 3. doctora ____ 6. pintor

4 **Ordenar** Number the following events from one to five, in the order they occur.

____ a. Marissa dice que no sabe cómo será su vida cuando tenga 30 años.

____ b. Miguel le da su currículum a la señora Díaz.

____ c. La señora Díaz dice que Miguel es un pintor talentoso y un excelente profesor.

____ d. Juan Carlos dice que estudia ciencias ambientales.

____ e. Marissa dice que Felipe será un excelente hombre de negocios.

Después de ver el video

5 **Preguntas** Answer the following questions in Spanish.

1. ¿Quiénes van a crear una compañía de asesores de negocios?

_____

2. ¿Qué será Jimena en el futuro?

_____

3. ¿Quién trabaja en el Palacio de Bellas Artes desde hace cinco años?

_____

4. ¿Quién quiere seguir estudiando historia del arte?

_____

5. ¿Quién fue aceptada en el Museo de Antropología?

_____

6 **En tu opinión** Answer the following questions in Spanish.

1. En tu opinión, ¿cuál de los personajes (*characters*) va a tener la profesión más interesante?

Explica tu respuesta. _____

_____

2. ¿Cuál de los personajes será el/la más rico/a? Explica tu opinión. _____

_____

3. ¿Cuál de los personajes será el/la más famoso/a? Explica tu opinión. _____

_____

4. ¿Cuál de los personajes será el/la más feliz? _____

_____

5. ¿Cuáles de los personajes van a lograr sus metas (*achieve their goals*)? Explica tu opinión.

_____

_____

7 **Tus planes** Write a description of what your life will be like in five years. Don't forget to mention your family, friends, residence, hobbies, and occupation.

_____

_____

_____

_____

_____

_____

_____

_____

Video Manual: *Escenas*

FLASH CULTURA   # Lección 1

Encuentros en la plaza
Antes de ver el video

1   **Vos**   Most Argentinians use the pronoun **vos** instead of **tú** when talking to friends. In some cases, the verb in the **vos** form is different from the **tú** form; in others, it is the same. Look at these questions with **vos**. Can you guess what the **tú** equivalent is?

> **modelo**
>
> Vos: ¿Cómo te llamás?
> Tú: ¿Cómo te llamas?

1. Y vos, ¿cómo estás?

_____

2. ¿De dónde sos?

_____

_____

2   **¡En español!**   Look at the video still. Imagine a conversation between two of these people.

¡Hola! ¿Cómo te va? _____

_____

_____

_____

_____

_____

Mientras ves el video

3   **Completar**   What does Silvina say when she meets her friends? Complete these conversations.

A. (3:42-3:51)

Chico: Hola.

Chica: ¿(1) _____?

Chica y chico: ¡Cuánto tiempo! (*It's been so long!*)

Silvina: Sí, hace mucho, ¿no?

Chica: ¡Qué (2) _____ verte (*to see you*)!

Silvina: ¿(3) _____ están ustedes? ¿Bien?

Chica y chico: (4) _____ .

B. (4:12-4:19)

Silvina: Quiero (*I want*) presentarles a mi (5) _____ Gonzalo.

Chica: Hola, ¿qué (6) _____?

Gonzalo: Hola. Gonzalo. ¿Tú cómo te (7) _____?

Chica: Mariana.

Gonzalo: (8) _____, Mariana.

Lección 1 Flash Cultura Video Activities   **33**

Después de ver el video

4 **Ordenar** Pay attention to Silvina's actions and put them in the correct order.

_____ a. presenta a un amigo

_____ b. dice (*she says*): ¿Cómo están ustedes? ¿Bien?

_____ c. da (*she gives*) un beso y un abrazo

_____ d. camina (*she walks*) por la Plaza de Mayo

_____ e. dice: ¡Hasta pronto!

5 **¿Quién?** Indicate who would make each of these statements.

Statements	Long-time friends at a plaza	People meeting for the first time
1. ¡Qué bueno verte!		
2. Sí, hace mucho, ¿no?		
3. Les presento a mi amigo.		
4. ¿Cómo estás?		
5. Mucho gusto.		

6 **¡Cuánto tiempo!** Write a conversation you would have with a friend whom you have not seen in a long time. Include the expressions provided.

> ¡Cuánto tiempo!   ¡Qué bueno verte!
> Hace mucho.   ¿Qué tal?

_____

_____

_____

_____

_____

7 **Encuentros en la plaza** Describe two aspects of this episode that caught your attention: people, their physical proximity, activities they do, etc. Then, explain how those aspects are similar or different in your own culture. You may use English.

_____

_____

_____

_____

_____

FLASH CULTURA

Lección 2

Los estudios
Antes de ver el video

1 **Más vocabulario** Look over these useful words before you watch the video.

Vocabulario útil	
las ciencias biológicas y de la salud *biological and health sciences*	el cuarto año de la carrera *the fourth year of college*
las ciencias físico-matemáticas *physics and math*	dé clases *teaches* los estudios superiores *higher education*
¿Conoces a algún ex alumno reconocido? *Do you know any renowned alumni?*	la psicoterapia *psychotherapy*

2 **¡En español!** Look at the video still and answer these questions in Spanish. Carlos is in Mexico City; can you guess where? Who is Carlos talking to? What do you think this person does?

Carlos López, México, D.F.

_____
_____
_____
_____
_____
_____
_____
_____

Mientras ves el video

3 **Conversaciones** Complete these conversations between Carlos López and two students.

CARLOS LÓPEZ ¿(1) _____ te llamas?

ESTUDIANTE Héctor.

CARLOS LÓPEZ Héctor. ¿Y qué estudias?

ESTUDIANTE (2) _____ .

CARLOS LÓPEZ ¿Y cuál es tu materia favorita?

ESTUDIANTE Este… ahorita, (3) _____ de Roma.

CARLOS LÓPEZ ¿De dónde (4) _____ ?

ESTUDIANTE De Corea.

CARLOS LÓPEZ De Corea. ¿Te gusta estudiar en la (5) _____ ?

ESTUDIANTE Sí, me gusta mucho (*I like it a lot*).

CARLOS LÓPEZ ¿Qué estudias?

ESTUDIANTE Estoy estudiando (6) _____ .

4 **Identificar** Indicate which area of study each of these students and alumni is likely to study or have studied.

> Ciencias Biológicas y de la Salud   Ciencias Sociales
> Ciencias Físico-Matemáticas   Humanidades

Octavio Paz
Escritor

1. _____   2. _____   3. _____

Después de ver el video

5 **Oraciones** Complete each statement with the correct option.

> autobuses   estudio   profesor
> derecho   ex alumno   residencia estudiantil
> estudiantes   México, D.F.   universidad

1. _____ es un importante centro económico y cultural.

2. La UNAM es una _____ en la Ciudad de México.

3. La UNAM es como (*like*) una ciudad con _____ , policía y gobierno (*government*) propios (*own*).

4. Los _____ de la UNAM son de diferentes países.

5. Hay cuatro áreas principales de _____ .

6. Manuel Álvarez Bravo es un _____ famoso de la UNAM.

6 **¡Carlos López de visita (*on a visit*)!** Imagine that Carlos López visits your school and wants to find out about the institution, campus or facilities, classes, and students. Write a brief paragraph about what you would say.

> **modelo**
>
> ¡Hola, Carlos! Me llamo Rosa Estévez y estudio en la Universidad del Valle en Colombia. Hay muchos estudiantes de diferentes países. Este (*This*) semestre tomo clases...

_____

_____

_____

_____

_____

Video Manual: *Flash Cultura*

FLASH CULTURA   # Lección 3

La familia
Antes de ver el video

1   **Más vocabulario** Look over these useful words before you watch the video.

Vocabulario útil	
el canelazo *typical drink from Ecuador*	¡Qué familia tan grande tiene! *Your family is so big!*
la casa *house*	¡Qué grande es tu casa… ! *Your house is so big!*
Día de la Madre *Mother's Day*	¿Quién pelea con quién? *Who fights with whom?*
Ésta es la cocina. *This is the kitchen.*	te muestro *I'll show you*
Éste es un patio interior.	Vamos. *Let's go.*
This is an interior patio.	

2   **¡En español!** Look at the video still. Imagine what Mónica will say about families in Ecuador, and write a two- or three-sentence introduction to this episode.

Mónica, Quito

¡Hola, amigos! Bienvenidos a otra aventura de *Flash Cultura*. Hoy

vamos (*we are going*) a hablar de… _____

_____

_____

_____

_____

_____

_____

Mientras ves el video

3   **Identificar** Identify which family these people belong to: **los Valdivieso, los Bolaños**, or both.

Personas	Los Valdivieso	Los Bolaños
1. abuelos	_____	_____
2. novia	_____	_____
3. esposo	_____	_____
4. esposa	_____	_____
5. sobrinos	_____	_____
6. dos hijos y una hija	_____	_____

Video Manual: *Flash Cultura*

4 **Emparejar** Watch as Mrs. Valdivieso gives Mónica a tour of the house. Match the captions to the appropriate images.

1. _____   2. _____   3. _____

a. Y éste es el comedor...
   Todos comemos aquí.

d. Finalmente, ésta es
   la cocina.

b. Vamos, te enseño el
   resto de la casa.

e. ¿Qué están haciendo
   hoy en el parque?

c. Éste es un patio interior. Aquí
   hacemos reuniones familiares.

Después de ver el video

5 **¿Cierto o falso?** Indicate whether each statement is **cierto** (*true*) or **falso** (*false*).

1. En el parque, una familia celebra el Día de la Madre. _____
2. La familia Valdivieso representa la familia moderna y la familia Bolaños representa la
   familia tradicional. _____
3. Los Bolaños no viven (*do not live*) en Quito. _____
4. Bernardo tiene animales en su casa. _____
5. Los Valdivieso toman canelazo. _____

6 **¿Qué te gusta?** Imagine that you are one of the Valdivieso children and that Mónica asks you about your likes and dislikes. Select one of the children and write a paragraph using the cues provided.

bailar   dibujar   hermanos   padres

_____
_____
_____
_____

7 **Andy, un chico con novia** Andy's parents just found out that he has a girlfriend. Imagine that they are being introduced to her for the first time. Write five questions they would ask her.

_____
_____
_____
_____

Video Manual: *Flash Cultura*

FLASH CULTURA   # Lección 4

¡Fútbol en España!
Antes de ver el video

1   **Más vocabulario** Look over these useful words before you watch the video.

Vocabulario útil		
la afición *fans*	nunca *never*	seguro/a *sure*
más allá *beyond*	se junta (con) *is tied up (with)*	la válvula de escape *outlet*

2   **¡En español!** Look at the video still. Imagine what Mari Carmen will say about soccer in Spain, and write a two- or three-sentence introduction to this episode.

Mari Carmen Ortiz, Barcelona

¡Hola, amigos! ¡Bienvenidos a *Flash Cultura*! Hoy vamos a

hablar de... _____

_____

_____

_____

_____

Mientras ves el video

3   **Identificar** You might see any of these actions in a video about soccer in Spain. Check off the items you see in this episode.

___ a. celebrar un gol (*goal*)   ___ d. hablar con un jugador famoso   ___ g. celebrar en las calles (*streets*)

___ b. comer churros   ___ e. jugar al fútbol   ___ h. jugar al fútbol americano

___ c. ganar un premio (*award*)   ___ f. pasear en bicicleta

4   **Emparejar** Indicate which teams these people are affiliated with.

○ Barça   ○ Barça   ○ Barça

○ Real Madrid ○ Real Madrid ○ Real Madrid

○ no corresponde ○ no corresponde ○ no corresponde

Video Manual: *Flash Cultura*

Lección 4 Flash Cultura Video Activities   **39**

Después de ver el video

5 **Completar** Complete each statement with the correct option.

| aficionados al fútbol | brasileños | feo | guapo | Red Sox |

1. En España hay muchos _____.

2. Ronaldinho y Ronaldo son dos futbolistas (*soccer players*) _____ famosos.

3. La rivalidad entre el Barça y el Real Madrid es comparable con la rivalidad entre los Yankees y los _____ en béisbol.

4. Mari Carmen piensa que David Beckham es _____.

6 **Aficionados** Who are these fans? Imagine what they would say if they introduced themselves. Write information like their name, age, origin, team affiliation, and any other details that come to mind.

> **modelo**
>
> **Aficionado:** ¡Hola! Soy José Artigas y soy de Madrid. Mi equipo favorito es el Real Madrid. Miro todos los partidos en el estadio. ¡VIVA EL REAL MADRID! ¡Nunca pierde!

_____

_____

_____

_____

_____

_____

_____

_____

_____

_____

7 **David Beckham** Imagine that you are Mari Carmen and you decide to interview David Beckham. Write five questions you would ask him.

> **modelo**
>
> ¿Dónde prefieres vivir: en España o en los Estados Unidos?

_____

_____

_____

FLASH CULTURA   # Lección 5

¡Vacaciones en Perú!
Antes de ver el video

1 **Más vocabulario** Look over these useful words before you watch the video.

Vocabulario útil		
aislado/a *isolated*	**disfrutar** *to enjoy*	**se salvó** *was saved*
andino/a *Andean*	**el esfuerzo** *effort*	**la selva** *jungle*
ayudó *helped*	**hemos contratado** *we have hired*	**subir** *to climb, to go up*
el cultivo *farming*	**la obra** *work (of art)*	**la vuelta al mundo** *around the world*

2 **Completar** Complete these sentences. Make the necessary changes.

1. Machu Picchu es una _____ muy importante de la civilización inca.

   Esta (*This*) ciudad inca está rodeada (*surrounded*) de una gran _____.

2. Los incas fueron (*were*) grandes artistas y expertos en técnicas de _____

   como el sistema de terrazas (*terraces*).

3. Hoy muchos turistas van a _____ de las ruinas incas y del maravilloso paisaje

   (*landscape*) andino.

4. Cada año miles de personas deciden _____ hasta Machu Picchu por el Camino Inca.

3 **¡En español!** Look at the video still. Imagine what Omar will say about Machu Picchu, and write a two- or three-sentence introduction to this episode.

Omar Fuentes, Perú

¡Bienvenidos a otra aventura de *Flash Cultura*! Hoy estamos en…

_____

_____

_____

_____

Mientras ves el video

4 **Descripción** What does Noemí say about the lost city of Machu Picchu? Complete this quote.

"Omar, te cuento (*let me tell you*) que Machu Picchu se salvó de la invasión (1) _____

gracias a que se encuentra (*it's located*) (2) _____ sobre esta (3) _____ ,

como tú puedes ver. Y también la (4) _____ ayudó mucho… lo cubrió (*covered*)

rápidamente, y eso también contribuye."

Video Manual: *Flash Cultura*

5 **Emparejar** Watch the tourists describe their impressions of Machu Picchu. Match the captions to the appropriate people.

1. _____ 2. _____

3. _____ 4. _____

a. enigma y misterio   b. magnífico y misterioso   c. algo esplendoroso, algo único…

d. ¡Fantástico!   e. Nos encanta muchísimo.

Después de ver el video

6 **¿Cierto o falso?** Indicate whether each statement is **cierto** or **falso**.
1. Las ruinas de Machu Picchu están al lado del mar.
2. Hay menos de (*less than*) cien turistas por día en el santuario (*sanctuary*) inca.
3. Cuando visitas Machu Picchu, puedes contratar a un guía experto.
4. Todos los turistas llegan a Machu Picchu en autobús.
5. Omar pregunta a los turistas por qué visitan Machu Picchu.

7 **¡La vuelta al mundo!** Imagine that you are a travel agent and that the French globetrotting family you saw in the video is planning their next destination. Write a conversation between you and the mother. Suggest an exciting destination, describe the activities the family can do together, and then work out how to get there, where to stay, and for how long.

_____

_____

_____

_____

_____

FLASH CULTURA

Lección 6

Comprar en los mercados
Antes de ver el video

1 **Más vocabulario** Look over these useful words before you watch the video.

Vocabulario útil		
las artesanías *handicrafts*	la heladería *ice-cream shop*	la soda (C.R.) *food stall*
el camarón *shrimp*	el helado *ice cream*	la sopa de mondongo *tripe soup*
la carne *meat*	el pescado *fish*	suave *soft*
la flor *flower*	¡Pura vida! *Cool!, Alright!*	el/la tico/a *person from Costa Rica*
la fruta *fruit*	el regateo *haggling, bargaining*	vale *it costs*

2 **¡En español!** Look at the video still. Imagine what Randy will say about markets in Costa Rica, and write a two- or three-sentence introduction to this episode.

Randy Cruz, Costa Rica

¡Hola a todos! Hoy estamos en… _____

_____

_____

_____

_____

_____

Mientras ves el video

3 **¿Qué compran?** Identify which item(s) these people buy at the market.

1. _____   2. _____   3. _____

  a. frutas   b. artesanías   c. carne y pescado

  d. camarones y flores   e. zapatos

Video Manual: Flash Cultura

     Lección 6 Flash Cultura Video Activities   **43**

4 **Completar** Watch Randy bargain, and complete this conversation.

RANDY ¿(1) _____ vale?

VENDEDOR Trescientos (*300*) (2) _____ .

RANDY Trescientos colones el kilo. Me puede hacer un (3) _____ , ¿sí?

VENDEDOR Perfecto.

VENDEDOR OK... (4) _____ cuatro ochenta... cuatro y medio.

RANDY Cuatrocientos (*400*).

VENDEDOR Cuatro (5) _____ .

RANDY Cuatrocientos cuarenta.

VENDEDOR Sí, señor.

Después de ver el video

5 **Ordenar** Put Randy's actions in the correct order.

_____ a. Busca la heladería en el Mercado Central.

_____ b. Regatea el precio de unas papayas.

_____ c. Va al mercado al aire libre.

_____ d. Entrevista a personas en el Mercado Central.

_____ e. Toma sopa de mondongo, un plato (*dish*) típico de Costa Rica.

6 **¡Aquí no hay descuentos!** Imagine that Randy wants to buy an item of clothing that he really likes, but he doesn't have enough money to pay the full price. Write a conversation between Randy and a salesperson in which Randy negotiates the price. Be creative!

_____

_____

_____

_____

_____

7 **Preguntas** Answer these questions.

1. ¿En qué lugares o tipos de tiendas haces las compras generalmente? ¿Pequeñas tiendas, grandes almacenes o centros comerciales?

_____

2. ¿Con quién(es) sales generalmente a comprar ropa: solo/a (*alone*), con amigos o con alguien (*someone*) de tu familia? ¿Por qué?

_____

3. ¿Cómo prefieres pagar tus compras: con dinero o con tarjeta de crédito? ¿Por qué?

_____

4. ¿Esperas las rebajas para comprar cosas que quieres o no te importa (*you don't mind*) pagar el precio normal?

FLASH CULTURA   # Lección 7

Tapas para todos los días
Antes de ver el video

1   **Más vocabulario**   Look over these useful words before you watch the video.

Vocabulario útil

aquí *here*	informal *casual, informal*	preparaban unos platillos
los caracoles *snails*	País Vasco *Basque Country*	*used to prepare little dishes*
Cataluña *Catalonia*	*(autonomous community*	las tortillas de patata *Spanish*
(autonomous community	*in Spain)*	*potato omelets*
in Spain)	el pan *bread*	el trabajo *job; work*
contar los palillos *counting*	las porciones de comida	único/a *unique*
the toothpicks	*food portions*	
la escalivada *grilled vegetables*		

2   **Completar**   Complete this paragraph about **tapas**.

Las tapas son pequeñas (1) _____ que se sirven en bares y restaurantes de España.
Hay diferentes tipos de tapas: los (2) _____ y las (3) _____ son
algunos ejemplos. En algunos bares, los camareros (*waiters*) traen la comida, pero en lugares más
(*more*) (4) _____ el cliente toma las tapas en la barra (*bar*). Es muy común ir de
tapas solo o con amigos después del trabajo. Sin duda, ¡salir de tapas en España es una experiencia
fantástica y (5) _____ !

3   **¡En español!**   Look at the video still. Imagine what Mari Carmen will say about **tapas** in
Barcelona, and write a two- or three-sentence introduction to this episode.

Mari Carmen, España

¡Hola! Hoy estamos en Barcelona. Esta bonita ciudad... _____

_____

_____

_____

_____

Mientras ves el video

4   **Montaditos**   Indicate whether these statements about **montaditos** are **cierto** or **falso**.

1. Los clientes cuentan los palillos para saber cuánto pagar. _____

2. Los montaditos son informales. _____

3. Los montaditos son caros. _____

4. Los montaditos se preparan siempre con pan. _____

5. Hay montaditos en bares al aire libre solamente. _____

Video Manual: *Flash Cultura*

5 **Completar** (03:13 -03:29) Watch these people talk about **tapas** and complete this conversation.

MARI CARMEN ¿Cuándo sueles venir a (1) _____ tapas?

HOMBRE Generalmente (2) _____ del trabajo. Cuando al salir de trabajar

(3) _____ hambre, vengo (4) _____.

MARI CARMEN ¿Y vienes solo, vienes con amigos, o da igual (*doesn't it matter*)?

HOMBRE Da igual. Si alguien (5) _____ conmigo, mejor; y si no, vengo solo.

Después de ver el video

6 **¿Cierto o falso?** Indicate whether these statements are **cierto** or **falso.**

1. Mari Carmen pasea en motocicleta por el centro de Barcelona. _____

2. Mari Carmen entrevista a personas sobre sus hábitos después de ir al trabajo. _____

3. Una versión sobre el origen de las tapas dice que un rey (*king*) necesitaba (*needed*) comer pocas veces al día. _____

4. Los restaurantes elegantes y caros sirven montaditos. _____

5. La tradición del montadito proviene (*comes from*) del País Vasco. _____

6. Los pinchos son sólo platos fríos. _____

7 **Un día en la vida de...** Select one of these people and imagine a typical workday. Consider his or her daily routine as well as the time he or she gets up, goes to work, spends with friends, goes back home, and goes to sleep. Use the words provided.

más tarde	se acuesta	se levanta
por la noche	se cepilla los dientes	va al trabajo

_____

_____

_____

_____

_____

_____

FLASH CULTURA

Lección 8

La comida latina
Antes de ver el video

1 **Más vocabulario** Look over these useful words before you watch the video.

Vocabulario útil		
el arroz congrí *mixed rice and beans from Cuba*	el frijol *bean*	la rebanada *slice*
el azafrán *saffron*	el perejil *parsley*	la ropa vieja *Cuban shredded beef*
la carne molida *ground beef*	el picadillo a la habanera *Cuban-style ground beef*	el taco al pastor *Shepherd-style taco*
la carne picada *diced beef*	el plátano *banana*	la torta al pastor *traditional sandwich from Tijuana*
el cerdo *pork*	el pollo *chicken*	

2 **¡En español!** Look at the video still. Imagine what Leticia will say about **la comida latina** in Los Angeles, and write a two- or three-sentence introduction to this episode.

Leticia, Estados Unidos

¡Hola! Soy Leticia Arroyo desde Los Ángeles. Hoy vamos a hablar sobre... _____

_____

_____

_____

_____

_____

_____

Mientras ves el video

3 **Completar** (04:15 -04:48) Watch Leticia ask for recommendations to other clients in the restaurant and complete this conversation.

LETICIA Señoritas, ¿qué estamos (1) _____ de rico?

CLIENTE 1 Mojito.

LETICIA ¿Y de qué se trata el (2) _____?

CLIENTE 1 Es pollo con cebolla, arroz blanco, (3) _____ negros y plátanos fritos. Es delicioso.

LETICIA Rico. ¿Y el tuyo?

CLIENTE 2 Yo estoy comiendo (4) _____ con pollo, que es arroz amarillo, pollo y plátanos fritos.

LETICIA ¿Y otras cosas en el (5) _____ que están ricas también?

CLIENTE 2 A mí me (6) _____ la ropa vieja.

Video Manual: Flash Cultura

4 **Ordenar** Put these events in the correct order.

_____ a. Toma un café en el restaurante cubano.

_____ b. Leticia habla con el gerente *(manager)* de un supermercado.

_____ c. Leticia come picadillo, un plato típico cubano.

_____ d. La dueña de una taquería mexicana le muestra a Leticia diferentes platos mexicanos.

_____ e. Leticia compra frutas y verduras en un supermercado hispano.

Después de ver el video

5 **Emparejar** Match these expressions to the appropriate situations.

_____ 1. ¿Qué me recomienda?   _____ 4. ¿Está listo/a para ordenar?

_____ 2. ¡Se me hace agua la boca!   _____ 5. A la orden.

_____ 3. ¡Que se repita!

a. Eres un(a) empleado/a de una tienda. Ayudaste a un(a) cliente/a a hacer una compra. Él/Ella se despide y te dice gracias. ¿Qué le respondes?

b. Estás en un restaurante. Miraste el menú pero todavía no sabes *(know)* qué quieres comer. ¿Qué le dices al/a la camarero/a?

c. El/La camarero/a te dio el menú hace cinco minutos y ahora se acerca para preguntarte si sabes lo que quieres pedir. ¿Qué pregunta te hace?

d. Terminas de comer y pagas, estás muy contento/a por la comida y el servicio que recibiste. ¿Qué le dices al/a la camarero/a?

e. Acabas de entrar en un supermercado. Tienes mucho hambre y ves unos postres que te parecen *(seem)* deliciosos. ¿Qué dices?

6 **Un plato típico** Research one of these typical dishes or drinks from the Hispanic world. Find out about its ingredients, where it is typical, and any other information that you find interesting.

ropa vieja	malta Hatuey
Inca Kola	horchata
picadillo a la habanera	mate

_____

_____

_____

_____

_____

_____

_____

_____

FLASH CULTURA

Lección 9

Las fiestas
Antes de ver el video

1 **Más vocabulario** Look over these useful words before you watch the video.

<table>
<tr><td colspan="3" align="center">**Vocabulario útil**</td></tr>
<tr>
<td>alegrar *to make happy*
las artesanías *handicrafts*
el/la artesano/a *craftsperson;
 artisan*
los cabezudos *carnival figures
 with large heads*
la canción de Navidad
 Christmas carol</td>
<td>el cartel *poster*
la clausura *closing ceremony*
destacarse *to stand out*
el Día de Reyes *Three
 Kings' Day*
las frituras *fried foods; fritters*
la madera *wood*
la misa *mass*</td>
<td>la parranda *party*
la pintura *painting*
el santo de palo *wooden
 sculpture of saint*
tocar el tambor
 to play drums
los Tres Santos Reyes/Reyes
 Magos *Three Kings*</td>
</tr>
</table>

2 **Completar** Complete this paragraph about **la Navidad** in Puerto Rico.

En Puerto Rico, las Navidades no terminan después del (1) _____ como en el resto de los países hispanos, sino después de las fiestas de la calle San Sebastián. Hay muchas expresiones artísticas de (2) _____ locales; entre ellas se destacan los (3) _____, que son pequeñas estatuas (*statues*) de madera de vírgenes y santos. La (4) _____ empieza por la noche cuando las personas salen a disfrutar del baile y la música con amigos y familiares.

3 **¡En español!** Look at the video still. What do you think this episode will be about? Imagine what Diego will say and write a two- or three-sentence introduction to this episode.

Diego Palacios, Puerto Rico

¡Bienvenidos! Soy Diego Palacios de Puerto Rico. Hoy les quiero

mostrar… _____

_____

_____

_____

_____

Mientras ves el video

4 **Ordenar** Put Diego's actions in the correct order.

_____ a. Les preguntó a personas qué disfrutaban más de las fiestas.

_____ b. Bailó con los cabezudos en la calle.

_____ c. Habló con artesanos sobre los santos de palo.

_____ d. Tomó un helado de coco.

_____ e. Comió unas frituras (*fried foods*).

Video Manual: *Flash Cultura*

5 **Emparejar** Match the captions to the appropriate elements.

1. ___   2. ___

3. ___   4. ___

a. el güiro   b. los cabezudos   c. los santos de palo   d. los panderos   e. los carteles

Después de ver el video

6 **¿Cierto o falso?** Indicate whether each statement is **cierto** or **falso**.

1. Las Navidades en Puerto Rico terminan con del Día de Reyes. _____

2. Los artistas hacen cuadros y carteles sobre la Navidad. _____

3. En Puerto Rico, las celebraciones navideñas son totalmente religiosas. _____

4. Los santos de palo representan a personajes puertorriqueños. _____

5. Según un artesano, la pieza de artesanía más popular es la de los Tres Santos Reyes.

   _____

6. El güiro y el pandero son algunos de los instrumentos típicos de la música de estas fiestas.

   _____

7 **¡De parranda!** Imagine that you are an exchange student in Puerto Rico and that you are attending this celebration. You are dancing on the street when suddenly Diego spots you and decides to interview you. Tell him how you feel and what cultural aspects catch your attention. Make sure to include these words.

| artistas | bailar | cabezudos | de parranda | en la calle | tocar el tambor |

_____

_____

_____

_____

Video Manual: *Flash Cultura*

FLASH CULTURA   # Lección 10

La salud
Antes de ver el video

1 **Más vocabulario** Look over these useful words before you watch the video.

Vocabulario útil		
atender *to treat; to see (in a hospital)*	cumplir (una función) *to fulfill (a function/role)*	gratuito *free (of charge)*
atendido/a *treated*	esperar *to wait*	herido/a *injured*
brindar *to offer*	estar de guardia *to be on call*	el reportaje *story*
chocar *to crash*	golpeado/a *bruised*	se atienden pacientes *patients are treated*

2 **¡En español!** Look at the video still. Imagine what Silvina will say about hospitals in Argentina, and write a two- or three-sentence introduction to this episode.

Silvina Márquez, Argentina

¡Hola a todos! Hoy estamos en… _____
_____
_____
_____
_____

Mientras ves el video

3 **Problemas de salud** Match these statements to their corresponding video stills.

  1. ___

  2. ___

  3. ___

a. Tengo dolor de cabeza y me golpeé la cabeza.
d. Me chocó una bici.

b. Mi abuela estaba con un poco de tos.
e. Me salió una alergia.

c. Estoy congestionada.

Video Manual: Flash Cultura

4 **Completar** Watch Silvina interview a patient, and complete this conversation.

SILVINA ¿Y a vos qué te pasa? ¿Por qué estás aquí en la (1) _____?

PACIENTE Porque me salió una (2) _____ en la (3) _____ hace dos días y quería (*wanted*) saber qué tenía (*had*). ¿Y a vos qué te pasó?

SILVINA Yo tuve un accidente. Me (4) _____ una bici en el centro y mirá cómo quedé...

PACIENTE ... toda lastimada (*hurt*)...

SILVINA Sí, y aquí también, aquí también... Estoy toda (5) _____.

Después de ver el video

5 **Ordenar** Put Silvina's actions in the correct order.

_____ a. Le dio sus datos personales a la enfermera.

_____ b. Llegó a la guardia del hospital.

_____ c. Fue atendida por el doctor.

_____ d. Tuvo un accidente con una bicicleta.

_____ e. Entrevistó a pacientes.

6 **El sistema de salud en Argentina** Identify the main characteristics of the health system in Argentina. Use these guiding questions.

1. ¿Cómo es el sistema de salud: público, privado o mixto?

2. ¿Hay que pagar en los hospitales públicos?

3. ¿Qué son las guardias?

4. ¿Hay que esperar mucho para ser atendido/a?

5. ¿Cómo es la carrera de medicina?

6. ¿Qué similitudes y diferencias existen entre el sistema de salud en Argentina y el de tu país?

7 **¿Un pequeño accidente?** You were exploring the city of Buenos Aires when an aggressive pedestrian knocked you to the ground. You arrived in great pain at the **guardia** only to find the wait very long. Write your conversation with a nurse in which you explain your symptoms to convince him/her that this is *not* a minor accident and you should receive immediate care.

_____

_____

_____

_____

_____

_____

_____

_____

_____

_____

Video Manual: Flash Cultura

FLASH CULTURA

Lección 11

Maravillas de la tecnología
Antes de ver el video

1   Más vocabulario   Look over these useful words before you watch the video.

Vocabulario útil		
la afirmación cultural *cultural affirmation*	el/la cuzqueño/a *person from Cuzco*	la masificación *spread*
alejado/a *remote*	el desarrollo *development*	mejorar *to improve*
beneficiarse *to benefit*	el esfuerzo *effort*	el/la proveedor(a) *supplier*
chatear (*Spanglish*) *to chat*	al extranjero *abroad*	servirse de *to make use of*
	mandar *to send*	

2   La tecnología   Complete this paragraph about technology in Peru.

En Perú, la (1) _____ de Internet benefició el (2) _____ de la agricultura en las comunidades indígenas. Para estas comunidades es una herramienta (*tool*) importante para obtener e intercambiar información. También, en ciudades como Cuzco, los artistas y comerciantes que (3) _____ de Internet pueden (4) _____ el nivel (*level*) de ventas porque se conectan (5) _____ y así pueden vender sus productos en otros países.

3   ¡En español!   Look at the video still. Imagine what Omar will say about technology in Peru and write a two- or three-sentence introduction to this episode.

Omar Fuentes, Perú

¡Hola a todos! ¿Saben de qué vamos a hablar hoy? _____

_____

_____

_____

_____

Mientras ves el video

4   Completar   Watch Omar interview a young man, and complete their conversation.

OMAR   ¿Qué haces en medio de la Plaza de Armas usando una (1) _____?

JOVEN   Estoy mandándole un (2) _____ a mi novia en Quito.

OMAR   … en Quito… ¿Así que tú eres (3) _____?

JOVEN   Sí, soy ecuatoriano.

OMAR   Y… ¿qué tal? ¿Qué te (4) _____ el Cuzco? ¿Qué te parece el Perú?

JOVEN   Me encanta Cuzco porque se parece mucho a mi ciudad, pero me gusta un poco más porque puedo usar (5) _____ en medio de la plaza y (6) _____ me molesta.

Lección 11 Flash Cultura Video Activities   **53**

5 **Emparejar** Identify why these people use cell phones and Internet.

1. ___

2. ___

3. ___

a. para escribir mensajes a su novia

b. para comunicarse con su proveedor

c. para vender sus productos en el extranjero

d. para hacer una videoconferencia y hablar con su familia

e. para chatear con amigos

Después de ver el video

6 **¿Cierto o falso?** Indicate whether each statement is **cierto** o **falso**.

1. En Perú, los cibercafés son lugares exclusivos para los turistas. _____

2. Los cibercafés son conocidos como cabinas de Internet en Perú y están por todo el país. _____

3. A diferencia de los cibercafés, los teléfonos celulares ayudan a la comunicación rápida y económica. _____

4. La comunidad indígena de Perú se beneficia de las ventajas que ofrecen los cibercafés. _____

5. En la Plaza de Armas de Cuzco es posible navegar en la red de manera inalámbrica. _____

6. Las nuevas tecnologías de la comunicación no permiten a las comunidades indígenas reafirmarse culturalmente. _____

7 **Preguntas** Answer these questions.

1. ¿Para qué usas Internet?

_____

2. ¿Cómo te comunicas con tu familia y tus amigos cuando viajas?

_____

3. ¿Piensas que la masificación de la tecnología es buena? ¿Por qué?

_____

4. ¿Piensas que el servicio de Internet debe ser gratuito para todas las personas? ¿Por qué?

_____

8 **Un email** Remember the young man who was writing an e-mail to his girlfriend at the Plaza de Armas in Cuzco? Imagine you are the young man, and write an e-mail to his girlfriend telling her about living in Cuzco and how technology is used here.

¡Hola, mi amor! En este momento estoy en la Plaza de Armas de Cuzco. _____

_____

_____

_____

_____

_____

_____

FLASH CULTURA

Lección 12

La casa de Frida
Antes de ver el video

1   **Más vocabulario**   Look over these useful words before you watch the video.

Vocabulario útil		
el alma *soul*	contar con *to have; to feature*	el relicario *locket*
la artesanía *crafts*	convertirse en *to become*	el retrato *portrait*
el barro *clay*	la muleta *crutch*	la urna *urn*
la ceniza *ash*	el recorrido *tour*	el vidrio soplado *blown glass*

2   **Emparejar**   Match each definition to the appropriate word.

1. Es un aparato que ayuda a caminar a las personas que no pueden hacerlo por sí solas (*by themselves*). _____

2. Es el recipiente (*container*) donde se ponen las cenizas de una persona muerta. _____

3. Es una pintura de una persona. _____

4. tener, poseer _____

5. camino o itinerario en un museo, un parque, etc. _____

6. Transformarse en algo distinto de lo que era antes. _____

3   **¡En español!**   Look at the video still. Imagine what Carlos will say about **La Casa de Frida** and write a two- or three-sentence introduction to this episode.

Carlos López, México

¡Bienvenidos a otro episodio de *Flash Cultura*! Soy Carlos López

desde… _____

_____

_____

_____

_____

Mientras ves el video

4   **¿Dónde están?**   Identify where these items are located in Frida's museum.

¿Dónde están?	La cocina	La habitación
1. barro verde de Oaxaca		
2. la urna con sus cenizas		
3. los aparatos ortopédicos		
4. vidrio soplado		
5. la cama original		
6. artesanía de Metepec		

   Lección 12 Flash Cultura Video Activities   **55**

5 | **Impresiones** Listen to what these people say, and match the captions to the appropriate person.

1. ____   2. ____

3. ____   4. ____

a. Me encanta que todavía (*still*) tienen todas las cosas de Frida en su lugar...

b. tenemos la gran bendición (*blessing*) de que contamos con un jardinero que... trabajó (*worked*) para ellos.

c. A mí lo que más me gusta es la cocina y los jardines.

d. El espacio más impresionante de esta casa es la habitación de Frida.

e. ... para mí fueron unas buenas personas...

Después de ver el video

6 | **Ordenar** Put Carlos' actions in the correct order.

_____ a. Habló con distintas personas sobre el museo y sus impresiones.

_____ b. Caminó por las calles de Coyoacán.

_____ c. Pasó por el estudio y terminó el recorrido en la habitación de Frida.

_____ d. Mostró el cuadro *Viva la vida* y otras pinturas de Frida.

_____ e. Recorrió la cocina.

_____ f. Llegó al museo Casa de Frida Kahlo.

7 | **¿Qué te gustó más?** Choose an aspect of Frida's house and describe it. Is it similar or different to your own house? What do you find interesting about it?

_____

_____

_____

_____

_____

_____

_____

_____

Video Manual: *Flash Cultura*

FLASH CULTURA

Lección 13

Naturaleza en Costa Rica
Antes de ver el video

1 **Más vocabulario** Look over these useful words before you watch the video.

Vocabulario útil		
el balneario *spa*	las faldas *foot (of a*	el piso *ground*
el Cinturón de Fuego	*mountain or volcano)*	la profundidad *depth*
Ring of Fire	lanzar *to throw*	refrescarse *to refresh oneself*
cuidadoso/a *careful*	mantenerse fuera *to keep outside*	el rugido *roar*
derramado/a *spilled*	el milagro *miracle*	el ruido *noise*

2 **Completar** Complete this paragraph about volcanoes in Central America.

Los países centroamericanos crearon "La Ruta Colonial y de los volcanes" para atraer turismo cultural y ecológico a esta región. El recorrido (*tour*) de los volcanes es el itinerario favorito de los visitantes ya que éstos pueden escuchar los (1) _____ volcánicos y sentir el (2) _____ vibrando cuando caminan cerca. Es posible caminar por las (3) _____ de los volcanes que no están activos y observar la lava (4) _____ en antiguas erupciones. ¡Centroamérica es un (5) _____ de la naturaleza!

3 **¡En español!** Look at the video still. Imagine what Alberto will say about volcanoes and hot springs in Costa Rica and write a two- or three-sentence introduction to this episode.

Alberto Cuadra, Costa Rica

¡Bienvenidos a Costa Rica! Hoy vamos a visitar…_____

_____

_____

_____

_____

_____

Mientras ves el video

4 **¿Qué ves?** Identify the items you see in the video.

____ 1. cuatro monos juntos   ____ 5. el mar

____ 2. las montañas   ____ 6. dos ballenas

____ 3. un volcán   ____ 7. las aguas termales

____ 4. una tortuga marina   ____ 8. muchos pumas

Video Manual: Flash Cultura

5 **Completar** Complete this conversation between Alberto and the guide.

ALBERTO ¿Qué tan activo es el (1) _____ Arenal?

GUÍA El volcán Arenal se encuentra dentro de los volcanes más (2) _____ en el mundo. Se pueden observar las (3) _____ incandescentes, sobre todo en la noche... y en este momento, el sonido que (4) _____ es efecto de la actividad activa del volcán.

ALBERTO ¿Por qué es que el volcán produce este sonido?

GUÍA Bueno, es el efecto de las erupciones; la combinación también del aire, del (5) _____; cuando la (6) _____ sale y tiene el contacto con la parte externa.

Después de ver el video

6 **Ordenar** Put Alberto's actions in the correct order.

_____ a. Se cubrió con una toalla porque tenía frío.

_____ b. Caminó hasta el Parque Nacional Volcán Arenal.

_____ c. Vio caer las rocas incandescentes desde la ventana de su hotel.

_____ d. Cuando sintió que se movía el piso, tuvo miedo y salió corriendo.

_____ e. Se bañó en las aguas termales de origen volcánico.

_____ f. Conversó con el guía sobre el volcán.

7 **¡Defendamos al volcán!** Imagine that you are a forest ranger at the **volcán Arenal** park and you just learned that a highly-polluting company plans to move its plant near the park. Write a conversation between you and your colleagues at work in which you try to convince them to take action to prevent it.

_____

_____

_____

_____

_____

_____

8 **Ecoturismo** Alberto says that ecotourism represents the fastest growing subsector of the tourist industry. Identify the positive and negative aspects of ecotourism and then write a brief paragraph about it. You may use examples from the video.

Aspectos positivos	Aspectos negativos

_____

_____

_____

_____

_____

_____

Video Manual: *Flash Cultura*

FLASH CULTURA   # Lección 14

El Metro del D.F.
Antes de ver el video

1 **Más vocabulario** Look over these useful words before you watch the video.

Vocabulario útil		
ancho/a *wide*	contar con *to have, to offer*	repartido/a *spread*
el boleto *ticket*	debajo *underneath*	el siglo *century*
el camión *bus (Mexico)*	gratuito/a *free*	superado/a *surpassed*
el castillo *castle*	imponente *impressive*	la superficie *surface*
construido/a *built*	recorrer *to cover (traveling)*	ubicado/a *located*

2 **Completar** Complete these sentences.

1. En México se le dice _____ a los autobuses.
2. Los autobuses _____ distintos puntos de México, D.F.
3. El Metro tiene estaciones _____ por toda la ciudad.
4. El Bosque de Chapultepec está _____ en el centro de México, D.F.
5. El Metro es un servicio _____ para personas de más de 60 años.

3 **¡En español!** Look at the video still. Imagine what Carlos will say about **el Metro** in Mexico City and write a two- or three-sentence introduction to this episode.

Carlos López, México

¡Hola! Hoy vamos a hablar de… _____

_____

_____

_____

_____

Mientras ves el video

4 **¿Qué les gusta?** Identify what each of these passengers likes about **el Metro**.

1. ___   2. ___   3. ___

a. Es útil para ir a la escuela y visitar a mis compañeros.   b. Hay una parada (*stop*) cerca de mi casa.
c. Es un transporte seguro, rápido y cómodo.   d. Es barato y siempre me dan un descuento.
e. Hay mucha variedad de gente.

Video Manual: *Flash Cultura*

5 **¿Qué dice?** Identify the places Carlos mentions in the video.

_____ 1. una joyería del siglo pasado

_____ 2. las estaciones de metro superficiales

_____ 3. la Catedral Metropolitana

_____ 4. una panadería

_____ 5. un castillo construido en la montaña

_____ 6. el correo

_____ 7. un zoológico

_____ 8. un bosque en el centro de la ciudad

Después de ver el video

6 **¿Cierto o falso?** Indicate whether these statements are **cierto** or **falso**.

1. Carlos dice que el Metrobús es el sistema favorito de los ciudadanos. _____

2. Los tranvías circulan bajo la superficie de la ciudad. _____

3. En el Metro puedes recorrer los principales atractivos de México, D.F. _____

4. El Zócalo es la plaza principal de la capital mexicana. _____

7 **¿Cómo llego?** Imagine that you are in Mexico City. You want to go to **Los Reyes** and decided to take the subway, but got confused and end up in **Camarones**, the other end of the city! On a separate piece of paper, write a conversation in which you ask a person for directions to help you get to your destination. Use some of these expressions. You can also find a map of the **Metro** online.

cambiar de tren
las estaciones
   de transbordo
estar perdido
hasta
al norte
seguir derecho

FLASH CULTURA

Lección 15

¿Estrés? ¿Qué estrés?
Antes de ver el video

1 **Más vocabulario** Look over these useful words before you watch the video.

Vocabulario útil		
el ambiente *atmosphere*	el/la madrileño/a	remontarse *to go back (in time)*
el descanso *rest*	*person from Madrid*	retirarse *to retreat*
el espectáculo *show*	mantenerse sano/a	*(to a peaceful place)*
el estanque *pond*	*to stay healthy*	el retiro *retreat*
judío/a *Jewish*	el paseo *walk*	trotar *to jog*
llevadero/a *bearable*	remar *to row*	el vapor *steam*

2 **Completar** Complete this paragraph about **baños árabes**.

Madrid fue lugar de encuentro de tres culturas: musulmana, cristiana y (1) _____.
Los musulmanes, por ejemplo, introdujeron los famosos baños árabes que eran lugares de
(2) _____ donde las personas iban a (3) _____ a lugares tranquilos
y a socializar. Aunque en la actualidad los (4) _____ continúan disfrutando de estos
baños, existen muchas otras alternativas para mantenerse sanos y sin estrés.

3 **¡En español!** Look at the video still. Imagine what Miguel Ángel will say about **el estrés** in
Madrid and write a two- or three-sentence introduction to this episode.

Miguel Ángel Lagasca, España

¡Bienvenidos a Madrid! Hoy les quiero mostrar... _____

_____

_____

_____

_____

_____

_____

Mientras ves el video

4 **Completar** Listen to a man talking about his dog, and complete the conversation.

HOMBRE Bueno, a mí me espera además un (1) _____. Yo tengo un perro que se
llama Curro, que es un fenómeno... Gracias a él, pues, aparte del (2) _____ de
Madrid, sirve para (3) _____ y dar un paseíto, ¿eh?, y resulta muy agradable.
Más (4) _____ [...] Yo insisto que lo mejor en Madrid es tener un perro, si es
(5) _____ que se llame Curro, y dar un (6) _____ con él, y es
muy divertido.

5 **¿Estrés en Madrid?** Being the capital of Spain, Madrid has the hustle and bustle of any big city. Identify why these madrileños are stressed out.

1. ____   2. ____   3. ____

a. Porque durmieron en el parque para conseguir boletos.

b. Porque hay mucho tráfico en la ciudad.

c. Porque hay personas que les quieren quitar el lugar en la cola.

d. Porque tiene un perro muy agresivo.

e. Porque tienen que hacer largas colas para todo, sobre todo para espectáculos culturales.

Después de ver el video

6 **Preguntas** Answer each of these questions.

1. ¿Qué problema tiene Madrid que es típico de una gran ciudad?

_____

2. Menciona dos lugares adonde los madrileños van para desestresarse.

_____

3. ¿Quién es Curro? ¿Qué opina su dueño?

_____

4. ¿Cuáles son tres actividades saludables que se pueden hacer en el Parque del Retiro?

_____

5. ¿Cuántas salas de baños árabes tiene el Medina Mayrit?

_____

7 **No hablo español** Remember the American who cut in line for the show? The couple behind him did not succeed in making him go to the back of the line. What would you say to him? Write a conversation in which you tell him to go to the back of the line!

_____

_____

_____

_____

_____

_____

_____

_____

_____

_____

Video Manual: Flash Cultura

FLASH CULTURA

Lección 16

El mundo del trabajo
Antes de ver el video

1 **Más vocabulario** Look over these useful words before you watch the video.

Vocabulario útil		
el desarrollo *development*	(ser) exitoso/a *(to be) successful*	la madera *wood*
el destino *destination*		el nivel *level*
la elevación *height*	la fidelidad *loyalty*	la oportunidad *opportunity*

2 **Emparejar** Match each definition to the appropriate word.

_____ 1. Alguien o algo que tiene muy buena aceptación.

_____ 2. Meta, punto de llegada.

_____ 3. Conveniencia de tiempo y de lugar.

_____ 4. Parte sólida de los árboles cubierta por la corteza (*bark*).

_____ 5. Altura que algo alcanza, o a la que está colocado.

_____ 6. Distancia vertical de un punto de la tierra respecto al nivel del mar.

_____ 7. Progresar, crecer económica, social, cultural o políticamente.

_____ 8. Lealtad que alguien debe a otra persona.

a. elevación

b. madera

c. desarrollo

d. exitoso

e. nivel

f. destino

g. fidelidad

h. oportunidad

3 **¡En español!** Look at the video still. Imagine what Mónica will say about jobs in Ecuador and write a two- or three-sentence introduction to this episode.

Mónica, Ecuador

Hola, les saluda Mónica... _____

_____

_____

_____

_____

_____

_____

Mientras ves el video

4 **Marcar** Check off what you see while watching the video.

_____ 1. vendedor de periódicos

_____ 2. payaso

_____ 3. dentista

_____ 4. heladero

_____ 5. barrendera

_____ 6. hombre policía

_____ 7. médico

_____ 8. pintora

_____ 9. artesano

_____ 10. mesero

Video Manual: *Flash Cultura*

5

Impresiones Listen to what these people say, and match the captions to the appropriate person.

1. ____   2. ____   3. ____

a. Claro que sí. Soy la jefa.

b. Odio mi trabajo. Me pagan poquísimo (*very little*) y aparte, mi jefa es súper fastidiosa...

c. Lo que más me gusta de trabajar en Klein Tours es que ayudamos al desarrollo de nuestro país.

d. Bueno, la persona que quiera estar conmigo deberá recibirme con mi profesión ya que yo no tengo un horario de oficina normal.

Después de ver el video

6

¿Cierto o falso? Indicate whether each statement is **cierto** or **falso**. Correct the false statements.

1. Quito es una de las capitales de mayor elevación del mundo.

_____

2. La mujer policía trabaja desde muy temprano en la mañana.

_____

3. La peluquería de don Alfredo está ubicada en la calle García Moreno, debajo del Mercado Central en el centro de Quito.

_____

4. La profesión de don Alfredo es una tradición familiar.

_____

5. Klein Tours es una agencia de viajes especializada en excursiones por todo el territorio de la ciudad de Quito.

_____

6. Las principales áreas de trabajo de Klein Tours son ventas, operaciones, marketing y el área administrativa.

_____

7

Escribir From the following list choose a profession that you would like to work in. Then, write three **ventajas** y three **desventajas** for that profession.

| artista | dentista | mesero/a | peluquero/a | vendedor/a |
| barrendero/a | enfermero/a | payaso/a | policía | |

Ventajas	Desventajas
1. _____	1. _____
2. _____	2. _____
3. _____	3. _____

¡VIVAN LOS PAÍSES HISPANOS!

Lección 2

Los Estados Unidos

Antes de ver el video

1 **Más vocabulario** Look over these useful words and expressions before you watch the video.

Vocabulario útil		
algunos *some, a few*	espectáculos *shows*	millón *million*
beisbolistas *baseball players*	estaciones *stations*	mucha *large*
comparsa *parade*	este *this*	muchos *many*
concursos *contests*	ligas mayores *major leagues*	por ciento *percent*
diseñador *designer*	más *more*	su *their*
disfraces *costumes*	mayoría *majority*	tiene *has*
escritora *writer*		

2 **Deportes** In this video, you are going to learn about some famous Dominican baseball players. In preparation, answer these questions about sports.

1. What sports are popular in the United States? _____

2. What is your favorite sport? _____

3. Do you play any sports? Which ones? _____

Mientras ves el video

3 **Cognados** Check off all the cognates you hear during the video.

___ 1. agosto   ___ 3. celebrar   ___ 5. democracia   ___ 7. festival   ___ 9. intuición

___ 2. carnaval   ___ 4. discotecas   ___ 6. famosos   ___ 8. independencia   ___ 10. populares

Después de ver el video

4 **Responder** Answer the questions in Spanish. Use complete sentences.

1. ¿Cuántos hispanos hay en Estados Unidos?

_____

2. ¿De dónde son la mayoría de los hispanos en Estados Unidos?

_____

3. ¿Quiénes son Pedro Martínez y Manny Ramírez?

_____

4. ¿Dónde hay muchas discotecas y estaciones de radio hispanas?

_____

5. ¿Qué son WADO y Latino Mix?

_____

6. ¿Es Julia Álvarez una escritora dominicana?

_____

Video Manual: *¡Vivan los países hispanos!*

¡VIVAN LOS PAÍSES HISPANOS!   Lección 2

Canadá
Antes de ver el video

1 **Más vocabulario** Look over these useful words and expressions before you watch the video.

Vocabulario útil		
bancos *banks*	hijas *daughters*	periódico *newspaper*
campo *field*	investigadora científica *research scientist*	que *that*
canal de televisión *TV station*	mantienen *maintain*	revista *magazine*
ciudad *city*	mayoría *majority*	seguridad *safety*
comunidad *community*	ofrecen *offer*	sus *her*
escuelas *schools*	otras *others*	trabajadores *workers*
estudia *studies*	pasa *spends*	vive *lives*

2 **Responder** This video talks about the Hispanic community in Montreal. In preparation for watching the video, answer the following questions about your family's background.

1. Where were your parents born? And your grandparents? _____

2. If any of them came to the United States from another country, when and why did they come here?

_____

3. Are you familiar with the culture of the country of your ancestors? What do you know about their culture? Do you follow any of their traditions? Which ones? _____

_____

Mientras ves el video

3 **Marcar** Check off the nouns you hear while watching the video.

___ 1. apartamento   ___ 3. periódico   ___ 5. horas   ___ 7. instituciones   ___ 9. lápiz

___ 2. comunidad   ___ 4. escuela   ___ 6. hoteles   ___ 8. laboratorio   ___ 10. programa

Después de ver el video

4 **¿Cierto o falso?** Indicate whether these statements are **cierto** or **falso.** Correct the false statements.

1. Los hispanos en Montreal son de Argentina. _____

2. En Montreal no hay canales de televisión en español. _____

3. En Montreal hay hispanos importantes. _____

4. Una hispana importante en el campo de la biología es Ana María Seifert. _____

5. Ella vive con sus dos hijas en una mansión en Montreal. _____

6. Ella pasa muchas horas en el museo. _____

7. En su casa se mantienen muchas tradiciones argentinas. _____

8. Ella participa en convenciones nacionales e internacionales. _____

¡VIVAN LOS PAÍSES HISPANOS!

Lección 4

México
Antes de ver el video

1 **Más vocabulario** Look over these useful words before you watch the video.

Vocabulario útil			
día *day*	estos *these*	gente *people*	sentir *to feel*
energía *energy*	fiesta *party, celebration*	para *to*	valle *valley*

2 **Describir** In this video, you will learn about the archaeological ruins of Teotihuacán, where the celebration of the equinox takes place every year. Do you know what the equinox is? In English, try to write a description.

equinoccio: _____

_____

3 **Categorías** Categorize the words listed in the word bank.

arqueológicos	gente	increíble	mexicanos	Teotihuacán
capital mexicana	hacen	interesante	moderno	tienen
celebrar	hombres	jóvenes	mujeres	Valle de México
ciudad	importante	Latinoamérica	niños	van
escalar				

Lugares	Personas	Verbos	Adjetivos

Mientras ves el video

4 **Marcar** Check off the pastimes you see while watching the video.

_____ 1. pasear   _____ 4. escalar (pirámides)   _____ 7. visitar monumentos

_____ 2. nadar   _____ 5. tomar el sol   _____ 8. bucear

_____ 3. patinar   _____ 6. ver películas

Después de ver el video

5 **Completar** Fill in the blanks with the appropriate word(s).

la capital mexicana	muy interesante
la celebración del *equinoccio*	pasean
celebrar	sentir
comienzan	sol
manos	el Valle de México

1. Teotihuacán está a cincuenta kilómetros de _____.

2. A _____ van muchos grupos de música tradicional.

3. Todos quieren _____ la energía del sol en sus _____.

4. Ir a las pirámides de Teotihuacán es una experiencia _____.

5. Las personas _____ por las ruinas.

6 **¿Cierto o falso?** Indicate whether each statement is **cierto** or **falso**. Correct the false statements.

1. Las pirámides de Teotihuacán están lejos del Valle de México.

   _____

2. Muchas personas van a Teotihuacán todos los años para celebrar el *equinoccio*.

   _____

3. Turistas de muchas nacionalidades van a la celebración.

   _____

4. La gente prefiere ir a Teotihuacán en sus ratos libres.

   _____

5. La celebración del equinoccio termina a las cinco de la mañana.

   _____

6. Las personas celebran la energía que reciben de Teotihuacán todos los años.

   _____

7 **Foto** Describe the video still. Write at least three sentences in Spanish.

_____

_____

_____

_____

¡VIVAN LOS PAÍSES HISPANOS!

Lección 6

Puerto Rico
Antes de ver el video

1   **Más vocabulario** Look over these useful words before you watch the video.

Vocabulario útil		
angosto *narrow*	calle *street*	plaza *square*
antiguo *old*	escultura *sculpture*	promocionar *to promote*
artesanías *handicrafts*	exposición *exhibition*	sitio *site*
bahía *bay*	fuente *fountain*	vender *to sell*
barrio *neighborhood*		

Mientras ves el video

2   **Cognados** Check off all the cognates you hear during the video.

_____ 1. aeropuerto   _____ 9. estrés

_____ 2. área   _____ 10. histórico

_____ 3. arte   _____ 11. información

_____ 4. artístico   _____ 12. nacional

_____ 5. cafés   _____ 13. permanente

_____ 6. calma   _____ 14. presidente

_____ 7. capital   _____ 15. restaurantes

_____ 8. construcciones

Después de ver el video

3   **Completar** Complete the sentences with words from the word bank.

camina	coloniales	excelente	galerías	plaza
capital	esculturas	exposición	hermoso	promociona

1. En la bahía de la _____ de Puerto Rico está el Castillo de San Felipe del Morro.

2. Muchas de las construcciones del Viejo San Juan son _____.

3. En la mayoría de los parques hay _____ inspiradas en la historia del país.

4. El Instituto de Cultura Puertorriqueña _____ eventos culturales en la isla.

5. Hay muchas _____ de arte y museos.

6. En el Museo de San Juan hay una _____ permanente de la historia de Puerto Rico.

     Lección 6 Video Activities   **69**

¡VIVAN LOS PAÍSES HISPANOS!

Cuba

Antes de ver el video

1 **Más vocabulario** Look over these useful words before you watch the video.

Vocabulario útil	
conversar *to talk*	relacionadas *related to*
imágenes *images (in this case, of a religious nature)*	relaciones *relationships*
miembro *member*	sacerdote *priest*

Mientras ves el video

2 **Marcar** Check off the activities you see while watching the video.

_____ 1. hombre escribiendo

_____ 2. hombre leyendo

_____ 3. mujer corriendo

_____ 4. mujer llorando (*crying*)

_____ 5. niño jugando

_____ 6. personas bailando

_____ 7. personas caminando

_____ 8. personas cantando

_____ 9. personas conversando

Después de ver el video

3 **¿Cierto o falso?** Indicate whether each statement is **cierto** or **falso.** Correct the false statements.

1. Cada tres horas sale un barco de La Habana con destino a Regla.

_____

2. Regla es una ciudad donde se practica la santería.

_____

3. La santería es una práctica religiosa muy común en algunos países latinoamericanos.

_____

4. Los santeros no son personas importantes en su comunidad.

_____

5. La santería es una de las tradiciones cubanas más viejas.

_____

¡VIVAN LOS PAÍSES HISPANOS!

Lección 6

La República Dominicana
Antes de ver el video

1   **Más vocabulario**   Look over these useful words and expressions before you watch the video.

Vocabulario útil	
crear *to create, to form*	**papel** *role*
emigrantes *emigrants*	**ritmos** *rhythms*
fiestas nacionales *national festivals*	**tocar (música)** *to play (music)*

2   **Preguntas**   This video talks about two musical genres famous in the Dominican Republic. In preparation for watching the video, answer these questions.

1. ¿Cuál es el género (*genre*) musical estadounidense con más fama internacional?

   _____

2. ¿Te gusta esta música? ¿Por qué?

   _____

Mientras ves el video

3   **Marcar**   Check off the activities, things, and places you see in the video.

_____ 1. niños sonriendo   _____ 6. espectáculo de baile en teatro

_____ 2. mujer vendiendo ropa   _____ 7. bandera (*flag*) de la República Dominicana

_____ 3. parejas bailando   _____ 8. mujer peinándose

_____ 4. hombre tocando acordeón   _____ 9. boulevard

_____ 5. niño jugando al fútbol   _____ 10. playa

Después de ver el video

4   **Corregir**   The underlined elements in the sentences are incorrect. Write the correct words in the spaces provided.

1. Uno de los mejores ejemplos de la mezcla (*mix*) de culturas en la República Dominicana es la <u>arquitectura</u>.

   La palabra correcta es: _____

2. El Festival del Merengue se celebra en las <u>plazas</u> de Santo Domingo todos los veranos.

   La palabra correcta es: _____

3. La música de República Dominicana está influenciada por la música tradicional de <u>Asia</u>.

   La palabra correcta es: _____

4. En todo el país hay discotecas donde se toca y se baila la bachata y el <u>jazz</u>.

La palabra correcta es: _____

5. El veintisiete de febrero de cada año los dominicanos celebran el día de la <u>madre</u>.

La palabra correcta es: _____

6. La bachata y el merengue son ritmos <u>poco</u> populares en la República Dominicana.

La palabra correcta es: _____

5 **Emparejar** Find the items in the second column that correspond to the ones in the first.

_____ 1. Aquí la gente baila la bachata y el merengue.

_____ 2. Este músico recibió en 1966 la medalla presidencial.

_____ 3. *El Bachatón*

_____ 4. Juan Luis Guerra, Johnny Ventura y Wilfredo Vargas

_____ 5. La música dominicana recibió la influencia de estas personas.

a. Johnny Pacheco

b. varios de los muchos músicos de bachata y merengue con fama internacional

c. los indígenas que vivían en la región

d. las discotecas de la ciudad

e. En este programa de televisión sólo se toca la bachata.

6 **Seleccionar** Select the sentence that best summarizes what you saw in this video.

_____ 1. Por muchos años, muchos emigrantes llegaron a la República Dominicana y crearon la actual cultura dominicana.

_____ 2. Todas las estaciones de radio tocan bachata y hay un programa de televisión muy popular dedicado exclusivamente a esta música, llamado *El Bachatón*.

_____ 3. Los ritmos más populares de la República Dominicana, la bachata y el merengue, son producto de varias culturas y forman parte integral de la vida de los dominicanos.

_____ 4. Una fiesta tradicional dominicana es el Festival del Merengue, que se celebra todos los veranos desde 1966 por las calles de Santo Domingo.

7 **Responder** Answer the questions in Spanish. Use complete sentences.

1. ¿Cuál es tu música favorita? ¿Por qué?

_____

2. ¿Dónde escuchas esta música? ¿Cuándo?

_____

3. ¿Quiénes son los intérpretes más famosos de esta música? ¿Cuál de ellos te gusta más?

_____

4. ¿Te gusta bailar? ¿Qué tipo de música bailas?

_____

5. ¿Es la música algo importante en tu vida? ¿Por qué?

_____

Video Manual: ¡Vivan los países hispanos!

¡VIVAN LOS PAÍSES HISPANOS!

Lección 8

Venezuela

Antes de ver el video

1 **Más vocabulario** Look over these useful words before you watch the video.

Vocabulario útil		
castillo *castle*	fuerte *fort*	plana *flat*
catarata *waterfall*	maravilla *wonder*	según *according to*
cima *top*	medir *to measure*	teleférico *cable railway*

Mientras ves el video

2 **Marcar** Check off the cognates you hear while watching the video.

_____ 1. animales

_____ 2. arquitectura

_____ 3. construcción

_____ 4. diversa

_____ 5. famoso

_____ 6. geológicas

_____ 7. horizontales

_____ 8. marina

_____ 9. mitología

_____ 10. naturales

_____ 11. plantas

_____ 12. verticales

Después de ver el video

3 **Completar** Complete the sentences with words from the word bank. Some words will not be used.

clase	islas	metros	río	verticales
fuertes	marina	planas	teleférico	

1. En Venezuela hay castillos y _____ que sirvieron para proteger al país hace muchos años.

2. En Venezuela hay más de 311 _____.

3. La isla Margarita tiene una fauna _____ muy diversa.

4. Los hoteles de isla Margarita son de primera _____.

5. El Parque Nacional Canaima tiene 38 grandes montañas de paredes _____ y cimas _____.

6. Venezuela también tiene el _____ más largo del mundo.

4 **Escribir** In Spanish, list the three things you found most interesting in this video and explain your choices. Use complete sentences.

_____

_____

_____

¡VIVAN LOS PAÍSES HISPANOS!

Lección 8

Colombia
Antes de ver el video

1 **Más vocabulario** Look over these useful words and expressions before you watch the video.

Vocabulario útil	
alrededores *surrounding area*	delfín *dolphin*
belleza natural *natural beauty*	desfile *parade*
campesinos *country/rural people*	disfrutar (de) *to enjoy*
carroza *float*	feria *fair*
cordillera *mountain range*	fiesta *festival*
costas *coasts*	orquídea *orchid*

Mientras ves el video

2 **Preguntas** Answer the question about the video still. Use complete sentences.

¿Cómo se llama esta celebración?

_____

_____

Después de ver el video

3 **Emparejar** Find the items in the second column that correspond to the ones in the first.

_____ 1. El grano colombiano que se exporta mucho.   a. el café
_____ 2. el Carnaval de Barranquilla   b. el Parque Amaracayu
_____ 3. En Colombia crecen muchas.   c. un desfile de carrozas decordas
_____ 4. Aquí vive el delfín rosado.   d. orquídeas
_____ 5. desfile de los silleteros   e. Feria de las Flores
_____ 6. Aquí vive el cóndor.   f. Nevado del Huila

4 **Responder** Answer these questions in Spanish. Use complete sentences.

1. ¿Cuál crees que es el carnaval más famoso del mundo? ¿Por qué?

_____

_____

2. ¿Cuál es el carnaval más famoso de los Estados Unidos? ¿Cómo se celebra?

_____

_____

¡VIVAN LOS PAÍSES HISPANOS!

Lección 8

Ecuador

Antes de ver el video

1   **Más vocabulario**   Look over these useful words and expressions before you watch the video.

Vocabulario útil		
algunas *some*	otro *other*	todo *every*
científico *scientist*	pingüino *penguin*	tomar fotografías *to take pictures*
guía *guide*	recurso *resource*	tortuga *turtle*

Mientras ves el video

2   **Marcar**   Check off the verbs you hear while watching the video.

_____ 1. aprender   _____ 5. escribir   _____ 9. tener

_____ 2. bailar   _____ 6. estudiar   _____ 10. tomar

_____ 3. beber   _____ 7. leer   _____ 11. vivir

_____ 4. comprar   _____ 8. recibir

Después de ver el video

3   **Responder**   Answer the questions in Spanish. Use complete sentences.

1. ¿En qué océano están las islas Galápagos?

_____

_____

2. ¿Qué hacen los científicos que viven en las islas?

_____

_____

3. ¿Qué hacen los turistas que visitan las islas?

_____

_____

4. ¿Qué proyectos tiene la Fundación Charles Darwin?

_____

_____

5. ¿Cuáles son los animales más grandes que viven en las islas?

_____

_____

6. ¿Por qué son importantes estas islas?

_____

_____

¡VIVAN LOS PAÍSES HISPANOS!

Lección 8

Perú

Antes de ver el video

1 **Más vocabulario** Look over these useful words and expressions before you watch the video.

Vocabulario útil		
canoa *canoe*	exuberante naturaleza	ruta *route, path*
dunas *sand dunes*	*lush countryside*	tabla *board*

Mientras ves el video

2 **Fotos** Describe the video stills. Write at least three sentences in Spanish for each still.

_____

_____

_____

_____

_____

_____

_____

_____

_____

_____

Después de ver el video

3 **Completar** Complete the sentences with words from the word bank.

aventura	kilómetros	pesca
excursión	llamas	restaurante
exuberante	parque	tradicional

1. En el Perú se practican muchos deportes de _____.

2. Pachamac está a 31 _____ de Lima.

3. La naturaleza en Santa Cruz es muy _____.

4. En el Perú, uno de los deportes más antiguos es la _____ en pequeñas canoas.

5. Caminar con _____ es uno de los deportes tradicionales en el Perú.

6. Santa Cruz es un sitio ideal para ir de _____.

¡VIVAN LOS PAÍSES HISPANOS!

Lección 10

Argentina
Antes de ver el video

1 **Más vocabulario** Look over these useful words and expressions before you watch the video.

Vocabulario útil		
actualmente *nowadays*	**gaucho** *cowboy*	**paso** *step*
barrio *neighborhood*	**género** *genre*	**salón de baile** *ballroom*
cantante *singer*	**homenaje** *tribute*	**suelo** *floor*
exponer *to exhibit*	**pareja** *partner*	**surgir** *to emerge*
extrañar *to miss*	**pintura** *paint*	**tocar** *to play*

2 **Completar** The previous vocabulary will be used in this video. In preparation for watching the video, complete the sentences using words from the vocabulary list. Conjugate the verbs as necessary. Some words will not be used.

1. Los artistas _____ sus pinturas en las calles.

2. Beyoncé es una _____ famosa.

3. El tango tiene _____ muy complicados.

4. El jazz es un _____ musical que se originó en los Estados Unidos.

5. El tango _____ en Buenos Aires, Argentina.

6. La gente va a los _____ a divertirse.

7. Las personas _____ mucho a su país cuando tienen que vivir en el extranjero.

Mientras ves el video

3 **Marcar** Check off the cognates you hear while watching the video.

_____ 1. adultos

_____ 2. aniversario

_____ 3. arquitectura

_____ 4. artistas

_____ 5. demostración

_____ 6. conferencia

_____ 7. dramático

_____ 8. exclusivamente

_____ 9. famosos

_____ 10. gráfica

_____ 11. impacto

_____ 12. musical

Después de ver el video

4 **¿Cierto o falso?** Indicate whether each statement is **cierto** or **falso**. Correct the false statements.

1. Guillermo Alio dibuja en el suelo una gráfica para enseñar a cantar.

_____

2. El tango es música, danza, poesía y pintura.

_____

3. Alio es un artista que baila y canta al mismo (*same*) tiempo.

_____

4. Alio y su pareja se ponen pintura verde en los zapatos.

_____

5. Ahora los tangos son historias de hombres que sufren por amor.

_____

6. El tango tiene un tono dramático y nostálgico.

_____

_____

5 **Completar** Complete the sentences with words from the word bank.

actualmente	compositor	fiesta	género	homenaje	pintor	surgió	toca

1. El tango es un _____ musical que se originó en Argentina en 1880.

2. El tango _____ en el barrio La Boca.

3. _____ este barrio se considera un museo al aire libre.

4. En la calle Caminito se _____ y se baila el tango.

5. Carlos Gardel fue el _____ de varios de los tangos más famosos.

6. En el aniversario de su muerte, sus aficionados le hacen un _____.

_____

6 **Responder** Answer the questions in Spanish. Use complete sentences.

1. ¿Por qué crees que el tango es tan famoso en todo el mundo?

_____

2. ¿Te gustaría (*Would you like*) aprender a bailar tango? ¿Por qué?

_____

3. ¿Qué tipo de música te gusta? Explica tu respuesta.

_____

¡VIVAN LOS PAÍSES HISPANOS!

Lección 10

Chile
Antes de ver el video

1 **Más vocabulario** Look over these useful words and expressions before you watch the video.

Vocabulario útil	
disfrutar (de) *to enjoy*	isla *island*
grados *degrees*	recursos naturales *natural resources*
hace miles de años *thousands of years ago*	repartidas *spread throughout, distributed*
indígena *indigenous*	vista *view*

Mientras ves el video

2 **Fotos** Describe the video stills. Write at least three sentences in Spanish for each still.

_____
_____
_____
_____
_____

_____
_____
_____
_____
_____

Después de ver el video

3 **Completar** Complete the sentences with words from the word bank.

atracción	diferente	escalan	llega	remoto
característico	difícil	indígena	recursos	repartidas

1. *Rapa Nui* es el nombre de la isla de Pascua en la lengua _____ de la región.

2. Esta isla está en un lugar _____.

3. Los habitantes de esta isla no tenían muchos _____ naturales.

4. En un día de verano la temperatura _____ a los 90°.

5. Las esculturas *moái* son el elemento más _____ de esta isla.

6. Hay más de novecientas esculturas _____ por toda la isla.

7. Otra gran _____ de la isla es el gran cráter Rano Kau.

8. Los visitantes _____ el cráter para disfrutar de la espectacular vista.

Video Manual: ¡Vivan los países hispanos!

¡VIVAN LOS PAÍSES HISPANOS!   Lección 10

Uruguay
Antes de ver el video

1   **Más vocabulario**   Look over these useful words and expressions before you watch the video.

Vocabulario útil		
asado *barbecue*	campos *rural areas*	jineteadas *rodeo*
cabalgatas colectivas *caravans*	ganadería *ranching*	ranchos ganaderos *cattle ranches*
caballos *horses*	gauchos *cowboys*	siglos *centuries*

2   **Predecir**   Based on the video stills, write what you think the video will be about.

_____

_____

_____

_____

Mientras ves el video

3   **Describir**   Write a short description of the items.

1. Las estancias son _____

2. Los gauchos son _____

3. Las cabalgatas colectivas son _____

4. Las jineteadas son _____

Después de ver el video

4   **Responder**   Answer the questions in Spanish.

1. ¿Te gustaría quedarte por unos días en una estancia? ¿Por qué?

_____

2. ¿Por qué crees que a los turistas les gustan estos lugares? ¿Por qué son tan especiales?

_____

3. ¿Hay en tu país hoteles parecidos a las estancias? ¿Cómo son?

_____

¡VIVAN LOS PAÍSES HISPANOS!　Lección 10

Paraguay

Antes de ver el video

1 **Más vocabulario** Look over these useful words and expressions before you watch the video.

Vocabulario útil			
alimento *food*	cortar *to cut*	hervir *to boil*	suplemento
amargo *bitter*	cultivar *to cultivate*	hojas *leaves*	alimenticio
asegurar *to maintain*	empresas *companies*	quemar *to burn*	*dietary*
calabaza *pumpkin*	fuente *source*	sagrada *sacred*	*supplement*

Mientras ves el video

2 **Ordenar** Number the sentences in the order in which they appear in the video.

_____ a. El mate es un alimento.

_____ b. Hay muchas técnicas para preparar el mate.

_____ c. Tomar mate era ilegal.

_____ d. El mate se toma a toda hora.

_____ e. La yerba mate crece en América del Sur.

_____ f. El mate tiene vitaminas, minerales y antioxidantes.

_____ g. El mate tiene un sabor amargo.

_____ h. Los indígenas guaraní creían que esta planta era un regalo de sus antepasados.

_____ i. El mate es típico de Paraguay, Argentina y Uruguay.

_____ j. El mate es usado por personas que quieren adelgazar.

Después de ver el video

3 **Fotos** Describe the video stills. Write at least three sentences in Spanish for each one.

_____

_____

_____

_____

_____

_____

_____

_____

¡VIVAN LOS PAÍSES HISPANOS!

Lección 10

Bolivia

Antes de ver el video

1 **Más vocabulario** Look over these useful words before you watch the video.

Vocabulario útil		
alimento *food*	particular *unique*	tratamiento *treatment*
enorme *enormous*	salar *salt flat*	

2 **Foto** Describe the video still. Write at least three sentences in Spanish.

_____

_____

_____

_____

_____

Mientras ves el video

3 **Marcar** Check off the cognates you hear while watching the video.

_____ 1. abundante   _____ 4. contacto   _____ 7. estrés   _____ 10. extraordinario

_____ 2. arte   _____ 5. cultura   _____ 8. exceso   _____ 11. presente

_____ 3. color   _____ 6. diversa   _____ 9. exótico   _____ 12. región

Después de ver el video

4 **Palabra correcta** The underlined elements in these statements are incorrect. Write the correct word on the space provided.

1. El salar de Uyuni está al <u>norte</u> de Bolivia. _____

2. La sal, sin exceso, es <u>mala</u> para las personas que sufren de enfermedades de los huesos.

   _____

3. Los hoteles de esta región se hicieron con cuidado porque el contacto en exceso con la sal es

   <u>excelente</u> para la salud. _____

4. Estos hoteles ofrecen a los huéspedes masajes y otros tratamientos para aliviar el <u>acné</u>.

   _____

5. La sal se usa en Uyuni para <u>dañar</u> los alimentos. _____

6. El salar de Uyuni parece un gran <u>parque</u> de color blanco. _____

¡VIVAN LOS PAÍSES HISPANOS!

Lección 12

Guatemala
Antes de ver el video

1 **Más vocabulario** Look over these useful words and expressions before you watch the video.

Vocabulario útil		
alfombra *rug*	destruir *to destroy*	ruinas *ruins*
artículos *items*	época colonial *colonial times*	sobrevivir *to survive*
calle *street*	indígenas *indigenous people*	terremoto *earthquake*

2 **Describir** In this video you are going to learn about an open-air market in Guatemala. In Spanish, describe one open-air market that you know.

mercado: _____

_____

_____

_____

_____

_____

3 **Categorías** Categorize the words listed in the word bank.

bonitas	espectaculares	indígenas	quieres
calles	grandes	mercado	región
colonial	habitantes	monasterios	sentir
conocer	iglesias	mujeres	vieja

Lugares	Personas	Verbos	Adjetivos

Mientras ves el video

4 **Marcar** Check off what you see while watching the video.

_____ 1. fuente (*fountain*)

_____ 2. hombres con vestidos morados

_____ 3. mujer bailando

_____ 4. mujer llevando bebé en el mercado

_____ 5. mujeres haciendo alfombras de flores

_____ 6. niñas sonriendo

_____ 7. niño dibujando

_____ 8. personas hablando

_____ 9. ruinas

_____ 10. turista mirando el paisaje

Después de ver el video

5 **Completar** Complete the sentences with words from the word bank.

| aire libre | alfombras | atmósfera | fijo | indígenas | regatear |

1. En Semana Santa las mujeres hacen _____ con miles de flores.

2. En Chichicastenango hay un mercado al _____ los jueves y domingos.

3. En el mercado los artículos no tienen un precio _____.

4. Los clientes tienen que _____ cuando hacen sus compras.

5. En las calles de Antigua, los turistas pueden sentir la _____ del pasado.

6. Muchos _____ de toda la región vienen al mercado a vender sus productos.

6 **¿Cierto o falso?** Indicate whether each statement is **cierto** or **falso**. Correct the false statements.

1. Antigua fue la capital de Guatemala hasta 1773.

_____

2. Una de las celebraciones más importantes de Antigua es la de Semana Santa.

_____

3. En esta celebración, muchas personas se visten con ropa de color verde.

_____

4. Antigua es una ciudad completamente moderna.

_____

5. Chichicastenango es una ciudad mucho más grande que Antigua.

_____

6. El terremoto de 1773 destruyó todas las iglesias y monasterios en Antigua.

_____

7 **Escribir** Write four sentences comparing the cities Antigua and Chichicastenango.

_____

_____

_____

_____

¡VIVAN LOS PAÍSES HISPANOS!

Lección 12

Honduras
Antes de ver el video

1 **Más vocabulario** Look over these useful words and expressions before you watch the video.

Vocabulario útil		
astrónomo *astronomer*	escala *scale*	quetzal *quetzal (a type of bird)*
clara *clear*	impresionante *amazing*	ruinas *ruins*
dentro de *inside*	piezas de arte *works of art*	serpiente *snake*

2 **Predecir** Do you remember the video from **Lección 4**? It was about the pyramids of Teotihuacán. In this lesson you are going to hear about other pyramids, those in the city of Copán, Honduras. Write a paragraph about the things you think you will see in this video.

_____

_____

_____

Mientras ves el video

3 **Marcar** Check off the words you hear while watching the video.

_____ 1. azteca   _____ 5. maya   _____ 9. Sol

_____ 2. bailes   _____ 6. ochocientos   _____ 10. Tegucigalpa

_____ 3. cultura precolombina   _____ 7. quetzal

_____ 4. grupos   _____ 8. Rosalila

Después de ver el video

4 **Seleccionar** Choose the option that best completes each sentence.

1. Una ciudad muy importante de la cultura _____ es Copán.
   a. olmeca   b. salvadoreña   c. azteca   d. maya

2. Desde mil novecientos _____ y cinco, científicos han trabajado en estas ruinas.
   a. cincuenta   b. setenta   c. sesenta   d. noventa

3. Los mayas fueron grandes artistas, _____, matemáticos, astrónomos y médicos.
   a. maestros   b. estudiantes   c. arquitectos   d. cantantes

4. Ricardo Agurcia descubrió un templo _____ una pirámide.
   a. afuera de   b. cerca de   c. dentro de   d. a un lado de

5. En Copán encontraron el texto más _____ que dejó la gran civilización maya.
   a. extenso   b. corto   c. interesante   d. divertido

6. En Copán está el Museo de _____ Maya.
   a. Arte   b. Pintura   c. Escultura   d. Texto

¡VIVAN LOS PAÍSES HISPANOS!   Lección 12

El Salvador
Antes de ver el video

1 **Más vocabulario** Look over these useful words before you watch the video.

Vocabulario útil			
alimento *food*	fuente *source*	grano *grain*	salsa *sauce*

Mientras ves el video

2 **Marcar** Check off the verbs you hear while watching the video.

_____ 1. bailar   _____ 5. describir   _____ 8. saber   _____ 11. usar

_____ 2. cocinar   _____ 6. hacer   _____ 9. servir   _____ 12. vender

_____ 3. comer   _____ 7. limpiar   _____ 10. tocar   _____ 13. vivir

_____ 4. decir

Después de ver el video

3 **Completar** Complete the sentences with words from the word bank.

aceite	fuente	pupusas
arroz	maíz	sal
camarón	postre	símbolo

1. En El Salvador el _____ es el alimento principal de la dieta diaria.

2. Las pupusas se comen a veces como _____ acompañadas de frutas.

3. En todos los lugares importantes de El Salvador se venden _____.

4. Para hacer las pupusas se usa maíz, agua, _____ y sal.

5. El maíz es una buena _____ de carbohidratos.

6. El maíz se ha usado como _____ religioso.

4 **Foto** Describe the video still. Write at least three sentences in Spanish.

_____

_____

_____

_____

_____

¡VIVAN LOS PAÍSES HISPANOS!   Lección 14

Nicaragua
Antes de ver el video

1   **Más vocabulario** Look over these useful words and expressions before you watch the video.

Vocabulario útil		
artesanías *handicrafts, craft work*	dioses *gods*	ofrendas *offerings*
atractivos *attractions*	laguna *lagoon*	venado *deer*
burlarse *to make fun (of)*	obras artesanales *handicrafts*	venerar *to worship*

Mientras ves el video

2   **Marcar** Check off the verbs you hear while watching the video.

_____ 1. bailan   _____ 4. comer   _____ 7. deriva   _____ 10. venden

_____ 2. burlan   _____ 5. correr   _____ 8. estudiar   _____ 11. veneraban

_____ 3. calmar   _____ 6. creían   _____ 9. jugar   _____ 12. ver

Después de ver el video

3   **Emparejar** Find the items in the second column that correspond to the ones in the first.

_____ 1. la más reciente erupción del Volcán Masaya   a. una celebración

_____ 2. Le daban esto a los dioses para calmar al volcán.   b. ofrendas

_____ 3. *Mazalt* y *yan*   c. el volcán hacía erupción

_____ 4. pasaba cuando los dioses estaban enojados   d. nombre *Masaya* en lengua indígena

_____ 5. el Torovenado   e. 1993

4   **Respuestas** Answer the questions in Spanish. Use complete sentences.

1. ¿Cómo se llama el pueblo donde está situada la laguna de Masaya?

   _____

2. ¿De dónde se deriva el nombre *Masaya*?

   _____

3. ¿Cuál es la fiesta más importante que se celebra en Masaya?

   _____

4. ¿De quiénes se burlan los habitantes en estas fiestas?

   _____

5. ¿Por qué se le conoce a Masaya como la capital del folklore nicaragüense?

   _____

6. ¿Qué venden en el mercado, además de frutas y verduras?

   _____

Lección 14 Video Activities   **87**

¡VIVAN LOS PAÍSES HISPANOS!   Lección 14

Costa Rica

Antes de ver el video

1 **Más vocabulario** Look over these useful words and expressions before you watch the video.

Vocabulario útil		
bosque *forest*	guía certificado *certified guide*	riqueza *wealth*
conservar *to preserve*	nuboso *cloudy*	tiendas de campaña *camping tents*
cubierto *covered*	permitir *to allow*	tocar *to touch*
entrar *to enter*	regla *rule*	

2 **Foto** Describe the video still. Write at least three sentences in Spanish.

_____

_____

_____

_____

_____

Mientras ves el video

3 **Marcar** While watching the video, check off the rules that have been put in place to protect nature.

_____ 1. En el parque Monteverde no pueden entrar más de 150 personas al mismo tiempo.

_____ 2. Los turistas tienen que dormir en tiendas de campaña.

_____ 3. Los turistas no pueden visitar Tortuguero en febrero.

_____ 4. Después de las seis no se permite ir a la playa sin un guía certificado.

_____ 5. Los turistas no pueden tocar las tortugas.

_____ 6. En Tortuguero está prohibido sacar fotografías.

Después de ver el video

4 **Completar** Complete the sentences with words from the word bank.

acampan	entrar	pasan	prohíbe
conservan	estudiar	prefieren	transportan

1. En Monteverde se _____ más de dos mil especies de animales.

2. En este parque no pueden _____ más de 150 personas al mismo tiempo.

3. Algunos turistas _____ en Monteverde.

4. Otros _____ ir a los hoteles de los pueblos que están cerca de Monteverde.

5. Se _____ sacar fotografías.

¡VIVAN LOS PAÍSES HISPANOS!

Lección 14

Panamá
Antes de ver el video

1 **Más vocabulario** Look over these useful words before you watch the video.

Vocabulario útil		
anualmente *annually*	impresionante *incredible*	según *according to*
arrecife *reef*	lado *side*	sitio *site*
disfrutar *to enjoy*	peces *fish*	torneo *tournament*
especies *species*	precioso *beautiful*	

2 **Responder** This video talks about the best places to dive and surf in Panama. In preparation for watching this video, answer these questions about surfing.

1. ¿Practicas el surf? ¿Conoces a alguien que lo practique? ¿Dónde lo practicas?

_____

2. ¿Te gusta este deporte? ¿Por qué?

_____

Mientras ves el video

3 **Ordenar** Number the items in the order in which they appear in the video.

a. _____

b. _____

c. _____

Después de ver el video

4 **Emparejar** Find the items in the second column that correspond to the ones in the first.

1. La isla Contadora es la más grande _____
2. Allí siempre hace calor _____
3. En Panamá, los visitantes pueden bucear en el océano Pacífico por la mañana, _____
4. Las islas de San Blas son 365, _____
5. En Santa Catarina los deportistas disfrutan de _____

a. por la noche.
b. del archipiélago.
c. la playa blanca y el agua color turquesa.
d. por eso se puede bucear en todas las estaciones.
e. una para cada día del año.
f. y en el mar Caribe por la tarde.

5 **Responder** Answer the questions in Spanish. Use complete sentences.

1. ¿Qué país centroamericano tiene costas en el océano Pacífico y en el mar Caribe?

_____

_____

2. ¿Por qué Las Perlas es un buen lugar para bucear?

_____

_____

3. ¿Cómo llegan los turistas a la isla Contadora?

_____

_____

4. ¿Cómo se llaman los indígenas que viven en las islas San Blas?

_____

_____

5. ¿Adónde van los mejores deportistas de surfing del mundo?

_____

_____

6 **Pasatiempos** Complete this chart in Spanish.

Mis deportes/ pasatiempos favoritos	Por qué me gustan	Dónde/cuándo los practico

¡VIVAN LOS PAÍSES HISPANOS!

Lección 16

España

Antes de ver el video

1 **Más vocabulario** Look over these useful words before you watch the video.

Vocabulario útil		
antiguo *ancient*	empezar *to start*	niños *children*
blanco *white*	encierro *running of bulls*	pañuelo *neckerchief, bandana*
cabeza *head*	esta *this*	peligroso *dangerous*
calle *street*	feria *fair, festival*	periódico *newspaper*
cohete *rocket (firework)*	fiesta *party, festival*	rojo *red*
comparsa *parade*	gente *people*	ropa *clothing*
correr *to run*	gigante *giant*	toro *bull*
defenderse *to defend oneself*	mitad *half*	ver *to see*

2 **Festivales** In this video, you are going to learn about a Spanish festival. List the things you would probably do and see at a festival.

_____

_____

_____

_____

Mientras ves el video

3 **Ordenar** Number the items in the order in which they appear in the video.

_____ a. cohete

_____ b. cuatro mujeres en un balcón

_____ c. gigante

_____ d. mitad hombre, mitad caballo (*horse*)

_____ e. muchas personas

_____ f. toro

Después de ver el video

4 **Fotos** Describe the video stills.

_____

_____

_____

_____

_____

_____

_____
_____
_____
_____
_____
_____

5 **Crucigrama** Complete these sentences and use the words to complete the crossword.

1. El Festival de San Fermín es la combinación de tres fiestas, una de ellas son las _____ comerciales.

2. Las _____ son los eventos favoritos de los niños.

3. La fiesta religiosa en honor a San Fermín, las ferias comerciales y los eventos taurinos son celebraciones _____.

4. Los Sanfermines es una de las _____ tradicionales españolas.

5. Las personas usan ropa blanca y _____ rojos.

6. En los encierros las personas corren delante de diecisiete _____.

7. En las comparsas hay figuras _____ hombre mitad animal.

8. En los días del festival, hay ocho _____ por día.

9. En las comparsas hay ocho _____.

10. Las comparsas pasan por las _____ de Pamplona.

11. Otras de las figuras tienen enormes _____.

[Crossword grid with vertical answer S-A-N-F-E-R-M-I-N-E-S]

PREPARACIÓN

1 **Saludos** For each question or expression, write the appropriate answer from the box in each blank.

De nada.	Encantada.	Muy bien, gracias.	Nos vemos.
El gusto es mío.	Me llamo Pepe.	Nada.	Soy de Ecuador.

1. ¿Cómo te llamas? _____

2. ¿Qué hay de nuevo? _____

3. ¿De dónde eres? _____

4. Adiós. _____

5. ¿Cómo está usted? _____

6. Mucho gusto. _____

7. Te presento a la señora Díaz. _____

8. Muchas gracias. _____

2 **Conversación** Complete this conversation by writing one word in each blank.

ANA Buenos días, señor González. ¿Cómo _____ 1 _____ 2?

SR. GONZÁLEZ _____ 3 bien, gracias. ¿Y tú, _____ 4 estás?

ANA Bien. _____ 5 presento a Antonio.

SR. GONZÁLEZ Mucho _____ 6, Antonio.

ANTONIO El gusto _____ 7 _____ 8.

SR. GONZÁLEZ ¿De dónde _____ 9, Antonio?

ANTONIO _____ 10 _____ 11 México.

ANA _____ 12 luego, señor González.

SR. GONZÁLEZ Nos _____ 13, Ana.

ANTONIO _____ 14, señor González.

3 **Saludos, despedidas y presentaciones** Complete these phrases with the missing words. Then write each phrase in the correct column of the chart.

1. ¿_____ pasa?
2. _____ luego.
3. _____ gusto.
4. Te _____ a Irene.
5. ¿_____ estás?
6. _____ días.
7. El _____ es mío.
8. Nos _____.

Saludos	Despedidas	Presentaciones

Workbook

4 **Los países** Fill in each blank with the name of the country that is highlighted in each map.

1. _____

2. _____

3. _____

4. _____

5. _____

5 **Diferente** Write the word or phrase that does not belong in each group.

1. Hasta mañana.
   Nos vemos.
   Buenos días.
   Hasta pronto.

   _____

2. ¿Qué tal?
   Regular.
   ¿Qué pasa?
   ¿Cómo estás?

   _____

3. Ecuador
   Washington
   México
   Estados Unidos

   _____

4. Muchas gracias.
   Muy bien, gracias.
   No muy bien.
   Regular.

   _____

5. ¿De dónde eres?
   ¿Cómo está usted?
   ¿De dónde es usted?
   ¿Cómo se llama usted?

   _____

6. Chau.
   Buenos días.
   Hola.
   ¿Qué tal?

   _____

2 **Lección 1** Workbook Activities

GRAMÁTICA

1.1 Nouns and articles

1 **¿Masculino o femenino?** Write the correct definite article before each noun. Then write each article and noun in the correct column.

1. _____ hombre   4. _____ pasajero   7. _____ chico

2. _____ profesora   5. _____ mujer   8. _____ pasajera

3. _____ chica   6. _____ conductora   9. _____ profesor

Masculino	Femenino
_____	_____
_____	_____
_____	_____
_____	_____
_____	_____

2 **¿El, la, los, o las?** Write the correct definite article before each noun.

1. _____ autobús   6. _____ mano

2. _____ maleta   7. _____ país

3. _____ lápices   8. _____ problema

4. _____ diccionario   9. _____ cosas

5. _____ palabras   10. _____ diarios

3 **Singular y plural** Give the plural form of each singular article and noun and the singular form of each plural article and noun.

1. unas capitales _____   6. unas escuelas _____

2. un día _____   7. unos mapas _____

3. un cuaderno _____   8. un programa _____

4. unos números _____   9. unos autobuses _____

5. una computadora _____   10. una palabra _____

4 **Las cosas** For each picture, provide the noun with its corresponding definite and indefinite articles.

1. _____   2. _____   3. _____   4. _____

_____   _____   _____   _____

Lección 1 Workbook Activities   **3**

1.2 Numbers 0–30

1 **Los números** Solve the math problems to complete the crossword puzzle.

1. (*Horizontal*) veinte más cinco
1. (*Vertical*) once más once
2. seis más tres
3. trece menos trece
4. veintiséis menos quince
5. doce más ocho

6. veintinueve menos diecinueve
7. treinta menos catorce
8. veintitrés menos dieciséis
9. siete más uno
10. veinticinco menos veintiuno
11. once más dos

2 **¿Cuántos hay?** Write questions and answers that indicate how many items there are. Write out the numbers.

> **modelo**
> 2 cuadernos
> ¿Cuántos cuadernos hay? Hay dos cuadernos.

1. 3 diccionarios _____

2. 12 estudiantes _____

3. 10 lápices _____

4. 7 maletas _____

5. 25 palabras _____

6. 21 países _____

7. 13 mochilas _____

8. 18 pasajeros _____

9. 15 computadoras _____

10. 27 fotografías _____

1.3 Present tense of ser

1 **Los pronombres** In the second column, write the subject pronouns that you would use when addressing the people listed in the first column. In the third column, write the pronouns you would use when talking about them.

Personas	Addressing them	Talking about them
1. el señor Varela	_____	_____
2. Claudia, Eva y Ana	_____	_____
3. un hombre y dos mujeres	_____	_____
4. la profesora	_____	_____
5. un estudiante	_____	_____
6. el director de una escuela	_____	_____
7. tres chicas	_____	_____
8. un pasajero de autobús	_____	_____
9. Antonio y Miguel	_____	_____
10. una turista	_____	_____

2 **Completar** Complete these sentences with the correct forms of **ser**.

1. Los pasajeros _____ de los Estados Unidos.

2. Nosotros _____ profesores.

3. La computadora _____ de Marisol.

4. La profesora _____ Elsa Jiménez.

5. Yo _____ de San Antonio.

6. ¿Quién _____ el conductor?

7. Tú _____ estudiante.

8. ¿De quiénes _____ las maletas?

3 **Nosotros somos...** Rewrite each sentence with the new subject. Change the verb **ser** as necessary.

> **modelo**
> Ustedes son profesores.
> Nosotros _somos profesores._

1. Nosotros somos estudiantes. Ustedes _____.

2. Usted es de Puerto Rico. Ella _____.

3. Nosotros somos conductores. Ellos _____.

4. Yo soy estudiante. Tú _____.

5. Ustedes son de Ecuador. Nosotras _____.

6. Ella es profesora. Yo _____.

7. Tú eres de España. Él _____.

8. Ellos son de México. Ellas _____.

Workbook

4 **¿De quién es?** Use **ser** + **de** (or **del**) to indicate that the objects belong to the people listed.

> **modelo**
> mochila / el hombre
> **Es la mochila del hombre.**

1. diccionario / el estudiante _____
2. cuadernos / las chicas _____
3. mano / Manuel _____
4. maletas / la turista _____
5. mapas / los profesores _____
6. libro / Francisco _____
7. lápices / la joven _____
8. fotografía / los chicos _____
9. computadora / la directora _____
10. capital / el país _____

5 **¿De dónde son?** Use **ser** + **de** to indicate where the people are from.

> **modelo**
> ustedes / Costa Rica
> **Ustedes son de Costa Rica.**

1. Lina y María / Colombia _____
2. el profesor / México _____
3. tú y los jóvenes / Argentina _____
4. las estudiantes / los Estados Unidos _____
5. ellos / Ecuador _____
6. la mujer / Puerto Rico _____
7. los turistas / España _____
8. él y yo / Chile _____
9. nosotras / Cuba _____
10. usted / Venezuela _____

6 **¡Pregunta!** Write questions for these answers.

> **modelo**
> **¿De dónde son ellos?**
> Ellos son de España.

1. _____
   Los lápices son de Ramón.
2. _____
   Lilia es de Ecuador.
3. _____
   Es una foto.
4. _____
   Ellas son Marisa y Susana.

1.4 Telling time

1   **La hora**   Give the time shown on each clock using complete sentences.

1. _____

2. _____

3. _____

4. _____

5. _____

6. _____

2   **¿Qué hora es?**   Use complete sentences to tell the time.

1. 3:40 p.m. _____

2. 6:00 a.m. _____

3. 9:15 p.m. _____

4. 12:00 p.m. _____

5. 1:10 p.m. _____

6. 10:45 a.m. _____

7. 5:05 p.m. _____

8. 11:50 p.m. _____

9. 1:30 a.m. _____

10. 10:00 p.m. _____

3   **El día de Marta** Use the schedule to answer the questions in complete sentences.

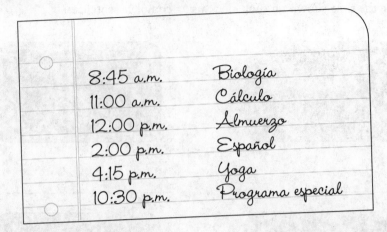

8:45 a.m.   Biología
11:00 a.m.   Cálculo
12:00 p.m.   Almuerzo
2:00 p.m.   Español
4:15 p.m.   Yoga
10:30 p.m.   Programa especial

1. ¿A qué hora es la clase de biología? _____

2. ¿A qué hora es la clase de cálculo? _____

3. ¿A qué hora es el almuerzo (*lunch*)? _____

4. ¿A qué hora es la clase de español? _____

5. ¿A qué hora es la clase de yoga? _____

6. ¿A qué hora es el programa especial? _____

4   **Síntesis** Answer the questions about yourself and your class using complete sentences.

1. ¿Cómo te llamas? _____

2. ¿De dónde eres? _____

3. ¿Qué hay de nuevo? _____

_____

4. ¿Qué hora es? _____

_____

5. ¿A qué hora es la clase de español? _____

_____

6. ¿Cuántos estudiantes hay en la clase de español? _____

_____

7. ¿Hay estudiantes de México en la clase? _____

_____

8. ¿A qué hora es tu (*your*) programa de televisión favorito? _____

_____

---

8   **Lección 1** Workbook Activities

PREPARACIÓN

Lección 2

1 **Categorías** Read each group of items. Then write the word from the list that relates to each group.

| biblioteca | clase | geografía |
| cafetería | cursos | laboratorio |

1. sándwiches, tacos, sodas, bananas _____

2. mapas, capitales, países, nacionalidades _____

3. historia, matemáticas, geografía, lenguas extranjeras _____

4. microscopios, experimentos, química, elementos _____

5. libros, mesas, computadoras, sillas _____

6. pizarras, tiza, borrador, profesora, escritorios _____

2 **Buscar** (*To search*) Find twelve school-related words in the grid, looking horizontally and vertically. Circle them in the puzzle, and write the words in the blanks.

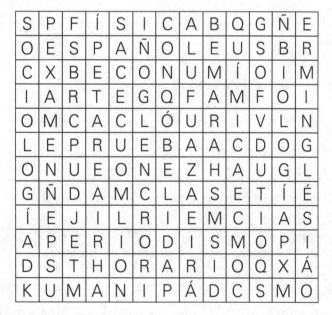

S	P	F	Í	S	I	C	A	B	Q	G	Ñ	E
O	E	S	P	A	Ñ	O	L	E	U	S	B	R
C	X	B	E	C	O	N	U	M	Í	O	I	M
I	A	R	T	E	G	Q	F	A	M	F	O	I
O	M	C	A	C	L	Ó	U	R	I	V	L	N
L	E	P	R	U	E	B	A	A	C	D	O	G
O	N	U	E	O	N	E	Z	H	A	U	G	L
G	Ñ	D	A	M	C	L	A	S	E	T	Í	É
Í	E	J	I	L	R	I	E	M	C	I	A	S
A	P	E	R	I	O	D	I	S	M	O	P	I
D	S	T	H	O	R	A	R	I	O	Q	X	Á
K	U	M	A	N	I	P	Á	D	C	S	M	O

Horizontales   **Verticales**

_____   _____

_____   _____

_____   _____

_____   _____

Lección 2 Workbook Activities   **9**

3   **El calendario**   Use the calendar to answer the questions with complete sentences.

marzo

L	M	M	J	V	S	D
		1	2	3	4	5
6	7	8	9	10	11	12
13	14	15	16	17	18	19
20	21	22	23	24	25	26
27	28	29	30	31		

abril

L	M	M	J	V	S	D
					1	2
3	4	5	6	7	8	9
10	11	12	13	14	15	16
17	18	19	20	21	22	23
24	25	26	27	28	29	30

> **modelo**
>
> ¿Qué día de la semana es el 8 de abril (*April*)?
> El *8 de abril es sábado.*/Es sábado.

1. ¿Qué día de la semana es el 21 de marzo (*March*)? _____

2. ¿Qué día de la semana es el 7 de abril? _____

3. ¿Qué día de la semana es el 2 de marzo? _____

4. ¿Qué día de la semana es el 28 de marzo? _____

5. ¿Qué día de la semana es el 19 de abril? _____

6. ¿Qué día de la semana es el 12 de marzo? _____

7. ¿Qué día de la semana es el 3 de abril? _____

8. ¿Qué día de la semana es el 22 de abril? _____

9. ¿Qué día de la semana es el 31 de marzo? _____

10. ¿Qué día de la semana es el 9 de abril? _____

4   **Completar**   Complete these sentences using words from the word bank.

arte	computación	geografía	laboratorio	tarea
biblioteca	examen	horario	profesora	universidad

1. La _____ de español es de México.

2. El _____ dice (*says*) a qué hora son las clases.

3. A las once hay un _____ de biología.

4. Martín es artista y toma (*takes*) una clase de _____.

5. Hay veinte computadoras en la clase de _____.

6. Los experimentos se hacen (*are made*) en el _____.

7. Hay muchos libros en la _____.

8. Los mapas son importantes en el curso de _____.

Workbook

GRAMÁTICA

2.1 Present tense of regular –ar verbs

1 **El presente** Write the missing forms of each verb.

Present tense					
Infinitivo	yo	tú	usted, él, ella	nosotros/as	ustedes, ellos
1. cantar	_____	_____	_____	_____	_____
2. _____	pregunto	_____	_____	_____	_____
3. _____	_____	contestas	_____	_____	_____
4. _____	_____	_____	practica	_____	_____
5. _____	_____	_____	_____	deseamos	_____
6. _____	_____	_____	_____	_____	llevan

2 **Completar** Complete these sentences using the correct form of the verb in parentheses.

1. Los turistas _____ (viajar) en un autobús.

2. Elena y yo _____ (hablar) español en clase.

3. Los estudiantes _____ (llegar) a la residencia estudiantil.

4. Yo _____ (dibujar) un reloj en la pizarra.

5. La señora García _____ (comprar) libros en la librería de la universidad.

6. Francisco y tú _____ (regresar) de la biblioteca.

7. El semestre _____ (terminar) en mayo (*May*).

8. Tú _____ (buscar) a tus (*your*) compañeros de clase en la cafetería.

3 **¿Qué hacen?** (*What do they do?*) Complete each sentence with the correct verb form so that the sentence makes sense.

busco	esperan	toman
conversas	regresamos	trabaja

1. Nosotras _____ a las seis de la tarde.

2. Muchos estudiantes _____ el curso de periodismo.

3. Rosa y Laura no _____ a Manuel.

4. Tú _____ con (*with*) los chicos en la residencia estudiantil.

5. El compañero de cuarto de Jaime _____ en el laboratorio.

6. Yo _____ un libro en la biblioteca.

Lección 2 Workbook Activities   **11**

Workbook

4   **Oraciones** Form sentences using the words provided. Use the correct present tense form or the infinitive of each verb.

1. una estudiante / desear / hablar / con su profesora de biología

_____

2. los profesores / contestar / las preguntas (*questions*) de los estudiantes

_____

3. (nosotros) / esperar / viajar / a Madrid

_____

4. (yo) / necesitar / practicar / los verbos en español

_____

5   **Negativo** Rewrite these sentences to make them negative.

1. Juanita y Raúl trabajan en la biblioteca.

_____

2. El conductor llega al mediodía.

_____

3. Deseo comprar tres cuadernos.

_____

4. El estudiante espera a la profesora.

_____

5. Estudiamos a las seis de la mañana.

_____

6. Te gusta usar (*use*) la computadora.

_____

6   **¿Y tú?** Use complete sentences to answer these yes or no questions.

> **modelo**
>
> ¿Bailas tango?
> *No, no bailo tango.*

1. ¿Estudias biología en la universidad?

_____

2. ¿Conversas mucho con los compañeros de clase?

_____

3. ¿Esperas estudiar administración de empresas?

_____

4. ¿Te gustan las lenguas extranjeras?

_____

5. ¿Te gusta escuchar música jazz?

_____

2.2 Forming questions in Spanish

1 **Las preguntas** Make questions out of these statements by inverting the word order.

1. Ustedes son de Puerto Rico.

_____

2. El estudiante dibuja un mapa.

_____

3. Los turistas llegan en autobús.

_____

4. La clase termina a las dos de la tarde.

_____

5. Samuel trabaja en la biblioteca.

_____

6. Los chicos miran un programa de televisión.

_____

7. El profesor Miranda enseña sociología.

_____

8. Isabel compra cinco libros de historia.

_____

9. Mariana y Javier estudian para (for) el examen.

_____

10. Ellas conversan en la cafetería de la universidad.

_____

2 **Seleccionar** Choose an interrogative word from the list to write a question that corresponds with each response.

Adónde	Cuántos	Dónde	Qué
Cuándo	De dónde	Por qué	Quién

1. _____

Paco y Rosa caminan a la biblioteca.

2. _____

El profesor de español es de México.

3. _____

Hay quince estudiantes en la clase.

4. _____

El compañero de cuarto de Jaime es Manuel.

5. _____

La clase de física es en el laboratorio.

6. _____

Julia lleva una computadora portátil.

7. _____

El programa de televisión termina a las diez.

8. _____

Estudio biología porque (because) me gusta trabajar en el laboratorio.

Workbook

3 **Muchas preguntas** Form three different questions from each statement.

> **modelo**
>
> Ana habla por teléfono.
> ¿Habla Ana por teléfono?
> Ana habla por teléfono, ¿no?
> Ana habla por teléfono, ¿verdad?

1. Sara canta en el coro (*choir*) de la universidad.

_____

_____

_____

2. Tú buscas el libro de arte.

_____

_____

_____

3. El profesor Gutiérrez enseña contabilidad.

_____

_____

_____

4. Ustedes necesitan hablar con el profesor de historia.

_____

_____

_____

4 **¿Qué palabra?** Write the interrogative word or phrase that makes sense in each question.

1. ¿_____ es la clase de administración de empresas?
   Es en la biblioteca.

2. ¿_____ estudias para los exámenes de matemáticas?
   Estudio por la noche (*at night*).

3. ¿_____ es el profesor de inglés?
   Es de los Estados Unidos.

4. ¿_____ libros hay en la clase de biología?
   Hay diez libros.

5. ¿_____ caminas con (*with*) Olga?
   Camino a la clase de biología con Olga.

6. ¿_____ enseña el profesor Hernández en la universidad?
   Enseña matemáticas.

7. ¿_____ llevas cinco libros en la mochila?
   Porque regreso de la biblioteca.

8. ¿_____ es la profesora de física?
   Es la señora Caballero.

2.3 The present tense of **estar**

1 **Están en...** Answer the questions based on the pictures. Write complete sentences.

1. ¿Dónde están Cristina y Bruno?

_____

2. ¿Dónde están la profesora y el estudiante?

_____

3. ¿Dónde está la puerta?

_____

4. ¿Dónde está la mochila?

_____

5. ¿Dónde está el pasajero?

_____

6. ¿Dónde está José Miguel?

_____

2 **¿Dónde están?** Use these cues and the correct form of **estar** to write complete sentences. Add any missing words.

1. libros / cerca / escritorio

_____

2. ustedes / al lado / puerta

_____

3. diccionario / entre / computadoras

_____

4. lápices / sobre / cuaderno

_____

5. estadio / lejos / residencias

_____

6. mochilas / debajo / mesa

_____

7. tú / en / clase de psicología

_____

8. reloj / a la derecha / ventana

_____

9. Rita / a la izquierda / Julio

_____

3 **¿Ser o estar?** Complete these sentences with the correct present-tense form of **ser** or **estar**.

1. Sonia _____ muy bien hoy.

2. Las sillas _____ delante del escritorio.

3. Ellos _____ estudiantes de sociología.

4. Alma _____ de un pueblo (*town*) de España.

5. _____ las diez y media de la mañana.

6. Nosotras _____ en la biblioteca.

4 **El libro** Complete this cell phone conversation with the correct forms of **estar**.

GUSTAVO Hola, Pablo. ¿_____ en la residencia estudiantil?
$\text{\hspace{12em}}_1$

PABLO Sí, _____ en la residencia.
$\text{\hspace{5em}}_2$

GUSTAVO Necesito el libro de física.

PABLO ¿Dónde _____ el libro?
$\text{\hspace{6em}}_3$

GUSTAVO El libro _____ en mi cuarto (*room*), al lado de la computadora.
$\text{\hspace{8em}}_4$

PABLO ¿Dónde _____ la computadora?
$\text{\hspace{6em}}_5$

GUSTAVO La computadora _____ encima del escritorio.
$\text{\hspace{8em}}_6$

PABLO ¡Aquí (*Here*) _____ el libro de física!
$\text{\hspace{6em}}_7$

5 **Conversación** Complete this conversation with the correct forms of **ser** and **estar**.

PILAR Hola, Irene. ¿Cómo _____?
$\text{\hspace{6em}}_1$

IRENE Muy bien, ¿y tú? ¿Qué tal?

PILAR Bien, gracias. Te presento a Pablo.

IRENE Encantada, Pablo.

PILAR Pablo _____ de México.
$\text{\hspace{3em}}_2$

IRENE ¿De qué ciudad de México _____?
$\text{\hspace{3em}}_3$

PABLO _____ de Monterrey. ¿Y tú, de dónde _____?
$\text{\hspace{3em}}_4 \text{\hspace{18em}}_5$

IRENE _____ de San Juan, Puerto Rico.
$\text{\hspace{3em}}_6$

PILAR ¿Dónde _____ Claudia, tu (*your*) compañera de cuarto?
$\text{\hspace{5em}}_7$

IRENE _____ en la residencia estudiantil.
$\text{\hspace{3em}}_8$

PABLO Nosotros vamos a (*are going to*) la librería ahora.

PILAR Necesitamos comprar el manual del laboratorio de física.

IRENE ¿A qué hora _____ la clase de física?
$\text{\hspace{5em}}_9$

PABLO _____ a las doce. ¿Qué hora _____ ahora?
$\text{\hspace{2em}}_{10} \text{\hspace{14em}}_{11}$

PILAR _____ las once y media.
$\text{\hspace{2em}}_{12}$

IRENE ¡Menos mal que (*Fortunately*) la librería _____ cerca del laboratorio!
$\text{\hspace{12em}}_{13}$

PILAR Sí, no _____ lejos de la clase. Nos vemos.
$\text{\hspace{4em}}_{14}$

IRENE Hasta luego.

PABLO Chau.

2.4 Numbers 31–100

1 **Números de teléfono** Provide the words for these telephone numbers.

> **modelo**
> 968-3659
> nueve, sesenta y ocho, treinta y seis, cincuenta y nueve

1. 776-7799

_____

2. 543-3162

_____

3. 483-4745

_____

4. 352-5073

_____

5. 888-7540

_____

6. 566-3857

_____

7. 492-6033

_____

8. 780-5770

_____

2 **¿Cuántos hay?** Use the inventory list to answer these questions about the number of items in stock at the school bookstore. Use complete sentences and write out the Spanish numbers in words.

Inventario			
lápices	91	mochilas	31
plumas	85	diccionarios	43
videos	72	computadoras	30
cuadernos	50	mapas	66

1. ¿Cuántos mapas hay? _____

2. ¿Cuántas mochilas hay? _____

3. ¿Cuántos diccionarios hay? _____

4. ¿Cuántos cuadernos hay? _____

5. ¿Cuántas plumas hay? _____

6. ¿Cuántos lápices hay? _____

7. ¿Cuántas computadoras hay? _____

8. ¿Cuántos videos hay? _____

Workbook

3 **Por ciento** Use the pie chart to complete these sentences. Write out the Spanish numbers in words.

física 17%

periodismo 18%

biología 18%

inglés 25%

español 22%

1. Un _____ por ciento de los estudiantes estudian biología o física.

2. Un _____ por ciento de los estudiantes estudian inglés o periodismo.

3. Un _____ por ciento de los estudiantes no estudian ciencias (*sciences*).

4. Un _____ por ciento de los estudiantes no estudian biología.

5. Un _____ por ciento de los estudiantes estudian inglés o español.

6. Un _____ por ciento de los estudiantes no estudian idiomas (*languages*).

4 **Síntesis** Imagine that a parent calls a college student during the second week of courses. Write questions that the parent might ask about the son or daughter's schedule, courses, and campus life. Use the cues provided. Then write possible answers.

> *modelo*
>
> ¿Cuándo termina la clase de español?
> La clase de español termina a las tres.

- ¿A qué hora…?
- ¿Dónde está…?
- ¿Qué cursos…?
- ¿Trabajas…?

- ¿Estudias…?
- ¿Qué días de la semana…?
- ¿Hay…?
- ¿Cuántos…?

_____

_____

_____

_____

_____

_____

_____

_____

¡VIVAN LOS PAÍSES HISPANOS!

Estados Unidos y Canadá

1   **Un mapa** Write each of these words in the appropriate country in the map.

Montreal	Sonia Sotomayor
50.480.000 hispanos	300.000 hispanos
dos lenguas oficiales	población total: 33.000.000
desfile de puertorriqueños	La Pequeña Habana

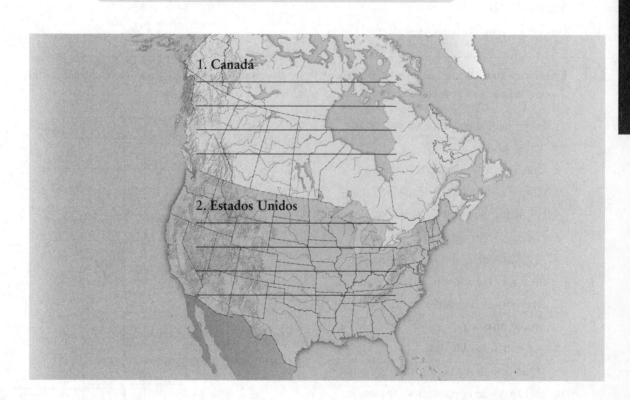

1. Canadá
_____
_____
_____
_____

2. Estados Unidos
_____
_____
_____
_____

2   **Hispanos en los Estados Unidos y Canadá** Where do most Hispanics in the U.S. come from? Which state has the largest Hispanic population? Rank the regions and states from 1 (most) to 5 (least).

Hispanos en EE.UU.	Hispanos en Canadá
_____ Cuba	_____ Chile
_____ Puerto Rico	_____ El Salvador
_____ México	_____ México
_____ Centroamérica y Sudamérica	_____ Otros países
_____ Otros países	

3 **Palabras** Unscramble the words about **¡Vivan los países hispanos!** to complete the sentences.

1. QIRRTUPOESORÑEU

El desfile de junio en Nueva York celebra a los _____ .

2. ÉXCOMI

Los tacos son platos de _____ .

3. IMIMA

La Pequeña Habana es un barrio de _____ .

4. XAOEMICN

John Quiñones es de origen _____ .

5. RFSACÉN

Una de las lenguas oficiales de Canadá es el _____ .

4 **Palabras cruzadas** (*crossed*) Write one letter in each square. Then complete the final sentence using the new words formed in bold.

1. Hay muchos hispanos en este estado de los EE.UU.

2. Una lengua oficial de Canadá.

3. Comida popular mexicana

4. Ciudad donde está La Pequeña Habana

5. ¿Qué es John Quiñones?

6. El 63,1% de la población hispana en los EE.UU. es de este país.

7. Apellido de una actriz famosa de origen hispano

8. ¿Qué es Ellen Ochoa?

9. ¿Qué tipo de comida son las quesadillas?

10. El 11,6% de la población hispana en Canadá es de este país.

11. Todos los años hay uno en Nueva York.

12. ¿Qué es la Pequeña Habana?

13. Nivel de estudios de muchos hispanos en Canadá.

En los _____ y en Canadá viven muchos hispanos.

PREPARACIÓN

1 **La familia** Look at the family tree and describe the relationships between these people.

modelo

Eduardo / Concha
Eduardo es el padre de Concha.

1. Juan Carlos y Sofía / Pilar

   _____

2. Pilar / Ana María y Luis Miguel

   _____

3. Eduardo / Raquel

   _____

4. José Antonio y Ramón / Concha

   _____

5. Raquel / Pilar

   _____

6. Concha, José Antonio y Ramón / Pilar

   _____

7. Ana María / Raquel

   _____

8. Joaquín / Ana María y Luis Miguel

   _____

2   **Diferente** Write the word that does not belong in each group.

1. ingeniera, médica, programadora, periodista, hijastra _____

2. cuñado, perro, yerno, suegra, nuera _____

3. sobrina, prima, artista, tía, hermana _____

4. padre, hermano, hijo, novio, abuelo _____

5. muchachos, tíos, niños, chicos, hijos _____

6. amiga, hermanastra, media hermana, madrastra _____

3   **Crucigrama** Complete this crossword puzzle.

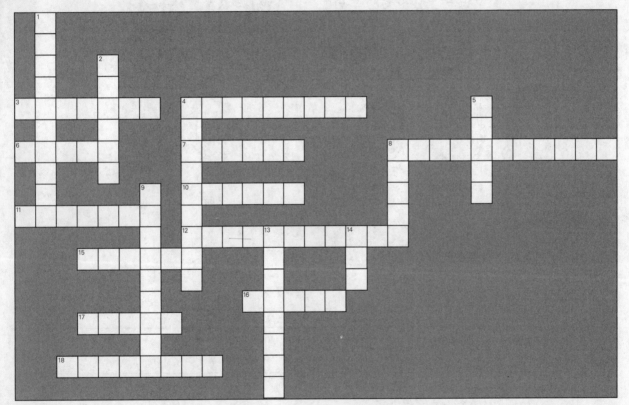

Horizontales

3. el hijo de mi hermano
4. la esposa de mi padre, pero no soy su hijo
6. el hijo de mi hija
7. el esposo de mi hermana
8. hombre que estudió (*studied*) computación
10. la madre de mi padre
11. padre, madre e (*and*) hijos
12. el hijo de mi madrastra, pero no de mi padre
15. doctor
16. tus nietos son los _____ de tus hijos
17. personas en general
18. la hija de mi esposa, pero no es mi hija

Verticales

1. mujer que escribe (*writes*) para el *New York Times*
2. compañeros inseparables
4. chicos
5. el esposo de mi madre es el _____ de mis abuelos
8. el hijo de mi tía
9. abuelos, primos, tíos, etc.
13. Pablo Picasso y Frida Kahlo
14. el hermano de mi madre

GRAMÁTICA

3.1 Descriptive adjectives

1 **¿Cómo son?** Choose the adjective in parentheses that agrees with each subject to write descriptive sentences about them.

> **modelo**
> gordo, delgada
> **Lidia:** Lidia *es delgada.*
> **El novio de Olga:** *El novio de Olga es gordo.*

(simpático, guapos, alta, bonitas)

1. la profesora de historia: _____

2. David y Simón: _____

3. el artista: _____

(trabajadora, viejo, delgadas, rubios)

4. esas (*those*) muchachas: _____

5. el abuelo de Alberto: _____

6. la programadora: _____

2 **Descripciones** Complete each sentence with the correct forms of the adjectives in parentheses.

1. Lupe, Rosa y Tomás son _____ (bueno) amigos.

2. Ignacio es _____ (alto) y _____ (guapo).

3. Lourdes y Virginia son _____ (bajo) y _____ (delgado).

4. Pedro y Vanesa son _____ (moreno), pero Diana es _____ (pelirrojo).

5. Nosotras somos _____ (inteligente) y _____ (trabajador).

6. Esos (*Those*) chicos son _____ (simpático), pero son _____ (tonto).

3 **No** Answer these questions using the adjective with the opposite meaning.

> **modelo**
> ¿Es alta Rosa?
> No, *es baja.*

1. ¿Es antipático el señor Lomas? _____

2. ¿Son morenas las hijas de Sara? _____

3. ¿Es fea la hermana de Eduardo? _____

4. ¿Son viejos los profesores de matemáticas? _____

5. ¿Son malos los nietos de la señora Sánchez? _____

6. ¿Es guapo el novio de Teresa? _____

4   **Origen y nacionalidad** Read the names and origins of the people in this tour group. Then write sentences saying what city they are from and their nationalities.

> **modelo**
> Álvaro Estrada / Miami, Estados Unidos
> Álvaro Estrada *es de* Miami. *Es* estadounidense.

1. Keiko y Benkei Taguchi / Tokio, Japón _____

2. Pierre y Marie Lebrun / Montreal, Canadá _____

3. Thomas Smith / Nueva York, Estados Unidos _____

4. Elizabeth Mitchell / Londres, Inglaterra (*England*) _____

5. Roberto Morales / Madrid, España _____

6. Andrés y Patricia Padilla / Quito, Ecuador _____

7. Paula y Cecilia Robles / San Juan, Puerto Rico _____

8. Conrad Schmidt / Berlín, Alemania (*Germany*) _____

9. Antoinette y Marie Valois / París, Francia _____

10. Marta Zedillo / Guadalajara, México _____

5   **Completar** Complete each sentence with the correct form of each adjective in parentheses.

(bueno)

1. La clase de matemáticas es muy _____.

2. Rogelio es un _____ compañero de cuarto.

3. Agustina compra una _____ mochila para los libros.

4. Andrés y Guillermo son muy _____ amigos.

(malo)

5. Federico es antipático y una _____ persona.

6. Ahora es un _____ momento para descansar.

7. La comida (*food*) de la cafetería es _____.

8. Son unas semanas _____ para viajar.

(grande)

9. Hay un _____ evento en el estadio hoy.

10. Los problemas en esa (*that*) familia son muy _____.

11. La biblioteca de la universidad es _____.

12. La prima de Irma es una _____ amiga.

3.2 Possessive adjectives

1 **¿De quién es?** Answer each question affirmatively using the correct possessive adjective.

> **modelo**
>
> ¿Es tu maleta?
> Sí, es mi maleta.

1. ¿Es la mochila de Adela? _____

2. ¿Es mi clase de español? _____

3. ¿Son los papeles de la profesora? _____

4. ¿Es el diccionario de tu compañera de cuarto? _____

5. ¿Es tu novia? _____

6. ¿Son los lápices de ustedes? _____

2 **Familia** Write the appropriate forms of the possessive adjectives indicated in parentheses.

1. _____ (*My*) cuñada, Isabella, es italiana.

2. _____ (*Their*) parientes están en Ecuador.

3. ¿Quién es _____ (*your* fam.) tío?

4. _____ (*Our*) padres regresan a las diez.

5. Es _____ (*his*) tarea de matemáticas.

6. Linda y María son _____ (*my*) hijas.

7. ¿Dónde trabaja _____ (*your* form.) esposa?

8. _____ (*Our*) familia es grande.

3 **Clarificar** Add a prepositional phrase that clarifies to whom the items belong.

> **modelo**
>
> ¿Es su libro? (ellos)
> ¿Es el libro de ellos?

1. ¿Cuál es su problema? (ella)

_____

2. Trabajamos con (*with*) su madre. (ellos)

_____

3. ¿Dónde están sus papeles? (ustedes)

_____

4. ¿Son sus plumas? (ella)

_____

5. ¿Quiénes son sus compañeros de cuarto? (él)

_____

6. ¿Cómo se llaman sus sobrinos? (usted)

_____

4   **Posesiones** Write sentences using possessive adjectives to indicate who owns these items.

> **modelo**
>
> Yo compro un escritorio.
> **Es mi** *escritorio.*

1. Ustedes compran cuatro sillas. _____

2. Tú compras una mochila. _____

3. Nosotros compramos una mesa. _____

4. Yo compro una maleta. _____

5. Él compra unos lápices. _____

6. Ellos compran una pizarra. _____

5   **Mi familia** Inés is talking about her family. Complete her description with the correct possessive adjectives.

Somos cinco hermanos. Graciela, Teresa y Carmen son _____ hermanas.
_____ 1

Francesca es _____ cuñada. Es la esposa de _____
2   3

hermano mayor, Pablo. Francesca es italiana. _____ papás viven en Roma. Vicente
4

es el hijo de _____ hermana mayor, Graciela. Él es _____ sobrino
5   6

favorito. _____ papá se llama Marcos y es español. Ellos viven con
7

_____ familia en Sevilla. Teresa estudia en Quito y vive con la tía Remedios y
8

_____ dos hijos, Carlos y Raquel, _____ primos. Carmen y yo
9   10

vivimos con _____ papás en Portoviejo. Los papás de _____
11   12

mamá viven también con nosotros. Nosotras compartimos _____ problemas con
13

_____ abuelos. Ellos son muy buenos. Y tú, ¿cómo es _____ familia?
14   15

6   **Preguntas** Answer these questions using possessive adjectives and the words in parentheses.

> **modelo**
>
> ¿Dónde está tu amiga? (Quito)
> **Mi** *amiga* **está en Quito.**

1. ¿Cómo es tu padre? (alto y moreno)

_____

2. José, ¿dónde están mis papeles? (en el escritorio)

_____

3. ¿Cómo es la escuela de Felipe? (pequeña y vieja)

_____

4. ¿Son mexicanos los amigos de ustedes? (puertorriqueños)

_____

5. Mami, ¿dónde está mi tarea? (en la mesa)

_____

3.3 Present tense of regular –er and –ir verbs

1 **Conversaciones** Complete these conversations with the correct forms of the verbs in parentheses.

(leer)

1. —¿Qué _____, Ana?

2. —_____ un libro de historia.

(vivir)

3. —¿Dónde _____ ustedes?

4. —Nosotros _____ en Nueva York. ¿Y tú?

(comer)

5. —¿Qué _____ ustedes?

6. —Yo _____ un sándwich y Eduardo _____ pizza.

(deber)

7. —Profesora, ¿_____ abrir nuestros libros ahora?

8. —Sí, ustedes _____ abrir los libros en la página (*page*) 87.

(escribir)

9. —¿_____ un libro, Melinda?

10. —Sí, _____ un libro para niños.

2 **Oraciones** Write complete sentences using the correct forms of the verbs in parentheses.

1. (Nosotros) (Escribir) muchas composiciones en la clase de inglés.

_____

2. Esteban y Luisa (aprender) a bailar tango.

_____

3. ¿Quién no (comprender) la lección de hoy?

_____

4. (Tú) (Deber) comprar un mapa de Quito.

_____

5. Ellos no (recibir) muchas cartas (*letters*) de sus padres.

_____

6. (Yo) (Buscar) unas fotos de mis primos.

_____

3 **¿Qué verbo es?** Choose the most logical verb to complete each sentence, using the correct form.

1. Tú _____ (abrir, correr, decidir) en el parque (*park*), ¿no?

2. Yo _____ (asistir, compartir, leer) a conciertos de Juanes.

3. ¿_____ (aprender, creer, deber) a leer tu sobrino?

4. Yo no _____ (beber, vivir, comprender) la tarea de física.

5. Los estudiantes _____ (escribir, beber, comer) hamburguesas en la cafetería.

6. Mi esposo y yo _____ (decidir, leer, deber) el *Miami Herald*.

Workbook

4 **Reescribir** Rewrite each sentence using the subject in parentheses. Change the verb form and possessive adjectives as needed.

> **modelo**
>
> No asistimos a clase los domingos. (yo)
> *No asisto a clase los domingos.*

1. Rubén cree que la lección 3 es fácil. (ellos)

_____

2. Mis hermanos comen hamburguesas en la cafetería. (la gente)

_____

3. Aprendemos a hablar, leer y escribir en la clase de español. (yo)

_____

4. Sandra escribe en su diario todos los días (*every day*). (tú)

_____

5. Comparto mis problemas con mis padres. (Víctor)

_____

6. Vives en una residencia interesante y bonita. (nosotras)

_____

5 **Descripciones** Look at the drawings and use these verbs to describe what the people are doing.

| abrir | aprender | comer | leer |

1. Nosotros _____

2. Yo _____

3. Mirta _____

4. Los estudiantes _____

3.4 Present tense of **tener** and **venir**

1   **Completar** Complete these sentences with the correct forms of **tener** and **venir**.

1. ¿A qué hora _____ ustedes al estadio?

2. ¿_____ tú a la universidad en autobús?

3. Nosotros _____ una prueba de psicología mañana.

4. ¿Por qué no _____ Juan a la clase de historia?

5. Yo _____ dos hermanos y mi prima _____ tres.

6. ¿_____ ustedes fotos de sus parientes?

7. Mis padres _____ unos amigos japoneses.

8. Inés _____ con su esposo y yo _____ con Ernesto.

9. Marta y yo no _____ al laboratorio los sábados.

10. ¿Cuántos nietos _____ tú?

11. Yo _____ una clase de contabilidad a las once de la mañana.

12. Mis amigos _____ a comer a la cafetería hoy.

2   **¿Qué tienen?** Rewrite each sentence, using the logical expression with **tener**.

1. Los estudiantes (tienen hambre, tienen miedo de) tomar el examen de química.

   _____

2. Las turistas (tienen sueño, tienen prisa) por llegar al autobús.

   _____

3. Mi madre (tiene cincuenta años, tiene razón) siempre (*always*).

   _____

4. Vienes a la cafetería cuando (*when*) (tienes hambre, tienes frío).

   _____

5. (Tengo razón, Tengo frío) en la biblioteca porque (*because*) abren las ventanas.

   _____

6. Rosaura y María (tienen calor, tienen ganas) de mirar la televisión.

   _____

7. Nosotras (tenemos cuidado, no tenemos razón) con el sol (*sun*).

   _____

8. David toma mucha agua cuando (*when*) (tiene miedo, tiene sed).

   _____

3 **Expresiones con _tener_** Complete each sentence with the correct expression and the appropriate form of **tener**.

tener cuidado	tener miedo	tener mucha suerte	tener que
tener ganas	tener mucha hambre	tener prisa	tener razón

1. Mis sobrinos _____ del perro de mis abuelos porque es muy grande.

2. Necesitas _____ con la computadora portátil (_laptop_). Es muy frágil (_fragile_).

3. Yo _____ practicar el vocabulario de español.

4. Lola y yo _____ de escuchar música latina.

5. Anita cree que (_that_) dos más dos son cinco. Ella no _____.

6. Ganas (_You win_) cien dólares en la lotería. Tú _____.

4 **Síntesis** Choose an interesting relative of yours and write a description of that person. Answer these questions in your description.

1. ¿Quién es?
2. ¿Cómo es?
3. ¿De dónde es?
4. ¿Cuántos hermanos/primos/hijos tiene?
5. ¿Cómo es su familia?
6. ¿Dónde vive?
7. ¿Cuántos años tiene?
8. ¿De qué tiene miedo?

_____

_____

_____

_____

_____

_____

_____

_____

_____

_____

_____

_____

_____

PREPARACIÓN

Lección 4

1 **Los deportes** Name the sport associated with each object. Include the definitive article.

1. _____

2. _____

3. _____

4. _____

5. _____

6. _____

2 **Una es diferente** Write the word that does not belong in each group.

1. pasatiempo, diversión, ratos libres, trabajar _____

2. patinar, descansar, esquiar, nadar, bucear _____

3. baloncesto, películas, fútbol, tenis, vóleibol _____

4. museo, equipo, jugador, partido, aficionados _____

5. correo electrónico, revista, periódico, tenis _____

6. cine, aficionado, gimnasio, piscina, restaurante _____

3 **¿Qué son?** Write each of these words in the appropriate column in the chart.

aficionado/a	excursionista	jugador(a)
baloncesto	fútbol	montañas
béisbol	gimnasio	restaurante

Deportes	Lugares	Personas

4 **El fin de semana** Complete the paragraph about Álex's weekend with the appropriate word from the word bank.

Álex

el cine	el monumento	una pelota
la ciudad	un museo	el periódico
deportes	la natación	la piscina
el gimnasio	el partido	un restaurante

Siempre leo _____ los domingos por la mañana. Después, me gusta practicar
_____ (2). A veces, nado en _____ (3) que hay en el parque.
Cuando no nado, hago ejercicio (*exercise*) en _____ (4). Cuando hay mucho
tráfico en _____ (5), voy al gimnasio en bicicleta.
Cuando no como en casa, como en _____ (6) con (*with*) mis amigos, y luego
nosotros vemos _____ (7) de béisbol. Algunos días, veo películas. Me gusta
más ver películas en _____ (8) que en mi casa.

GRAMÁTICA

4.1 The present tense of ir

1 **Vamos a la universidad** Complete the paragraph with the correct forms of **ir**.

Alina, Cristina y yo somos buenas amigas. (Nosotras) _____ a la universidad a las
ocho de la mañana todos los días (*every day*). Ellas y yo _____ al centro de
computación y leemos el correo electrónico. A las nueve Alina y Cristina _____
a su clase de psicología y yo _____ a mi clase de historia. A las diez y media yo
_____ a la biblioteca a estudiar. A las doce (yo) _____ a la
cafetería y como con ellas. Luego (*Afterward*), Alina y yo _____ a practicar
deportes. Yo _____ a practicar fútbol y Alina _____ a la piscina.
Cristina _____ a trabajar en la librería. Los fines de semana Alina, Cristina y yo
_____ al cine.

2 **Sujetos diferentes** Rewrite each sentence using the subject in parentheses. Change the forms of **ir** as needed.

1. Sergio y yo vamos a casa de Pablo el viernes. (Tomás)

   _____

2. Ustedes van a la librería a comprar unos cuadernos. (Los estudiantes)

   _____

3. Voy a la residencia estudiantil a buscar la mochila. (Tú)

   _____

4. Susana va al estadio a practicar hockey. (Yo)

   _____

5. Vas al museo en autobús. (Nosotras)

   _____

6. El papá de Javier va mucho al cine. (Mario y tú)

   _____

3   **Preguntas** Answer these questions in complete sentences using the words in parentheses.

1. ¿Adónde va Ana hoy? (al laboratorio)

_____

2. ¿Cuándo van a bailar tus amigos? (mañana)

_____

3. ¿A qué hora vas a la clase de música? (a las 10:45)

_____

4. ¿Cuándo va José a Boston? (en septiembre)

_____

5. ¿Dónde vas a leer el correo electrónico? (en la residencia estudiantil)

_____

6. ¿Dónde va a nadar el novio de Silvia? (en la piscina)

_____

7. ¿Adónde va el autobús número diez? (al parque municipal)

_____

8. ¿Dónde vas a trabajar los sábados? (en la biblioteca)

_____

4   **¡Vamos!** Rewrite these sentences using **ir a** + *infinitive* to say what activities these people are going to do tomorrow.

1. La familia García va al parque.

_____

2. Los jugadores ganan el partido.

_____

3. Los excursionistas escalan montañas.

_____

4. Gisela lee su correo electrónico.

_____

5. Tú vas al laboratorio de química.

_____

6. Mis compañeros de clase y yo visitamos la biblioteca del Congreso en Washington, D.C.

_____

7. El profesor de historia prepara un examen difícil.

_____

8. Escribo postales.

_____

4.2 Stem-changing verbs: e→ie, o→ue

1   **Los verbos** Complete these sentences with the correct forms of the verbs in parentheses.

1. Mi abuelo _____ (pensar) que la educación es muy importante.

2. El equipo de béisbol de mi residencia no _____ (perder) nunca (*never*).

3. Marcelo _____ (volver) a la universidad el lunes.

4. ¿A qué hora _____ (empezar) los partidos?

5. (Nosotros) _____ (dormir) en la montaña cuando vamos de excursión.

6. Mis padres _____ (cerrar) las ventanas porque tienen frío.

7. El ilustrador _____ (mostrar) sus dibujos en la galería.

8. (Yo) _____ (recordar) el primer (*first*) día de clases en la universidad.

9. ¿_____ (querer) (tú) ir a visitar los monumentos con nosotros?

10. (Yo) No _____ (encontrar) mis notas para el examen de mañana.

2   **Oraciones** Write complete sentences using the cues provided.

1. Vicente y Francisco / jugar / al vóleibol los domingos

_____

2. Adela y yo / empezar / a tomar clases de tenis

_____

3. ustedes / volver / de Cancún el viernes

_____

4. los jugadores de béisbol / recordar / el partido importante

_____

5. la profesora / querer / leer el periódico

_____

6. el excursionista / preferir / escalar la montaña de noche

_____

7. (yo) / dormir / ocho horas al día

_____

8. Miguel / poder / salir / a las seis

_____

9. Silvina y Carlos / no encontrar / el museo

_____

10. (tú) / cerrar / los libros y te vas a dormir

_____

Workbook

3 **No, no quiero** Answer these questions negatively, using complete sentences.

> modelo
>
> ¿Puedes ir a la biblioteca a las once?
> No, no puedo ir a la biblioteca a las once.

1. ¿Quieren ustedes patinar en línea con nosotros?

   _____

2. ¿Empiezan ellas a practicar deportes mañana?

   _____

3. ¿Prefieres jugar al fútbol a nadar en la piscina?

   _____

4. ¿Duermen tus sobrinos en casa de tu abuela?

   _____

5. ¿Juegan ustedes al baloncesto en la universidad?

   _____

6. ¿Piensas que la clase de química orgánica es difícil?

   _____

7. ¿Encuentras el programa de computadoras en la librería?

   _____

8. ¿Vuelven ustedes a casa los fines de semana?

   _____

9. ¿Puedo tomar el autobús a las once de la noche?

   _____

10. ¿Entienden ustedes la tarea de psicología?

    _____

4 **Correo electrónico** Complete this e-mail message with the correct form of the logical verb. Use each verb once.

comprar
dormir
empezar
entender
jugar
pensar
poder
preferir
querer
volver

Para Daniel Moncada	De Raúl	Asunto Saludo

Daniel:

¿Qué tal? Estoy con Mario en el centro de computación de la universidad. Los exámenes _____1_____ mañana. Mario y yo no _____2_____ muchas horas por la noche porque tenemos que estudiar mucho. Tú _____3_____ cómo estamos, ¿no?

Yo _____4_____ que los exámenes serán (will be) muy difíciles. Tengo muchas ganas de volver al pueblo. Cuando _____5_____ al pueblo puedo descansar. Yo _____6_____ el pueblo a la ciudad. _____7_____ volver pronto. Si (If) Mario y yo _____8_____ pasajes (tickets) de autobús el viernes, _____9_____ pasar el fin de semana contigo y con mi familia. En casa (At home) mis hermanos y yo _____10_____ al fútbol en nuestro tiempo libre.

Nos vemos,
Raúl

4.3 Stem-changing verbs: e→i

1 **Completar** Complete these sentences using the correct form of the verb provided.

1. Mis hermanos siempre (*always*) _____ (pedir) ver una película de acción.

2. Yo no _____ (conseguir) películas de acción en la biblioteca.

3. Mis hermanos y yo _____ (conseguir) entradas (*tickets*) al cine

   para estudiantes.

4. Al entrar al cine, mi hermano David _____ (pedir) una soda.

5. Yo _____ (repetir) el diálogo para mis hermanos.

6. Mis hermanos son pequeños y no _____ (seguir) bien la película.

2 **Conversaciones** Complete these conversations with the correct form of the verbs in parentheses.

(pedir)

1. —¿Qué _____ para comer, José?

2. —_____ pollo (*chicken*) con ensalada (*salad*).

(conseguir)

3. —¿Dónde _____ ustedes entradas para estudiantes?

4. —Nosotros las _____ en la oficina de la escuela.

(repetir)

5. —¿Quién _____ el poema que voy a leer?

6. —Yo _____ el poema, profesora.

(seguir)

7. —¿Qué equipo _____ Manuel y Pedro?

8. —Pedro _____ a los Red Sox y Manuel

   _____ a los Yankees de Nueva York.

3 **¿Qué haces?** Imagine that you are writing in your diary. Choose at least five of these phrases and describe what you do on any given day. You should add details you feel are necessary.

> conseguir hablar español   pedir una pizza
> conseguir el periódico   repetir una pregunta (*question*)
> pedir un libro   seguir instrucciones

_____

_____

_____

_____

_____

_____

   Lección 4 Workbook Activities   **37**

Workbook

4   **Las películas** Read the paragraph. Then answer the questions using complete sentences.

Gastón y Lucía leen el periódico y deciden ir al cine. Un crítico dice (*says*) que *El café en el centro* es buena. Ellos siguen la recomendación. Quieren conseguir entradas para estudiantes, que son más baratas. Para conseguir entradas para estudiantes, deben ir a la oficina de la escuela antes de (*before*) las seis de la tarde. La oficina cierra a las seis. Ellos corren para llegar a tiempo. Cuando (*When*) llegan, la oficina está cerrada y la secretaria está afuera (*outside*). Ellos le piden un favor a la secretaria. Explican que no tienen mucho dinero y necesitan entradas para estudiantes. La secretaria sonríe (*smiles*) y dice: "Está bien, pero es la última vez (*last time*)".

1. ¿Qué deciden hacer Gastón y Lucía?

_____

2. ¿De quién siguen la recomendación?

_____

3. ¿Por qué Gastón y Lucía quieren conseguir entradas para estudiantes?

_____

4. ¿Cuándo y dónde pueden conseguir entradas para estudiantes?

_____

5. ¿Qué ocurre cuando llegan a la oficina de la escuela?

_____

_____

6. ¿Qué le piden a la secretaria? ¿Consiguen las entradas?

_____

_____

_____

5   **Contestar** Answer these questions, using complete sentences.

1. ¿Cómo consigues buenas calificaciones (*grades*)?

_____

2. ¿Dónde pides pizza?

_____

3. ¿Sigues a algún (*any*) equipo deportivo?

_____

4. ¿Consigues entender la televisión en español?

_____

5. ¿Qué programas repiten en la televisión?

_____

4.4 Verbs with irregular yo forms

1 **Hago muchas cosas** Complete each sentence by choosing the best verb and writing its correct form.

1. (Yo) _____ (oír, suponer, salir) un disco de música latina.

2. (Yo) _____ (poner, oír, suponer) la hamburguesa y la soda sobre la mesa.

3. (Yo) _____ (salir, hacer, suponer) la tarea porque hay un examen mañana.

4. (Yo) _____ (traer, salir, hacer) a mi sobrina a mi clase de baile.

5. (Yo) _____ (salir, suponer, ver) una película sobre un gran equipo de béisbol.

6. (Yo) _____ (ver, salir, traer) a bailar los jueves por la noche.

7. (Yo) _____ (hacer, poner, suponer) que la película es buena, pero no estoy seguro (*sure*).

8. (Yo) _____ (traer, salir, hacer) mi computadora portátil (*laptop*) a clase en la mochila.

2 **Completar** Complete these sentences with the correct verb. Use each verb in the **yo** form once.

hacer	suponer
oír	traer
salir	ver

1. _____ para la clase a las dos.

2. Los fines de semana _____ mi computadora a casa.

3. _____ que tu novio es muy simpático, ¿no?

4. Por las mañanas _____ música en la radio.

5. Cuando tengo hambre, _____ un sándwich.

6. Para descansar, _____ películas en la televisión.

3 **Preguntas** Answer these questions, using complete sentences.

1. ¿Adónde sales a bailar con tus amigos?

_____

2. ¿Ves partidos de béisbol todos los fines de semana?

_____

3. ¿Oyes música clásica?

_____

4. ¿Traes una computadora portátil (*laptop*) a clase?

_____

5. ¿Cómo supones que va a ser el examen de español?

_____

6. ¿Adónde sales a comer los sábados?

_____

Lección 4 Workbook Activities **39**

4   **La descripción** Read this description of Marisol. Then imagine that you are Marisol, and write a description of yourself based on the information you read. The first sentence has been done for you.

Marisol es estudiante de biología en la universidad. Hace sus tareas todas (*every*) las tardes y sale por las noches a bailar o a comer en un restaurante cerca de la universidad. Los fines de semana, Marisol va a su casa a descansar, pero (*but*) trae sus libros. En sus ratos libres, oye música o ve una película en el cine. Si hay un partido de fútbol, Marisol pone la televisión y ve los partidos con su papá. Hace algo (*something*) de comer y pone la mesa (*sets the table*).

Soy estudiante de biología en la universidad. _____

_____

_____

_____

_____

_____

_____

5   **Síntesis** Interview a classmate about his or her pastimes, weekend activities, and favorite sports. Use these questions as a guideline, and prepare several more before the interview. Then, write it up in a question-and-answer format, using your subject's exact words.

- ¿Cuáles son tus pasatiempos? ¿Dónde los practicas?

- ¿Cuál es tu deporte favorito? ¿Practicas ese deporte? ¿Eres un(a) gran aficionado/a? ¿Tu equipo favorito pierde muchas veces? ¿Quién es tu jugador(a) favorito/a?

- ¿Adónde vas los fines de semana? ¿Qué piensas hacer el viernes?

- ¿Duermes mucho durante los fines de semana? ¿Vuelves a casa muy tarde (*late*)?

_____

_____

_____

_____

_____

_____

Workbook

¡VIVAN LOS PAÍSES HISPANOS!

México

1 **Completar** Complete the following sentences using the correct words.

1. El 16 de septiembre en México celebran _____ .

2. A las celebraciones del 16 de septiembre se les llama _____ .

3. Diego Rivera y Frida Kahlo son los _____ mexicanos más famosos.

4. Los dos se interesaron en _____ de la gente indígena y los campesinos.

5. Los pueblos mayas habitaron el _____ de México y _____ .

6. Los mayas crearon templos religiosos en forma de _____ .

7. México es el país que produce más (*most*) _____ en el mundo (*world*).

8. _____ y Durango son dos estados que tienen yacimientos (*deposits*) de plata.

2 **¿Qué hacen?** Write complete sentences using the cues below.

1. la moneda mexicana / ser / ¿? _____

2. los descendientes de los mayas / seguir / ¿? _____

3. en el Museo de Arte Moderno de la Ciudad de México / tú / poder / ¿?

_____

4. en Acapulco miles de turistas / visitar / ¿? _____

5. los mexicanos / celebrar / ¿? _____

6. la capital de México / tener una población / ¿?

_____

3 **Palabras** Using the clues, rearrange the letters to spell words from ¡Vivan los países hispanos!

1. AL EUQDABAR _____
   Lugar de Acapulco donde saltan los clavadistas.

2. EMACONIX _____
   Un hombre nacido en México.

3. DACUDI ZÁUJER _____
   Ciudad que está en la frontera (*border*) entre México y los Estados Unidos.

4. MÁPEDIRI _____
   Forma de los templos religiosos mayas.

5. NGADORU _____
   Estado mexicano que produce mucha plata.

6. ALETAGAUM _____
   País que tiene frontera con México.

Workbook

Workbook

4 **Las fotos** Identify each photo.

1. _____

2. _____

3. _____

4. _____

5 **Preguntas** Answer the following questions in complete sentences.

1. ¿Cuáles son las cuatro ciudades principales de México?

_____

2. ¿Qué países hacen frontera (*border*) con México?

_____

3. ¿Cuál es un río importante de México?

_____

4. ¿Qué ciudad mexicana importante está en la frontera con los Estados Unidos?

_____

5. ¿En qué se interesaron Frida Kahlo y Diego Rivera?

_____

6. ¿Dónde hay exhibiciones de algunas de las obras de Frida Kahlo y Diego Rivera?

_____

7. ¿Cómo celebran los mexicanos la independencia de su país?

_____

8. ¿Qué día celebran los mexicanos la independencia de su país?

_____

REPASO   **Lecciones 1-4**

1 **¿Ser o estar?** Complete each sentence with the correct form of **ser** or **estar**.

1. Los abuelos de Maricarmen _____ de España.

2. La cafetería de la universidad _____ cerca del estadio.

3. Gerónimo y Daniel _____ estudiantes de sociología.

4. —Hola, Gabriel. _____ María. ¿Cómo _____?

5. El cuaderno de español _____ debajo del libro de química.

6. Victoria no viene a clase hoy porque _____ enferma (*sick*).

2 **¿Quiénes son?** Read the clues and complete the chart. Write out the numbers.

1. La persona de los Estados Unidos tiene treinta y dos años.
2. David es de Canadá.
3. La programadora no es la persona de Ecuador.
4. El conductor tiene cuarenta y cinco años.
5. Gloria es artista.
6. La médica tiene cincuenta y un años.
7. La persona de España tiene ocho años menos que el conductor.
8. Ana es programadora.

Nombre	Profesión	Edad (*Age*)	Nacionalidad
Raúl	estudiante	diecinueve	mexicano
Carmen			
			estadounidense
David			
	programadora		

3 **Oraciones** Form complete sentences using the words provided. Write out the words for numbers.

1. Juan Carlos y Beto / jugar / fútbol

   _____

2. estudiante / llegar / grande / biblioteca / 5:30 p.m.

   _____

3. hay / 15 / cuadernos / sobre / escritorio

   _____

4. yo / aprender / español / escuela

   _____

5. Me / gustar / viajar en autobús

   _____

6. ¿te / gustar / las novelas de terror?

   _____

4   **Conversación** Complete this conversación with the correct form of the verbs provided.

ALICIA   ¿Qué _____ (hacer) este fin de semana?
                              1

PACO   No _____ (tener) planes. ¿Y tú?
                        2

ALICIA   El sábado _____ (ir) al cine con David.
                              3

PACO   ¿A qué hora _____ (empezar) la película?
                                4

ALICIA   _____ (Suponer) que empieza a las nueve.
                    5

PACO   ¿_____ (Querer) ir al restaurante El Dorado a las siete?
              6

ALICIA   No, gracias. No me _____ (gustar) ese restaurante.
                                        7

5   **Preguntas** Read the answers and ask the appropriate questions.

1. _____

Vivo en la residencia estudiantil.

2. _____

Tomo cinco clases.

3. _____

Estudio periodismo.

4. _____

Mi profesor favorito es el señor Zamora.

6   **Tu familia** Imagine that these people are your relatives. Choose one and write several sentences about that person. First, say where the person is located in the photo. Include this information: name, relationship to you, profession, age, place of origin, likes and dislikes. Describe the person and his or her weekend activities using the adjectives and verbs you have learned.

_____

_____

_____

_____

_____

PREPARACIÓN

1 **Viajes** Complete these sentences with the logical words.

1. Una persona que tiene una habitación en un hotel es _____.

2. El lugar donde los pasajeros esperan el tren es _____.

3. Para viajar en avión, tienes que ir _____.

4. Antes de entrar en el avión, tienes que mostrar _____.

5. La persona que lleva el equipaje a la habitación del hotel es _____.

6. Para planear (*plan*) tus vacaciones, puedes ir a _____.

7. Cuando entras a un país diferente, tienes que pasar por _____.

8. Para abrir la puerta de la habitación, necesitas _____.

9. Hay habitaciones baratas (*cheap*) en _____.

10. Cuando una persona entra en un país, tiene que mostrar _____.

2 **De vacaciones** Complete this conversation with the logical words.

aeropuerto	equipaje	llegada	playa
agente de viajes	habitación	pasajes	sacar fotos
cabaña	hotel	pasaportes	salida
confirmar	llave	pasear	taxi

ANTONIO ¿Llevas todo (*everything*) lo que vamos a necesitar para el viaje, Ana?

ANA Sí. Llevo los _____ para subir (*get on*) al avión. También llevo
          1
los _____ para entrar en Ecuador.
          2

ANTONIO Y yo tengo el _____ con todas (*all*) nuestras cosas.
                             3

ANA ¿Tienes la cámara para _____?
                                  4

ANTONIO Sí, está en mi mochila.

ANA ¿Vamos al _____ en metro?
                      5

ANTONIO No, vamos a llamar a un _____. Nos lleva directamente al aeropuerto.
                                       6

ANA Voy a llamar al aeropuerto para _____ la reservación.
                                          7

ANTONIO La _____ dice que ya (*already*) está confirmada.
                 8

ANA Muy bien. Tengo muchas ganas de _____ por Quito.
                                           9

ANTONIO Yo también. Quiero ir a la _____ y nadar en el mar.
                                          10

ANA ¿Cuál es la hora de _____ al aeropuerto de Quito?
                               11

ANTONIO Llegamos a las tres de la tarde y vamos directamente al _____.
                                                                       12

Lección 5 Workbook Activities   **45**

Workbook

3   **Los meses** Write the appropriate month next to each description or event.

1. el Día de San Valentín _____
2. el tercer mes del año _____
3. Hannukah _____

4. el Día de las Madres _____
5. el séptimo mes del año _____
6. el Día de Año Nuevo (*New*) _____

4   **Las estaciones** Answer these questions using complete sentences.

1. ¿Qué estación sigue al invierno? _____
2. ¿En qué estación va mucha gente a la playa? _____
3. ¿En qué estación empiezan las clases? _____

5   **El tiempo** Answer these questions with complete sentences on the weather map.

1. ¿Hace buen tiempo en Soria? _____
2. ¿Llueve en Teruel? _____
3. ¿Hace sol en Girona? _____
4. ¿Está nublado en Murcia? _____
5. ¿Nieva en Cáceres? _____
6. ¿Qué tiempo hace en Salamanca? _____
7. ¿Hace viento cerca de Castellón? _____
8. ¿Qué tiempo hace en Almería? _____
9. ¿Está nublado en Las Palmas? _____
10. ¿Hace buen tiempo en Lleida? _____

GRAMÁTICA

5.1 Estar with conditions and emotions

1 **¿Por qué?** Choose the best phrase to complete each sentence.

1. José Miguel está cansado porque...
   a. trabaja mucho.
   b. su familia lo quiere.
   c. quiere ir al cine.

2. Los viajeros están preocupados porque...
   a. es la hora de comer.
   b. va a venir un huracán (*hurricane*).
   c. estudian matemáticas.

3. Maribel y Claudia están tristes porque...
   a. nieva mucho y no pueden salir.
   b. van a salir a bailar.
   c. sus amigos son simpáticos.

4. Los estudiantes están equivocados porque...
   a. estudian mucho.
   b. pasean en bicicleta.
   c. su respuesta es incorrecta.

5. Laura está enamorada porque...
   a. tiene que ir a la biblioteca.
   b. su novio es simpático, inteligente y guapo.
   c. sus amigas ven una película.

6. Mis abuelos están felices porque...
   a. vamos a pasar el verano con ellos.
   b. mucha gente toma el sol.
   c. el autobús no llega.

2 **Completar** Complete these sentences with the correct form of **estar** + condition or emotion.

1. No tenemos nada que hacer; _____ muy _____.

2. Humberto _____ muy _____ en su gran cama nueva (*new*).

3. Los estudiantes de filosofía no _____ _____; ellos tienen razón.

4. Cuando Estela llega a casa a las tres de la mañana, _____ muy _____.

5. La habitación _____ _____ porque no tengo tiempo (*time*) de organizar los libros y papeles.

6. Son las once de la noche; no puedo ir a la biblioteca ahora porque _____ _____.

7. El auto de mi tío _____ muy _____ por la nieve y el lodo (*mud*) que hay esta semana.

8. Mi papá canta en la casa cuando _____ _____.

9. Alberto _____ _____ porque sus amigos están muy lejos.

10. Las ventanas _____ _____ porque hace buen tiempo.

Workbook

3 **Marta y Juan** Complete this e-mail using **estar** + the correct forms of the following emotions and conditions. Try to use each term once.

abierto	cómodo	enojado	ocupado
aburrido	contento	feliz	seguro
avergonzado	desordenado	limpio	triste
cansado	enamorado	nervioso	

Querida Marta:

¿Cómo estás? Yo _____ porque mañana vuelvo a Puerto Rico y por fin te
                           1
voy a ver. Sé (*I know*) que tú _____ porque tenemos que estar separados durante
                                       2
el semestre, pero _____ de que (*that*) te van a aceptar en la universidad
                            3
y que vas a venir en septiembre. La habitación en la residencia estudiantil no es grande,
pero mi compañero de cuarto y yo _____ aquí. Las ventanas son grandes
                                           4
y _____ siempre (*always*) porque el tiempo es muy bueno en California.
        5
El cuarto no _____ porque mi compañero de cuarto es muy ordenado. En
                    6
la semana mis amigos y yo _____ porque trabajamos y estudiamos muchas
                                    7
horas al día. Cuando llego a la residencia estudiantil por la noche, _____ y
                                                                          8
me voy a dormir. Los fines de semana no _____ porque hay muchas cosas
                                                  9
que hacer en San Diego. Ahora _____ porque mañana tengo que llegar al
                                       10
aeropuerto a las cinco de la mañana y tengo miedo de quedarme dormido (*fall asleep*).
Pero tengo ganas de estar contigo (*with you*) porque _____ de ti (*you*) y
                                                              11
_____ porque te voy a ver mañana.
        12

Te quiero mucho,

Juan

4 **¿Cómo están?** Read each sentence, then write a new one for each, using **estar** + an emotion or condition to tell how these people are doing or feeling.

> **modelo**
> Pepe tiene que trabajar muchas horas.
> *Pepe está ocupado.*

1. Vicente y Mónica tienen sueño. _____
2. No tenemos razón. _____
3. El pasajero tiene miedo. _____
4. Paloma se quiere casar con (*marry*) su novio. _____
5. Los abuelos de Irene van de vacaciones a Puerto Rico. _____
6. No sé (*I don't know*) si el examen va a ser fácil o difícil. _____

5.2 The present progressive

1 **Completar** Complete these sentences with the correct form of **estar** + the present participle of the verbs in parentheses.

1. Ana _____ (buscar) un apartamento en el centro de la ciudad.

2. Mis primos _____ (comer) en el café de la esquina.

3. (Yo) _____ (empezar) a entender muy bien el español.

4. Miguel y Elena _____ (vivir) en un apartamento en la playa.

5. El amigo de Antonio _____ (trabajar) en la oficina hoy.

6. (Tú) _____ (jugar) al Monopolio con tu sobrina y su amiga.

7. Muchas familias _____ (tener) problemas con sus hijos adolescentes.

8. El inspector de aduanas _____ (abrir) las maletas de Ramón.

9. (Nosotros) _____ (pensar) en ir de vacaciones a Costa Rica.

10. Mi compañera de cuarto _____ (estudiar) en la biblioteca esta tarde.

2 **Están haciendo muchas cosas** Look at the illustration and label what each person is doing. Use the present progressive.

1. El señor Rodríguez _____

_____.

2. Pepe y Martita _____

_____.

3. Paquito _____

_____.

4. Kim _____

_____.

5. Tus abuelos _____

_____.

6. (Yo) _____

_____.

7. La madre de David _____

_____.

8. (Tú) _____

_____.

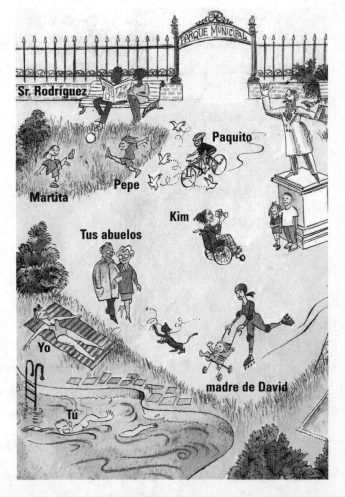

Workbook

5.3 Comparing ser and estar

1 **Usos de *ser* y *estar*** Complete these sentences with **ser** and **estar**. Then write the letter that corresponds to the correct use of the verb in the blank at the end of each sentence.

Uses of *ser*	Uses of *estar*
a. Nationality and place of origin	i. Location or spatial relationships
b. Profession or occupation	j. Health
c. Characteristics of people and things	k. Physical states or conditions
d. Generalizations	l. Emotional states
e. Possession	m. Certain weather expressions
f. What something is made of	n. Ongoing actions (progressive tenses)
g. Time and date	
h. Where or when an event occurs	

1. El concierto de jazz _____ a las ocho de la noche. _____

2. Inés y Raúl _____ preocupados porque el examen va a ser difícil. _____

3. La playa _____ sucia porque hay muchos turistas. _____

4. No puedo salir a tomar el sol porque _____ nublado. _____

5. En el verano, Tito _____ botones del hotel Brisas de Loíza. _____

6. Rita no puede venir al trabajo hoy porque _____ enferma. _____

7. La motocicleta nueva _____ de David. _____

8. (Yo) _____ estudiando en la biblioteca porque tengo un examen mañana. _____

9. La piscina del hotel _____ grande y bonita. _____

10. _____ importante estudiar, pero también tienes que descansar. _____

2 **¿Ser o estar?** In each of the following pairs, complete one sentence with the correct form of **ser** and the other with the correct form of **estar.**

1. Irene todavía no _____ lista para salir.

    Ricardo _____ el chico más listo de la clase.

2. Tomás no es un buen amigo porque _____ muy aburrido.

    Quiero ir al cine porque _____ muy aburrida.

3. Mi mamá está en cama (*in bed*) porque _____ mal del estómago (*stomach*).

    El restaurante que está cerca del laboratorio _____ muy malo.

4. La mochila de Javier _____ verde (*green*).

    No me gustan las bananas cuando _____ verdes.

5. Elena _____ más (*more*) rubia por tomar el sol.

    La hija de mi profesor _____ rubia.

6. Gabriela _____ muy delgada porque está enferma (*sick*).

    Mi hermano _____ muy delgado.

3 **Escribir** Write sentences using these cues and either **ser** or **estar** as appropriate.

1. el escritorio / limpio y ordenado

_____

2. el restaurante japonés / excelente

_____

3. la puerta del auto / abierta

_____

4. Marc y Delphine / franceses

_____

5. (yo) / cansada de trabajar

_____

6. Paula y yo / buscando un apartamento

_____

7. la novia de Guillermo / muy simpática

_____

8. la empleada del hotel / ocupada

_____

9. ustedes / en la ciudad de San Juan

_____

10. (tú) / José Javier Fernández

_____

4 **La familia Piñero** Complete this paragraph with the correct forms of **ser** and **estar.**

Los Piñero _____ 1 de Nueva York pero _____ 2 de vacaciones en

Puerto Rico. _____ 3 en un hotel grande en el pueblo de Dorado. Los padres

_____ 4 Elena y Manuel y, ahora, _____ 5 comiendo en el restaurante

del hotel. Los hijos _____ 6 Cristina y Luis y _____ 7 nadando en la

piscina. Ahora mismo _____ 8 lloviendo pero el sol va a salir

muy pronto (*soon*). Hoy _____ 9 lunes y la familia _____ 10

muy contenta de poder descansar. El señor Piñero _____ 11 profesor y la señora

Piñero _____ 12 médica. Los Piñero dicen: «¡Cuando no _____ 13

de vacaciones, _____ 14 todo el tiempo muy ocupados!»

Workbook

5.4 Direct object nouns and pronouns

1 **Oraciones** Complete these sentences with the correct direct object pronouns.

1. ¿Trae Daniel su pasaporte? No, Daniel no _____ trae.

2. ¿Confirma la reservación el agente de viajes? Sí, el agente de viajes _____ confirma.

3. ¿Hacen las maletas Adela y Juan José? Sí, Adela y Juan José _____ hacen.

4. ¿Buscas el pasaje en tu mochila? Sí, _____ busco en mi mochila.

5. ¿Compra Manuela una casa nueva (*new*)? Sí, Manuela _____ compra.

6. ¿Necesita lápices especiales el estudiante? No, el estudiante no _____ necesita.

7. ¿Cierran las puertas cuando empieza el examen? Sí, _____ cierran cuando empieza el examen.

8. ¿Ves mi computadora nueva? Sí, _____ veo.

9. ¿Escuchan el programa de radio David y Sonia? Sí, David y Sonia _____ escuchan.

10. ¿Oyen ustedes a los niños en el patio? No, no _____ oímos.

2 **Quiero verlo** Rewrite each of these sentences in two different ways, using direct object pronouns.

> **modelo**
> Quiero ver la película esta tarde.
> La quiero ver esta tarde.
> Quiero verla esta tarde.

1. Preferimos reservar una habitación hoy.

_____

_____

2. Ana y Alberto pueden pedir las llaves de la pensión.

_____

_____

3. Rosario tiene que conseguir un pasaje de ida y vuelta a Miami.

_____

_____

4. Vas a perder el tren si no terminas a las cinco.

_____

_____

5. Mis abuelos deben tener cuatro maletas en su casa.

_____

_____

6. La chica piensa tomar el metro por la mañana.

_____

_____

PREPARACIÓN

Lección 6

1 El almacén Look at the department store directory. Then complete the sentences with terms from the word list.

Almacén Gema

PRIMER PISO	Departamento de caballeros
SEGUNDO PISO	Zapatos y ropa de invierno
TERCER PISO	Departamento de damas y óptica
CUARTO PISO	Ropa interior, ropa de verano y trajes de baño

abrigos	calcetines	gafas de sol	sandalias
blusas	cinturones	guantes	trajes de baño
bolsas	corbatas	medias	trajes de hombre
botas	faldas	pantalones de hombre	vestidos

1. En el primer piso puedes encontrar _____

2. En el segundo piso puedes encontrar _____

3. En el tercer piso puedes encontrar _____

4. En el cuarto piso puedes encontrar _____

5. Quiero unos pantalones cortos. Voy al _____ piso.

6. Buscas unas gafas. Vas al _____ piso.

7. Arturo ve una chaqueta en el _____ piso.

8. Ana ve los bluejeans en el _____ piso.

2 Necesito muchas cosas Complete these sentences with the correct terms.

1. Voy a nadar en la piscina. Necesito _____.

2. Está lloviendo mucho. Necesito _____.

3. No puedo ver bien porque hace sol. Necesito _____.

4. Voy a correr por el parque. Necesito _____.

5. Queremos entrar en muchas tiendas diferentes. Vamos al _____.

6. No tengo dinero en la cartera. Voy a pagar con la _____.

3 **Los colores** Answer these questions in complete sentences.

1. ¿De qué color es el chocolate?

_____

2. ¿De qué color son las bananas?

_____

3. ¿De qué color son las naranjas (*oranges*)?

_____

4. ¿De qué colores es la bandera (*flag*) de los Estados Unidos?

_____

5. ¿De qué color son las nubes (*clouds*) cuando está nublado?

_____

6. ¿De qué color son los bluejeans?

_____

7. ¿De qué color es la nieve?

_____

8. ¿De qué color son las palabras de los libros?

_____

4 **¿Qué lleva?** Look at the illustration and fill in the blanks with the names of the numbered items.

GRAMÁTICA

6.1 Numbers 101 and higher

1 **La lotería** Read the following lottery winnings list. Then answer the questions, writing the Spanish words for numbers. Remember to use **de** after the number whenever necessary.

LOTERÍA NACIONAL	SORTEO° DEL DÍA 24 DE JUNIO Diez series de 100.000 billetes° cada una	SORTEO 49 00	Lista acumulada° de las cantidades que han correspondido a los números premiados, clasificados por su cifra° final Estos premios° podrán cobrarse hasta el día 25 de septiembre, INCLUSIVE

2		3		4		5		6		7	
Números	Pesos	Números	Pesos	Números	Pesos	Números	Pesos	Números	Pesos	Números	Pesos
43402	100.000	43403	110.000	43404	110.000	43405	100.000	43406	100.000	43407	100.000
43412	100.000	43413	110.000	43414	110.000	43415	100.000	43416	100.000	43417	100.000
43422	100.000	43423	110.000	43424	130.000	43425	100.000	43426	100.000	43427	100.000
43432	100.000	43433	110.000	43434	110.000	43435	100.000	43436	100.000	43437	100.000
43442	100.000	43443	110.000	43444	110.000	43445	100.000	43446	100.000	43447	100.000
43452	100.000	43453	110.000	43454	110.000	43455	100.000	43456	100.000	43457	100.000
43462	100.000	43463	110.000	43464	110.000	43465	100.000	43466	100.000	43467	100.000
43472	100.000	43473	110.000	43474	160.000	43475	100.000	43476	100.000	43477	100.000
43482	100.000	43483	110.000	43484	110.000	43485	100.000	43486	1.280.000	**43487**	**20.000.000**
43492	100.000	43493	110.000	43494	110.000	43495	100.000	43496	100.000	43497	100.000
98302	100.000	98303	110.000	98304	110.000	98305	100.000	98306	100.000	98307	100.000
98312	100.000	98313	110.000	98314	110.000	98315	100.000	98316	100.000	98317	100.000
98322	100.000	98323	110.000	98324	130.000	98325	100.000	98326	100.000	98327	100.000
98332	100.000	98333	110.000	98334	110.000	98335	100.000	98336	100.000	98337	100.000
98342	100.000	98343	110.000	98344	110.000	98345	100.000	98346	100.000	98347	100.000
98352	100.000	98353	110.000	98354	110.000	98355	100.000	98356	100.000	98357	100.000
98362	100.000	98363	110.000	98364	110.000	98365	100.000	98366	100.000	98367	100.000
98372	100.000	98373	2.110.000	**98374**	**100.110.000**	98375	2.100.000	98376	2.100.000	98377	2.100.000
98382	100.000	98383	110.000	98384	110.000	98385	100.000	98386	100.000	98387	100.000
98392	100.000	98393	110.000	98394	110.000	98395	100.000	98396	100.000	98397	100.000
		Terminaciones		**Terminaciones**		**Terminaciones**		**Terminaciones**		**Terminaciones**	
		4333	260.000	374	160.000	175	50.000	776	260.000	9957	250.000
		233	60.000	24	30.000	255	50.000			147	50.000
		733	60.000	74	60.000						
		3	10.000	4	10.000						

ESTE SORTEO ADJUDICA° 3.584.100 DÉCIMOS° PREMIADOS° POR UN IMPORTE° TOTAL DE 7.000.000.000 DE PESOS

PREMIO ESPECIAL 490.000.000 Pesos Núm. 98374 PRIMER PREMIO	FRACCIÓN 6.ª	SERIE 7.ª	PREMIO ACUMULADO 500.000.000

sorteo *lottery drawing*   acumulada *cumulative*   premio *prize*   cifra *figure*   billetes *tickets*   adjudica *awards*
décimos *lottery tickets*   premiados *awarded*   importe *quantity*

1. El sorteo tiene diez series de _____ billetes cada una.

2. El número 43403 gana _____ pesos.

3. El número 98373 gana _____ pesos.

4. El número 98374 gana _____ pesos.

5. El número 43487 gana _____ pesos.

6. La terminación _____ gana ciento sesenta mil pesos.

7. El sorteo adjudica _____ décimos premiados.

8. El importe total es de _____ pesos.

9. El premio especial es de _____ pesos.

10. El premio acumulado es de _____ pesos.

Workbook

Workbook

2 **¿Cuántos hay?** Use **Hay** + the cues to write complete sentences.

> **modelo**
> 450 / personas en la compañía
> Hay *cuatrocientas cincuenta personas en la compañía.*

1. 275.000.000 / habitantes en mi país

_____

2. 827 / pasajeros en el aeropuerto

_____

3. 25.350 / estudiantes en la universidad

_____

4. 3.930.000 / puertorriqueños en Puerto Rico

_____

5. 56.460 / libros en la biblioteca de mi pueblo

_____

6. 530.000 / turistas en la ciudad en el verano

_____

3 **¿Cuánto cuesta?** Two friends are shopping in a very expensive store. Finish the questions adding the name of each item with its article and then complete each answer writing out the corresponding amount.

1. $537

3. $169

5. $202

2. $123

4. $312

6. $480

1. ¿Cuánto cuestan _____?   4. ¿Cuánto cuesta _____?

Cuestan _____.   Cuesta _____.

2. ¿Cuánto cuestan _____?   5. ¿Cuánto cuesta _____?

Cuestan _____.   Cuesta _____.

3. ¿Cuánto cuestan _____?   6. ¿Cuánto cuesta _____?

Cuestan _____.   Cuesta _____.

6.2 The preterite tense of regular verbs

1 **El pretérito** Complete these sentences with the preterite tense of the indicated verb.

1. Marcela _____ (encontrar) las sandalias debajo de la cama.

2. Gustavo _____ (recibir) el dinero para comprar los libros.

3. Sara y Viviana _____ (terminar) el libro al mismo (*same*) tiempo.

4. La agente de viajes _____ (preparar) un itinerario muy interesante.

5. (Yo) _____ (volver) de la ciudad en bicicleta.

6. Los dependientes _____ (escuchar) el partido por la radio.

7. Patricia y tú _____ (viajar) a México el verano pasado.

8. (Nosotras) _____ (comprar) abrigos para el frío.

9. (Tú) _____ (regresar) del centro comercial a las cinco de la tarde.

10. Ustedes _____ (vivir) en casa de sus padres hasta el año pasado.

2 **Ahora y en el pasado** Rewrite these sentences in the preterite tense.

1. Ramón escribe una carta.

   _____

2. Mi tía trabaja de dependienta en un gran almacén.

   _____

3. Comprendo el trabajo de la clase de biología.

   _____

4. La familia de Daniel vive en Argentina.

   _____

5. Virginia y sus amigos comen en el café de la librería.

   _____

6. Los ingenieros terminan la construcción de la tienda en junio.

   _____

7. Llevas ropa muy elegante.

   _____

8. Los turistas caminan, compran y descansan.

   _____

9. Corremos por el estadio antes (*before*) del partido.

   _____

Workbook

3 **Ya pasó** Answer these questions negatively, indicating that what is being asked already happened.

> **modelo**
>
> ¿Va a comprar ropa Silvia en el centro comercial?
> No, Silvia ya *compró ropa en el centro comercial.*

1. ¿Va a viajar a Perú tu primo Andrés?

_____

2. ¿Vas a buscar una tienda de computadoras?

_____

3. ¿Vamos a encontrar muchas rebajas en el centro?

_____

4. ¿Va a pagar las sandalias María en la caja?

_____

5. ¿Van a regatear con el vendedor Mónica y Carlos?

_____

6. ¿Va a pasear por la playa tu abuela?

_____

4 **La semana pasada** Your friend asks you whether you did these activities last week. Write each question, then answer it affirmatively or negatively.

> **modelo**
>
> sacar fotos de amigos
> —¿Sacaste fotos de amigos?
> —Sí, saqué fotos de amigos./No, no saqué fotos de amigos.

1. pagar el abrigo con la tarjeta de crédito

_____

_____

2. jugar al tenis

_____

_____

3. buscar un libro en la biblioteca

_____

_____

4. llegar tarde (*late*) a clase

_____

_____

5. empezar a escribir una carta

_____

_____

6.3 Indirect object pronouns

1 **¿A quién?** Complete these sentences with the correct indirect object pronouns.

1. _____ doy a la profesora los libros.

2. Amelia _____ pregunta a nosotras si (*if*) queremos ir al cine.

3. El empleado _____ busca trabajo a sus primas en el almacén.

4. Julio _____ quiere traer un televisor nuevo a sus padres.

5. Los clientes _____ dicen a nosotros que todo está muy caro.

6. Tu hermano no _____ presta la ropa a ti (*you*).

7. La empleada de la tienda _____ cerró la puerta a mi tía.

8. La mamá no _____ hace las tareas a sus hijos.

9. _____ deben pagar mucho dinero porque llevas ropa muy cara.

10. Las dependientas _____ dan el vestido rosado a mí.

2 **¿A quién?** Use the cues in parentheses to rewrite the sentences using indirect object pronouns.

1. Llevo unos zapatos de tenis. (a mi hermano)

_____

2. Compré un impermeable. (a ella)

_____

3. Ellos traen trajes de baño. (a nosotros)

_____

4. No escribimos las cartas de recomendación. (a Gerardo y Marta)

_____

5. Ustedes dan un vestido. (a Marisela)

_____

6. Pides un descuento. (al dependiente)

_____

7. Conseguimos unas gafas en rebaja. (a ustedes)

_____

8. Hacemos muchas preguntas. (al vendedor)

_____

9. Doy información. (a un amigo)

_____

10. Ustedes venden unos libros. (a mi compañero de cuarto)

_____

Lección 6 Workbook Activities   **59**

3 **Escribir** Rewrite these sentences, using an alternate placement for the indirect object pronouns.

> **modelo**
> Me quiero comprar un coche nuevo.
> *Quiero comprarme un coche nuevo.*

1. Les vas a dar muchos regalos a tus padres.

_____

2. Quiero comprarles unos guantes a mis sobrinos.

_____

3. Clara va a venderle sus libros de francés a su amiga.

_____

4. Los clientes nos pueden pagar con tarjeta de crédito.

_____

4 **De compras** Complete the paragraph with the correct indirect object pronouns.

Isabel y yo vamos de compras al centro comercial. Yo _____ tengo que comprar
₁

unas cosas a mis parientes porque voy a viajar a mi ciudad este fin de semana. A mi hermana Laura

_____ quiero comprar unas gafas de sol, pero ella _____ tiene
₂   ₃

que comprar un traje de baño a mí. A mis dos sobrinos _____ voy a comprar
₄

una pelota de béisbol. A mi padre _____ llevo un libro, y a mi madre
₅

_____ quiero conseguir una blusa. _____ quiero llevar camisas
₆   ₇

con el nombre de mi universidad a todos. _____ quiero mostrar que pienso
₈

mucho en ellos.

5 **Respuestas** Answer these questions negatively. Use indirect object pronouns in the answer.

> **modelo**
> ¿Le compraste una camisa al vendedor?
> *No, no le compré una camisa.*

1. ¿Le escribió Rolando un correo electrónico a Miguel?

_____

2. ¿Nos trae el botones las maletas a la habitación?

_____

3. ¿Les venden gafas de sol los vendedores a los turistas?

_____

4. ¿Te da regalos tu hermano?

_____

5. ¿Les dicen mentiras sus amigos a ustedes?

_____

6. ¿Me buscaste la revista en la librería?

_____

Workbook

6.4 Demonstrative adjectives and pronouns

1 **Completar** Complete these sentences with the correct form of the adjective in parentheses.

1. Me quiero comprar _____ (*these*) zapatos porque me gustan mucho.

2. Comimos en _____ (*that*) restaurante la semana pasada.

3. _____ (*that over there*) tienda vende las gafas de sol a un precio muy alto.

4. Las rebajas en _____ (*this*) almacén son legendarias.

5. _____ (*those*) botas hacen juego con tus pantalones negros.

6. Voy a llevar _____ (*these*) pantalones con la blusa roja.

2 **Preguntas** Answer these questions negatively, using the cues in parentheses and the corresponding demonstrative adjectives.

> **modelo**
> ¿Compró esas medias Sonia? (cartera)
> No, *compró esa cartera.*

1. ¿Va a comprar ese suéter Gloria? (pantalones)

_____

2. ¿Llevaste estas sandalias? (zapatos de tenis)

_____

3. ¿Quieres ver esta ropa interior? (medias)

_____

4. ¿Usa aquel traje David? (chaqueta negra)

_____

5. ¿Decidió Silvia comprar esas gafas de sol? (sombrero)

_____

6. ¿Te mostró el vestido aquella vendedora? (dependiente)

_____

3 **Ésos no** Complete these sentences using demonstrative pronouns. Choose a pronoun for each sentence, paying attention to agreement.

1. Aquellas sandalias son muy cómodas, pero _____ son más elegantes.

2. Esos vestidos largos son muy caros; voy a comprar _____.

3. No puedo usar esta tarjeta de crédito; tengo que usar _____.

4. Esos zapatos tienen buen precio, pero _____ no.

5. Prefiero este sombrero porque _____ es muy grande.

6. Estas medias son buenas; las prefiero a _____.

4 **Éstas y aquéllas** Look at the illustration and complete this conversation with the appropriate demonstrative adjectives and pronouns.

CLAUDIA ¿Te gusta _____ corbata, Gerardo?
                                    1

GERARDO No, no me gusta _____. Prefiero _____ que está sobre
                                              2   3

el escaparate (*display case*).

CLAUDIA _____ es bonita, pero no hace juego con tu chaqueta.
                    4

GERARDO Mira _____ chaqueta. Me gusta y está a buen precio.
                           5

Puedo usar _____ y darle ésta a mi hermano.
                        6

CLAUDIA ¿Y _____ cinturón?
                      7

GERARDO _____ es muy elegante. ¿Es caro?
                    8

CLAUDIA Es más barato que _____ tres del escaparate.
                                         9

5 **Síntesis** Imagine that you went with your brother to an open-air market last weekend. This weekend you take a friend there. Write a conversation between you and your friend, using as many different verbs as you can from those you have learned. Follow the guide.

• Indicate to your friend the items you liked and didn't like, the items that you bought, how much you paid for them, and for whom you bought the items.

• Suggest items that your friend might buy and for whom he or she might buy them.

_____

_____

_____

_____

_____

¡VIVAN LOS PAÍSES HISPANOS!

El Caribe

1 | **El mapa** Write each of these words in the appropriate country in the map.

La Habana Vieja	población: 11.075.000	El Morro
Fajardo	Pedro Martínez	Palacio de los Capitanes Generales
Mayagüez	Guantánamo	Santo Domingo
Santiago de los Caballeros	el merengue	la isla de Vieques

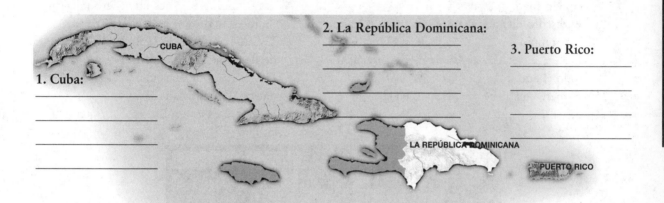

2. La República Dominicana:
_____
_____
_____

3. Puerto Rico:
_____
_____
_____

1. Cuba:
_____
_____
_____

2 | **Completar** Select the option that best completes each sentence.

1. Tres de las ciudades principales de Puerto Rico
   son Mayagüez, Ponce y _____.

2. Las aguas del Caribe son _____.

3. Puerto Rico, Cuba y la República Dominicana
   están en _____.

4. La capital de Cuba es _____.

5. Juan Luis Guerra es un cantante
   de la _____.

6. El sitio más fotografiado de
   Puerto Rico es _____.

7. El Morro está en la Bahía
   de _____.

8. Una de las ciudades principales dominicanas
   es Santiago de los _____.

9. La Habana _____ fue (*was*) declarada
   Patrimonio de la Humanidad en 1982.

10. La moneda de Cuba es _____.

a. el Caribe
b. Caguas
c. El Morro
d. Camagüey
e. San Juan
f. cálidas y transparentes
g. el peso cubano
h. Caballeros
i. República Dominicana
j. Vieja
k. La Habana

3 Crucigrama Complete this crossword puzzle based on the clues provided.

Horizontales

1. El Caribe tiene una enorme variedad de _____ y animales exóticos.

4. La salsa nació en _____.

6. _____ es una ciudad puertorriqueña que está entre Mayagüez y Fajardo.

8. _____ y Santiago de los Caballeros son dos ciudades de la República Dominicana.

10. _____ se construyó en el siglo XVI en San Juan.

11. El distrito de La Habana Vieja fue declarado Patrimonio _____ de la Humanidad.

14. El _____ goza de un clima tropical todo el año.

15. El merengue tiene sus orígenes en el _____.

Verticales

1. El Morro fue construido por los españoles para defenderse de los _____.

2. Actualmente, El Morro es un _____ que atrae a miles de turistas.

3. La ciudad de Cuba que está cerca de la Sierra Maestra es _____.

5. Antes las canciones del merengue hablaban de problemas _____.

7. La _____ es un género musical latino que proviene de Nueva York.

9. El _____ es la música tradicional de República Dominicana.

12. El _____ es una afición nacional dominicana.

13. El Morro es un _____ que está en Puerto Rico.

4 Las fotos Write complete sentences describing the activities or places in the photos.

1. _____   2. _____   3. _____

PREPARACIÓN   # Lección 7

---

1   **Las rutinas** Complete each sentence with a word from **Preparación**.

1. Susana se lava el pelo con _____.

2. Elena usa el _____ para maquillarse.

3. Manuel se lava las manos con _____.

4. Después de lavarse las manos, usa la _____.

5. Luis tiene un _____ para levantarse temprano.

---

2   **¿En el baño o en la habitación?** Write **en el baño** or **en la habitación** to indicate where each activity takes place.

1. bañarse _____

2. levantarse _____

3. ducharse _____

4. lavarse la cara _____

5. acostarse _____

6. afeitarse _____

7. cepillarse los dientes _____

8. dormirse _____

---

3   **Ángel y Lupita** Look at the drawings, and choose the appropriate phrase to describe what Ángel or Lupita is doing in a complete sentence.

| afeitarse por la mañana | cepillarse los dientes después de comer |
| bañarse por la tarde | ducharse antes de salir |

1. _____   2. _____

_____   _____

Lección 7 Workbook Activities   **65**

3. _____   4. _____

_____   _____

4   **La palabra diferente** Fill in the blank with the word that doesn't belong in each group.

1. luego, después, más tarde, entonces, antes _____

2. maquillarse, cepillarse el pelo, despertarse, peinarse, afeitarse _____

3. bailar, despertarse, acostarse, levantarse, dormirse _____

4. champú, despertador, jabón, maquillaje, crema de afeitar _____

5. entonces, bañarse, lavarse las manos, cepillarse los dientes, ducharse _____

6. pelo, vestirse, dientes, manos, cara _____

5   **La rutina de Silvia** Rewrite this paragraph, selecting the correct sequencing words from
the parentheses.

(Por la mañana, Durante el día) Silvia se prepara para salir. (Primero, Antes de) se levanta y se ducha.
(Después, Antes) de ducharse, se viste. (Entonces, Durante) se maquilla. (Primero, Antes) de salir come
algo y bebe un café. (Durante, Por último) se peina y se pone una chaqueta. (Durante el día, Antes de)
Silvia no tiene tiempo (*time*) de volver a su casa. (Más tarde, Antes de) come algo en la cafetería de la
universidad y estudia en la biblioteca. (Por la tarde, Por último), Silvia trabaja en el centro comercial.
(Por la noche, Primero) llega a su casa y está cansada. (Más tarde, Después de) prepara algo de comer y
mira la televisión un rato. (Antes de, Después de) acostarse a dormir siempre estudia un rato.

_____

_____

_____

_____

_____

_____

_____

_____

_____

_____

GRAMÁTICA

7.1 Reflexive verbs

1   **Se hace**   Complete each sentence with the correct present tense forms of the verb in parentheses.

1. Marcos y Gustavo _____ (enojarse) con Javier.

2. Mariela _____ (maquillarse) todas las mañanas después de ducharse.

3. (Yo) _____ (acostarse) temprano porque tengo clase por la mañana.

4. Los jugadores _____ (ducharse) en el baño después del partido.

5. Irma y yo _____ (ponerse) los vestidos nuevos.

6. (Tú) _____ (preocuparse) por tu novio porque siempre pierde las cosas.

7. Usted _____ (lavarse) la cara con un jabón especial.

2   **Lo hiciste**   Answer the questions positively, using complete sentences.

1. ¿Te cepillaste los dientes después de comer?

_____

2. ¿Se maquilla Julia antes de salir a bailar?

_____

3. ¿Se duchan ustedes antes de entrar en la piscina?

_____

4. ¿Se ponen sombreros los turistas cuando van a la playa?

_____

5. ¿Nos ponemos los vestidos en la habitación del hotel?

_____

3   **Terminar**   Complete each sentence with the correct reflexive verbs. You may use some verbs more than once.

acordarse	cepillarse	enojarse	maquillarse
acostarse	dormirse	levantarse	quedarse

1. Mi mamá _____ porque no queremos _____ temprano.

2. La profesora _____ con nosotros cuando no _____ de los verbos.

3. Mi hermano _____ los dientes cuando _____.

4. Mis amigas y yo _____ estudiando en la biblioteca por la noche y por la mañana _____ muy cansadas.

5. Muchas noches _____ delante del televisor, porque no quiero _____.

Workbook

4 **Escoger** Choose the correct verb from the parentheses, then fill in the blank with its correct form.

(lavar/lavarse)

1. Josefina _____ las manos en el baño.

   Josefina _____ la ropa en casa de su mamá.

(peinar/peinarse)

2. (Yo) _____ a mi hermana todas las mañanas.

   (Yo) _____ en el baño, delante del espejo.

(quitar/quitarse)

3. (Nosotros) _____ los abrigos al entrar en casa.

   (Nosotros) _____ los libros de la mesa para comer.

(levantar/levantarse)

4. Los estudiantes _____ muy temprano.

   Los estudiantes _____ la mano para hacer preguntas.

5 **El incidente** Complete the paragraph with reflexive verbs from the word bank. Use each verb only once.

acordarse	enojarse	levantarse	ponerse	quedarse
afeitarse	irse	llamarse	preocuparse	sentarse
despertarse	lavarse	maquillarse	probarse	vestirse

Luis _____ todos los días a las seis de la mañana. Luego entra en la ducha y
                        1
_____ el pelo con champú. Cuando sale de la ducha usa la crema de afeitar
        2
para _____ delante del espejo. Come algo con su familia y él y sus hermanos
            3
_____ hablando un rato.
        4

Cuando sale tarde, Luis _____ porque no quiere llegar tarde a la clase de
                                5
español. Los estudiantes _____ nerviosos porque a veces (*sometimes*) tienen
                            6
pruebas sorpresa en la clase.

Ayer por la mañana, Luis _____ con su hermana Marina porque ella
                                7
_____ tarde y pasó mucho tiempo en el baño con la puerta cerrada.
        8

—¿Cuándo sales, Marina? —le preguntó Luis.

—¡Tengo que _____ porque voy a salir con mi novio y quiero estar bonita!
                    9

—dijo Marina.

—¡Tengo que _____ ya, Marina! ¿Cuándo terminas?
                    10

—Ahora salgo, Luis. Tengo que _____. Me voy a poner mi vestido favorito.
                                11

—Tienes que _____ de que viven muchas personas en esta casa, Marina.
                    12

7.2 Indefinite and negative words

1 Alguno o ninguno Complete the sentences with indefinite and negative words from the word bank.

> alguien   algunas   ninguna
> alguna   ningún   tampoco

1. No tengo ganas de ir a _____ lugar hoy.

2. ¿Tienes _____ ideas para el proyecto?

3. ¿Viene _____ a la fiesta de mañana?

4. Nunca voy a _____ estadio.

5. ¿Te gusta _____ de estas corbatas?

6. Jorge, tú no eres el único. Yo _____ puedo ir de vacaciones.

2 Palabras negativas Complete the sentences with negative words.

1. No me gustan estas gafas. _____ quiero comprar _____ de ellas.

2. Estoy muy cansado. _____ quiero ir a _____ restaurante.

3. No tengo hambre. _____ quiero comer _____.

4. A mí no me gusta la playa. _____ quiero ir a la playa _____.

5. Soy muy tímida. _____ hablo _____ con _____.

6. No me gusta el color rojo, _____ _____ el color rosado.

3 Lo contrario Make each sentence negative.

> **modelo**
> Buscaste algunos vestidos en la tienda.
> **No buscaste ningún vestido en la tienda.**

1. Las dependientas venden algunas blusas.

_____

2. Alguien va de compras al centro comercial.

_____

3. Siempre me cepillo los dientes antes de salir.

_____

4. Te traigo algún programa de la computadora.

_____

5. Mi hermano prepara algo de comer.

_____

6. Quiero tomar algo en el café de la librería.

_____

4 **No, no es cierto** Answer the questions negatively.

> **modelo**
>
> ¿Comes siempre en casa?
> No, nunca como en casa./No, no como en casa nunca.

1. ¿Tiene Alma alguna falda?

_____

2. ¿Sales siempre los fines de semana?

_____

3. ¿Quiere comer algo Gregorio?

_____

4. ¿Le prestaste algunos discos de jazz a César?

_____

5. ¿Podemos o ir a la playa o nadar en la piscina?

_____

6. ¿Encontraste algún cinturón barato en la tienda?

_____

7. ¿Buscaron ustedes a alguien en la playa?

_____

8. ¿Te gusta alguno de estos trajes?

_____

5 **Lo opuesto** Rewrite the paragraph, changing the indefinite words to negative ones.

Rodrigo siempre está leyendo algún libro. También le gusta leer el periódico. Siempre lee algo. Alguien le pregunta si leyó una novela de Mario Vargas Llosa. Leyó algunos libros de Vargas Llosa el año pasado. También leyó algunas novelas de Gabriel García Márquez. Algunos libros le encantan. Le gusta leer o libros de misterio o novelas fantásticas.

_____

_____

_____

_____

_____

_____

_____

_____

_____

7.3 Preterite of **ser** and **ir**

1   **¿Ser o ir?** Complete the sentences with the preterite of **ser** or **ir**. Then write the infinitive form of the verb you used.

1. Ayer María y Javier _____ a la playa con sus amigos. _____

2. La película de ayer _____ muy divertida. _____

3. El fin de semana pasado (nosotros) _____ al centro comercial. _____

4. La abuela y la tía de Maricarmen _____ doctoras. _____

5. (Nosotros) _____ muy simpáticos con la familia de Claribel. _____

6. Manuel _____ a la universidad en septiembre. _____

7. Los vendedores _____ al almacén muy temprano. _____

8. Lima _____ la primera ciudad que visitaron en el viaje. _____

9. (Yo) _____ a buscarte a la cafetería, pero no te encontré. _____

10. Mi compañera de cuarto _____ a la tienda a comprar champú. _____

2   **Viaje a Perú** Complete the paragraph with the preterite of **ser** and **ir**. Then fill in the chart with the infinitive form of the verbs you used.

El mes pasado mi amiga Clara y yo _____ de vacaciones a Perú. El vuelo

(*flight*) _____ un miércoles por la mañana, y _____

cómodo. Primero Clara y yo _____ a Lima, y _____

a comer a un restaurante de comida peruana. La comida _____ muy buena.

Luego _____ al hotel y nos _____ a dormir. El jueves

_____ un día nublado. Nos _____ a Cuzco, y el viaje en

autobús _____ largo. Yo _____ la primera en despertarme

y ver la ciudad de Cuzco. La visita a la ciudad _____ impresionante. Luego

Clara y yo _____ de excursión a Machu Picchu. El cuarto día nos levantamos

muy temprano y nos _____ a la antigua ciudad inca. El amanecer sobre

Machu Picchu _____ hermoso. La excursión _____ una

experiencia inolvidable (*unforgettable*). ¿_____ tú a Perú el año pasado?

1. _____	7. _____	13. _____
2. _____	8. _____	14. _____
3. _____	9. _____	15. _____
4. _____	10. _____	16. _____
5. _____	11. _____	17. _____
6. _____	12. _____	18. _____

Workbook

7.4 Gustar and verbs like gustar

1 **¿Uno o varios?** Rewrite each sentence, choosing the correct form of the verb in parentheses.

1. Te (quedan, queda) bien las faldas y los vestidos.

_____

2. No les (molesta, molestan) la lluvia.

_____

3. No les (gusta, gustan) estar enojados.

_____

4. Les (aburre, aburren) probarse ropa en las tiendas.

_____

5. Le (fascina, fascinan) las tiendas y los almacenes.

_____

6. Le (falta, faltan) dos años para terminar la carrera (*degree*).

_____

7. Nos (encanta, encantan) pescar y nadar en el mar.

_____

8. Me (interesan, interesa) las ruinas peruanas.

_____

2 **Nos gusta el fútbol** Complete the paragraph with the correct forms of the verbs in parentheses.

A mi familia le _____ (fascinar) el fútbol. A mis hermanas les
                       1

_____ (encantar) los jugadores porque son muy guapos. También les
        2

_____ (gustar) la emoción (*excitement*) de los partidos. A mi papá le
        3

_____ (interesar) mucho los partidos y cuando puede los sigue por Internet.
        4

A mi mamá le _____ (molestar) nuestra afición porque no hacemos las tareas
                     5

de la casa cuando hay un partido. A ella generalmente le _____ (aburrir) los
                                                              6

partidos. Pero cuando le _____ (faltar) un gol al equipo argentino para ganar, le
                           7

_____ (encantar) los minutos finales del partido.
        8

3 **Los otros** Rewrite each sentence, substituting the subject with the one in parentheses.

1. Le quedan bien los vestidos largos. (la blusa cara)

_____

2. Les molesta la música moderna. (las canciones populares)

_____

3. No te interesa bailar salsa. (caminar por la playa)

_____

4. Me gusta esa toalla de playa. (aquellas gafas de sol)

_____

5. Les encantan las tiendas. (el centro comercial)

_____

6. Nos falta practicar el español. (unas semanas de clase)

_____

7. No les gusta el ballet. (las películas)

_____

8. No les importa esperar un rato. (buscar unos libros nuestros)

_____

4 **¿Qué piensan?** Complete the sentences with the correct pronouns and forms of the verbs in parentheses.

1. A mí _____ (encantar) las películas de misterio.

2. A Gregorio _____ (molestar) mucho la nieve y el frío.

3. A mi sobrina _____ (gustar) leer y escribir.

4. A ustedes _____ (faltar) un libro de esa colección.

5. ¿_____ (quedar) bien los sombreros a ti?

6. A nosotros _____ (fascinar) la historia peruana.

7. A ella no _____ (importar) las apariencias (*appearances*).

8. Los deportes por televisión a mí _____ (aburrir) mucho.

5 **Mi rutina diaria** Answer these questions about your daily routine, using verbs like **gustar** in complete sentences.

1. ¿Te molesta levantarte temprano durante la semana?

_____

2. ¿Qué te interesa hacer por las mañanas?

_____

3. ¿Te importa despertarte temprano los fines de semana?

_____

4. ¿Qué te encanta hacer los domingos?

_____

Lección 7 Workbook Activities   **73**

6   **Síntesis** Interview a classmate or relative about an interesting vacation he or she took. Then gather the answers into a report. Answer the following questions:

- Where did he or she go, what were the tours like, what were the tour guides like, and what were his or her traveling companions like?
- Where did he or she stay, what were the accommodations like, and what was his or her daily routine like during the trip?
- What did he or she like or love about the vacation? What interested him or her?
- What bothered or angered him or her? What bored him or her during the vacation?
- Be sure to address the negative and positive aspects of the vacation.

_____

_____

_____

_____

_____

_____

_____

_____

_____

_____

_____

_____

_____

_____

_____

_____

_____

_____

_____

_____

_____

_____

_____

PREPARACIÓN

1 **¿Qué comida es?** Read the descriptions and write the name of the food in the blank.

1. Son rojos y se sirven (*they are served*) en las ensaladas. _____

2. Se come (*It is eaten*) antes del plato principal; es líquida y caliente (*hot*). _____

3. Son unas verduras anaranjadas, largas y delgadas. _____

4. Hay de naranja y de manzana; se bebe en el desayuno. _____

5. Son dos rebanadas (*slices*) de pan con queso y jamón. _____

6. Es comida rápida; se sirven con hamburguesas y se les pone sal. _____

7. Son pequeños y rosados; viven en el mar. _____

8. Son frutas amarillas; con agua y azúcar se hace una bebida de verano. _____

2 **Categorías** Categorize the foods listed in the word bank.

aceite	camarones	jamón	mantequilla	pimienta	tomates
arvejas	cebollas	langosta	manzanas	pollo	uvas
atún	champiñones	leche	margarina	queso	vinagre
azúcar	chuletas de	lechuga	naranjas	sal	zanahorias
bananas	cerdo	limones	papas	salchichas	
bistec	hamburguesas	maíz	pavo	salmón	

Verduras y granos	Productos lácteos (*dairy*)	Condimentos	Carnes y aves (*poultry*)	Pescado y mariscos	Frutas

3 **¿Qué es?** Label the item of food shown in each drawing.

1. _____   2. _____

3. _____   4. _____

4 **¿Cuándo lo comes?** Read the lists of meals, then categorize when the meals would be eaten.

1. un sándwich de jamón y queso, unas chuletas de cerdo con arroz y frijoles, fruta y un café con leche

Desayuno _____

Almuerzo _____

Cena _____

2. una langosta con papas, huevos fritos y jugo de naranja, una hamburguesa y un refresco

Desayuno _____

Almuerzo _____

Cena _____

3. pan tostado con mantequilla, un sándwich de atún y té helado, un bistec con cebolla y arroz

Desayuno _____

Almuerzo _____

Cena _____

4. una sopa y una ensalada, cereales con leche, pollo asado con ajo y champiñones y vino blanco

Desayuno _____

Almuerzo _____

Cena _____

GRAMÁTICA

8.1 Preterite of stem-changing verbs

1 **En el pasado** Rewrite each sentence, conjugating the verb in the preterite tense.

1. Ana y Enrique piden unos refrescos fríos.

_____

2. Mi mamá nos sirve arroz con frijoles y carne.

_____

3. Tina y yo dormimos en una pensión de Lima.

_____

4. Las flores (*flowers*) de mi tía mueren durante el otoño.

_____

5. Ustedes se sienten bien porque ayudan a esas personas.

_____

_____

2 **¿Qué hicieron?** For each sentence, choose the correct verb from those in parentheses. Then complete the sentence by writing the preterite form of the verb.

1. Rosana y Héctor _____ las palabras del profesor. (repetir, dormir, morir)

2. El abuelo de Luis _____ el año pasado. (sentirse, morir, servir)

3. (Yo) _____ camarones y salmón de cena en mi casa. (morir, conseguir, servir)

4. Lisa y tú _____ pan tostado con queso y huevo. (sentirse, seguir, pedir)

5. Ana y yo _____ muy tarde los sábados. (dormirse, pedir, repetir)

6. Gilberto y su familia _____ ir al restaurante de mariscos. (servir, preferir, vestirse)

3 **Sujetos diferentes** Rewrite each sentence, using the subject in parentheses.

1. Anoche conseguimos los pasajes. (mis primos)

_____

2. Melinda y Juan siguieron a Carmen por la ciudad en el auto. (yo)

_____

3. Alejandro prefirió quedarse en casa. (ustedes)

_____

4. Pedí un plato de langosta con salsa de mantequilla. (ellas)

_____

5. Los camareros les sirvieron una ensalada con atún y tomate. (tu esposo)

_____

4 **En el restaurante** Create sentences from the elements provided. Use the preterite form of the verbs.

1. (nosotros) / preferir / este restaurante al restaurante italiano

_____

2. mis amigos / seguir / a Gustavo para encontrar el restaurante

_____

3. la camarera / servirte / huevos fritos y café con leche

_____

4. ustedes / pedir / ensalada de mariscos y vino blanco

_____

5. Carlos / preferir / las papas fritas

_____

6. (yo) / conseguir / el menú del restaurante

_____

5 **La planta de la abuela** Complete the letter with the preterite form of the verbs from the word bank. Use each verb only once.

conseguir	morir	preferir	seguir	servir
dormir	pedir	repetir	sentirse	vestirse

Querida mamá:

El fin de semana pasado fui a visitar a mi abuela Lilia en el campo. (Yo)

Le _____ unos libros que ella me _____ de la
         1   2

librería de la universidad. Cuando llegué, mi abuela me _____ un
                                                              3

plato sabroso de arroz con frijoles. La encontré triste porque la semana pasada su

planta de tomates _____, y ahora tiene que comprar los tomates en el
                        4

mercado. Me invitó a quedarme, y yo _____ en su casa. Por la
                                          5

mañana, abuela Lilia se despertó temprano, _____ y salió a comprar
                                                  6

huevos para el desayuno. Me levanté inmediatamente y la _____
                                                              7

para ir con ella al mercado. En el mercado, ella me _____ que
                                                        8

estaba triste por la planta de tomates. Le pregunté: ¿Debemos comprar otra planta

de tomates?, pero ella _____ esperar hasta el verano. Después del
                            9

desayuno volví a la universidad. _____ feliz después de ver a mi
                                      10

abuela. La quiero mucho. ¿Cuándo la vas a visitar?

Chau,

Mónica

8.2 Double object pronouns

1 **Buena gente** Rewrite each sentence, replacing the direct objects with direct object pronouns.

1. La camarera te sirvió el plato de pasta con mariscos.

_____

2. Isabel nos trajo (*brought*) la sal y la pimienta a la mesa.

_____

3. Javier me pidió el aceite y el vinagre anoche.

_____

4. El dueño nos busca una mesa para seis personas.

_____

5. Tu madre me consigue unas uvas deliciosas.

_____

6. ¿Te recomendaron este restaurante Lola y Paco?

_____

2 **Pronombres** Rewrite each sentence, using double object pronouns.

1. Le pidieron los menús al camarero.

_____

2. Nos buscaron un lugar cómodo para sentarnos.

_____

3. Les sirven papas fritas con el pescado a los clientes.

_____

4. Le llevan unos entremeses a la mesa a Marcos.

_____

5. Me trajeron (*brought*) una ensalada de lechuga y tomate.

_____

6. El dueño le compra la carne al señor Gutiérrez.

_____

7. Ellos te muestran los vinos antes de servirlos.

_____

8. La dueña nos abre la sección de no fumar.

_____

Workbook

3 **¿Quiénes son?** Answer the questions, using double object pronouns.

1. ¿A quiénes les escribiste las cartas? (a ellos) _____

2. ¿Quién le recomendó ese plato? (su tío) _____

3. ¿Quién nos va a abrir la puerta a esta hora? (Sonia) _____

4. ¿Quién les sirvió el pescado asado? (Miguel) _____

5. ¿Quién te llevó los entremeses? (mis amigas) _____

6. ¿A quién le ofrece frutas Roberto? (a su familia) _____

4 **La cena** Read the two dialogues. Then answer the questions, using double object pronouns.

CELIA (*A Tito*) Rosalía me recomendó este restaurante.

DUEÑO Buenas noches, señores. Les traigo unos entremeses, cortesía del restaurante.

CAMARERO Buenas noches. ¿Quieren ver el menú?

TITO Sí, por favor. ¿Está buena la langosta?

CAMARERO Sí, es la especialidad del restaurante.

TITO Entonces queremos pedir dos langostas.

CELIA Y yo quiero una copa (*glass*) de vino tinto, por favor.

CAMARERO De postre (*for dessert*) tenemos flan y fruta.

CELIA Perdón, ¿me lo puede repetir?

CAMARERO Tenemos flan y fruta.

CELIA Yo no quiero nada de postre, gracias.

DUEÑO ¿Les gustó la cena?

TITO Sí, nos encantó. Muchas gracias. Fue una cena deliciosa.

1. ¿Quién le recomendó el restaurante a Celia? _____

2. ¿Quién les sirvió los entremeses a Celia y a Tito? _____

3. ¿Quién les trajo (*brought*) los menús a Celia y a Tito? _____

4. ¿Quién le recomendó a Tito la langosta? _____

5. ¿Quién le pidió las langostas al camarero? _____

6. ¿Quién le pidió un vino tinto al camarero? _____

7. ¿Quién le repitió a Celia la lista de postres (*desserts*)? _____

8. ¿A quién le dio (*gave*) las gracias Tito cuando se fueron? _____

8.3 Saber and conocer

1 **¿Saber o conocer?** Complete the sentences, using **saber** and **conocer**.

1. (Yo) No _____ a los padres de Arturo y Gustavo.

2. Carolina _____ varias ciudades de Canadá.

3. ¿(Tú) _____ las preguntas que nos van a dar en el examen?

4. Jorge _____ preparar un pollo a la parmesana delicioso.

5. (Nosotros) _____ a la dueña del restaurante más caro de la ciudad.

6. Julio y tú _____ que estoy trabajando en mi casa hoy.

2 **¿Qué hacen?** Complete the sentences, using the verbs from the word bank. Use each verb only once.

conducir	ofrecer	saber
conocer	parecer	traducir

1. Gisela _____ una motocicleta por las calles (*streets*) de la ciudad.

2. Tú _____ servir el vino de una manera elegante.

3. El novio de Aurelia _____ ser inteligente y simpático.

4. En ese restaurante ya los _____ porque siempre van a comer allí (*there*).

5. Los vendedores del mercado al aire libre nos _____ rebajas.

6. (Yo) _____ libros de historia y de sociología al español.

3 **Oraciones completas** Create sentences, using the elements and **saber** or **conocer**.

1. Eugenia / mi amiga Alejandra

_____

2. tú / hablar español muy bien

_____

3. el sobrino de Rosa / leer y escribir

_____

4. José y Laura / la ciudad de Barcelona

_____

5. nosotros no / cuántas manzanas debemos comprar

_____

6. (yo) / al dueño del café La Paz

_____

7. Elena y María Victoria / patinar en línea

_____

Lección 8 Workbook Activities

8.4 Comparatives and superlatives

1 **¿Cómo se comparan?** Complete the sentences with the Spanish of the comparatives in parentheses.

1. Puerto Rico es _____ (*smaller than*) Guatemala.

2. Los limones son _____ (*more sour than*) las naranjas.

3. Los champiñones son _____ (*as tasty as*) las arvejas.

4. Los jugadores de baloncesto son _____ (*taller than*) los otros estudiantes.

5. Jimena es _____ (*more hard-working than*) su novio Pablo.

6. Marisol es _____ (*less intelligent than*) su hermana mayor.

7. La nueva novela de ese escritor es _____ (*as bad as*) su primera novela.

8. Agustín y Mario están _____ (*less fat than*) antes.

2 **Es obvio** Write sentences that compare the two items, using the adjectives in parentheses.

> **modelo**
> (inteligente) Albert Einstein / Homer Simpson
> *Albert Einstein es más inteligente que Homer Simpson.*

1. (famoso) Salma Hayek / mi hermana

_____

2. (difícil) estudiar química orgánica / leer una novela

_____

3. (malo) el tiempo en Boston / el tiempo en Florida

_____

4. (barato) los restaurantes elegantes / los restaurantes de comida rápida

_____

5. (grande) mi abuelo / mi sobrino

_____

3 **¿Por qué?** Complete the sentences with the correct comparatives.

> **modelo**
> Darío juega mejor al fútbol que tú.
> Es porque Darío practica <u>más que tú</u>.

1. Mi hermano es más gordo que mi padre. Es porque mi hermano come _____.

2. Natalia conoce más países que tú. Es porque Natalia viaja _____.

3. Estoy menos cansado que David. Es porque duermo _____.

4. Rolando tiene más hambre que yo. Va a comer _____.

5. Mi vestido favorito es más barato que el tuyo (*yours*). Voy a pagar _____.

6. Julia gana más dinero que Lorna. Es porque Julia trabaja _____.

4 **Facilísimo** Rewrite each sentence, using absolute superlatives.

1. Javier y Esteban están muy cansados. _____

2. Tu padre es muy joven. _____

3. La profesora es muy inteligente. _____

4. Las clases son muy largas. _____

5. La madre de Irene está muy feliz. _____

6. Estoy muy aburrido. _____

5 **El más...** Answer the questions affirmatively using the superlative with the words in parentheses.

> **modelo**
>
> El auto está sucísimo, ¿no? (ciudad)
>
> *Sí, es el más sucio de la ciudad.*

1. Esos vestidos son carísimos, ¿no? (tienda)

_____

2. El almacén Velasco es buenísimo, ¿no? (centro comercial)

_____

3. La cama de tu madre es comodísima, ¿no? (casa)

_____

4. Ángel y Julio están nerviosísimos por el examen, ¿no? (clase)

_____

5. Sara es jovencísima, ¿no? (mis amigas)

_____

6 **¿Más o menos?** Read the pairs of sentences. Then write a new sentence that compares the pairs.

> **modelo**
>
> Ese hotel tiene cien habitaciones. El otro hotel tiene cuarenta habitaciones.
>
> *Ese hotel tiene más habitaciones que el otro.*

1. La biblioteca tiene ciento cincuenta sillas. El laboratorio de lenguas tiene treinta sillas.

_____

2. Ramón compró tres corbatas. Roberto compró tres corbatas.

_____

3. Yo comí un plato de pasta. Mi hermano comió dos platos de pasta.

_____

4. Anabel durmió ocho horas. Amelia durmió ocho horas.

_____

5. Mi primo toma seis clases. Mi amiga Tere toma ocho clases.

_____

Workbook

7 **Síntesis** Conduct a survey of several people about a recent experience they had at a restaurant.

- What did they order?
- Who served them?
- Did they prefer this restaurant to others they had eaten at before?
- What did their dining companions think?

Then, ask them to review the restaurant for you. Ask them to compare the service, the food, the prices, and the ambience of the restaurant to those of others.

- How does it compare to other restaurants in the city and to other restaurants of its type?

- Ask them about some restaurants you know. Do they know these restaurants? Do they know where they are located?

When you are finished with the survey, prepare a report of the restaurants in your area, comparing them on the basis of the data you collected. Use as many different types of comparatives and superlative phrases as possible in your report.

_____

_____

_____

_____

_____

_____

_____

_____

_____

_____

_____

_____

_____

_____

_____

_____

¡VIVAN LOS PAÍSES HISPANOS!

Suramérica I

1 **El mapa** Fill in the blanks with the population and the name of the capital of each country.

1._____

Venezuela

2._____

Colombia

3._____

Ecuador

Perú

4._____

2 **¿De qué país es?** Write each of these words in the appropriate column in the chart.

bolívar	los Andes	El Salto Ángel	García Márquez
población indígena	Cartagena	tejidos	población: 28.048.000
área: 1.285.220 km^2	capital Bogotá	capital Lima	quechua
Canaima	lana de alpaca	dólar estadounidense	Barranquilla

Venezuela	Colombia	Ecuador	Perú
_____	_____	_____	_____
_____	_____	_____	_____
_____	_____	_____	_____
_____	_____	_____	_____

3 **Palabras cruzadas** (*crossed*) Write one letter in each square. Then answer the final question, using the new word that is formed.

1. moneda de Perú
2. nombre que los indígenas le dan al Parque Nacional Canaima
3. Las alpacas viven en los Andes de este país.
4. país suramericano con un área de 912.050 km^2
5. estilo literario de Gabriel García Márquez
6. Las alpacas hacen ésto para defenderse.
7. capital de Venezuela
8. Son de Ecuador y son famosos en todo el mundo por sus colores vivos.
9. El Salto Ángel es una.
10. capital de Perú
11. Lima tiene playas en este océano.
12. el río más caudaloso del mundo
13. moneda de Colombia

Venezuela, Colombia, Ecuador y Perú son países _____ .

4 **¡A viajar!** Imagine that you won a trip to South America. Choose one of the countries described: **Venezuela, Colombia, Ecuador,** or **Perú**. Write a paragraph explaining your reasons for choosing that country.

Quiero ir a _____ porque (*because*) _____

_____

_____

_____

_____

_____

REPASO

1 **¿Son o están?** Form complete sentences using the words provided and **ser** or **estar**.

1. Paloma y Carlos / en la agencia de viajes

_____

2. sus padres / del Perú

_____

3. nosotros / alegres por el viaje a Lima

_____

4. su primo / esperándolos en el aeropuerto

_____

5. Paloma / una turista amable

_____

2 **¿Te importa?** Complete the sentences with the correct pronoun and the form of the verb in parentheses.

1. A nosotros _____ (gustar) la comida cubana.

2. A mí _____ (encantar) los huevos fritos.

3. A mi hermano _____ (molestar) el olor a pescado.

4. A ustedes no _____ (importar) esperar un rato para sentarse, ¿no?

5. A ti _____ (fascinar) los restaurantes franceses.

6. A ellos _____ (faltar) tiempo para beber el café.

3 **Las vacaciones** Complete the paragraph with the correct preterite forms of the verbs in parentheses.

Ignacio y yo _____ (ir) de viaje a Viña del Mar, en Chile. Nosotros _____
               1   2
(comprar) pasajes baratos el mes pasado. Yo _____ (buscar) precios de pasajes para Chile
                                              3
en Internet. Los padres de Ignacio _____ (llegar) la semana pasada a Viña del Mar. Su
                                     4
padre _____ (preferir) llegar antes que nosotros para regresar más temprano. El primer
       5
día, ellos _____ (dormir) hasta tarde. Ignacio _____ (ir) al hotel donde sus
            6   7
padres se _____ (quedar). Su madre se _____ (aburrir) un poco los primeros
           8   9
días. Pero después, ella se _____ (interesar) más en la cultura local. Los padres de Ignacio
                             10
_____ (repetir) una y otra vez lo mucho que les _____ (gustar) Viña del Mar.
11   12
Nosotros _____ (ir) a comer al restaurante del hotel y _____ (pedir) machas
          13   14
a la parmesana, un plato típico de Chile. El camarero _____ (servir) vino. La noche
                                                        15
_____ (ser) muy divertida.
16

Workbook

4 **No son éstos** Answer these questions negatively using demonstrative pronouns.

> **modelo**
>
> ¿Les vas a prestar esos programas a ellos? (*those over there*)
> No, les voy a prestar aquéllos.

1. ¿Me vas a vender esa pelota de fútbol? (*this one*)

_____

2. ¿Van ustedes a mostrarle ese traje al cliente? (*that one over there*)

_____

3. ¿Va a llevarles estas bolsas Marisol? (*those ones*)

_____

4. ¿Les van a vender esos guantes a los estudiantes? (*these ones*)

_____

5 **No, nada, nunca** Answer the questions negatively, using negative words.

1. ¿Llegó José con alguna amiga a la cena?

_____

2. ¿Te enojaste con alguien en el restaurante?

_____

3. ¿Les gustó la comida a los otros invitados?

_____

4. ¿Siempre se van tan tarde de las fiestas Raúl y su esposa?

_____

6 **La compra** Look at the photo and imagine everything that led up to the woman's purchase. What did she need? Why did she need it? What kind of weather is it for? Where did she decide to buy it? Where did she look for it? Who helped her, and what did she ask them? Did she bargain with anyone? Was she undecided about anything? How did she pay for the purchase? Who did she pay? Answer these questions in a paragraph, using the preterite of the verbs that you know.

_____
_____
_____
_____
_____
_____
_____
_____
_____
_____

PREPARACIÓN

Lección 9

1 **Identificar** Label the following terms as **estado civil, fiesta,** or **etapa de la vida.**

1. casada _____

2. adolescencia _____

3. viudo _____

4. juventud _____

5. Navidad _____

6. niñez _____

7. vejez _____

8. aniversario de bodas _____

9. divorciado _____

10. madurez _____

11. cumpleaños _____

12. soltera _____

2 **Las etapas de la vida** Label the stages of life on the timeline.

0 5 10 15 20 25 30 35 40 45 50 55 60 65 70 75 80 85 90 95 100

4. _____

1. _____

2. _____

3. _____

5. _____

6. _____

3 **Escribir** Fill in the blank with the stage of life in which these events would normally occur.

1. jubilarse _____

2. graduarse en la universidad _____

3. cumplir nueve años _____

4. conseguir el primer trabajo _____

5. graduarse en la escuela secundaria _____

6. morir o quedar viudo _____

7. casarse (por primera vez) _____

8. tener un hijo _____

9. celebrar el cincuenta aniversario de bodas _____

10. tener la primera cita _____

4 **Información personal** Read the descriptions and answer the questions.

"Me llamo Jorge Rosas. Nací el 26 de enero de 1948. Mi esposa murió el año pasado. Tengo dos hijos: Marina y Daniel. Terminé mis estudios de sociología en la Universidad Interamericana en 1970. Me voy a jubilar este año. Voy a celebrar este evento con una botella de champán".

1. ¿Cuál es la fecha de nacimiento de Jorge? _____

2. ¿Cuál es el estado civil de Jorge? _____

3. ¿En qué etapa de la vida está Jorge? _____

4. ¿Cuándo es el cumpleaños de Jorge? _____

5. ¿Cuándo se graduó Jorge? _____

6. ¿Cómo va a celebrar la jubilación (*retirement*) Jorge? _____

"Soy Julia Jiménez. Nací en 1980. Me comprometí a los veinte años, pero rompí con mi novio antes de casarme. Ahora estoy saliendo con un músico cubano. Soy historiadora del arte desde que terminé mi carrera (*degree*) en la Universidad de Salamanca en 2002. Mi cumpleaños es el 11 de marzo. Mi postre favorito es el flan".

7. ¿Cuál es la fecha de nacimiento de Julia? _____

8. ¿Cuál es el estado civil de Julia? _____

9. ¿En qué etapa de la vida está Julia? _____

10. ¿Cuándo es el cumpleaños de Julia? _____

11. ¿Cuándo se graduó Julia? _____

12. ¿Cuál es el postre favorito de Julia? _____

"Me llamo Manuel Blanco y vivo en Caracas. Mi esposa y yo nos comprometimos a los veintiséis años, y la boda fue dos años después. Pasaron quince años y tuvimos tres hijos. Me gustan mucho los dulces".

13. ¿Dónde vive Manuel? _____

14. ¿En qué etapa de la vida se comprometió Manuel? _____

15. ¿Cuál es el estado civil de Manuel? _____

16. ¿A qué edad se casó Manuel? _____

17. ¿Cuántos hijos tiene Manuel? _____

18. ¿Qué le gusta comer a Manuel? _____

GRAMÁTICA

9.1 Irregular preterites

1 **¿Hay o hubo?** Complete these sentences with the correct tense of **haber**.

1. Ahora _____ una fiesta de graduación en el patio de la universidad.

2. _____ muchos invitados en la fiesta de aniversario anoche.

3. Ya _____ una muerte en su familia el año pasado.

4. Siempre _____ galletas y dulces en esas conferencias.

5. _____ varias botellas de vino, pero los invitados se las tomaron.

6. Por las mañanas _____ unos postres deliciosos en esa tienda.

2 **¿Cómo fue?** Complete these sentences with the preterite of the verb in parentheses.

1. Cristina y Lara te _____ (estar) buscando en la fiesta anoche.

2. (Yo) _____ (Tener) un problema con mi pasaporte y lo pasé mal en la aduana.

3. Rafaela _____ (venir) temprano a la fiesta y conoció a Humberto.

4. El padre de la novia _____ (hacer) un brindis por los novios.

5. Tus padres _____ (tener) un divorcio relativamente amistoso (*friendly*).

6. Román _____ (poner) las maletas en el auto antes de salir.

3 **¿Qué hicieron?** Complete these sentences, using the preterite of **decir, conducir, traducir,** and **traer.**

1. Felipe y Silvia _____ que no les gusta ir a la playa.

2. Claudia le _____ unos papeles al inglés a su hermano.

3. David _____ su motocicleta nueva durante el fin de semana.

4. Rosario y Pepe me _____ un pastel de cumpleaños de regalo.

5. Cristina y yo les _____ a nuestras amigas que vamos a bailar.

6. Cuando fuiste a Guatemala, (tú) nos _____ regalos.

4 **Es mejor dar...** Rewrite these sentences in the preterite tense.

1. Antonio le da un beso a su madre.

_____

2. Los invitados le dan las gracias a la familia.

_____

3. Tú les das una sorpresa a tus padres.

_____

4. Rosa y yo le damos una sorpresa al profesor.

_____

Workbook

5 **El pasado** Create sentences using the elements provided. Use the preterite tense of the verbs.

1. Rosalía / hacer / galletas

_____

2. mi tía / estar / en Perú

_____

3. (yo) / venir / a este lugar

_____

4. Rita y Sara / decir / la verdad

_____

5. ustedes / poner / la televisión

_____

6. ellos / traducir / el libro

_____

7. (nosotras) / traer / una cámara

_____

8. (tú) / tener / un examen

_____

6 **Ya lo hizo** Answer the questions negatively, indicating that the action has already occurred. Use the words in parentheses.

> **modelo**
> ¿Quiere Pepe cenar en el restaurante japonés? (restaurante mexicano)
> No, Pepe ya cenó en el restaurante mexicano.

1. ¿Vas a estar en la biblioteca hoy? (ayer)

_____

2. ¿Quieren dar una fiesta Elena y Miguel este fin de semana? (el sábado pasado)

_____

3. ¿Debe la profesora traducir esa novela este semestre? (el año pasado)

_____

4. ¿Va a haber un pastel de limón en la cena de hoy? (anoche)

_____

5. ¿Deseas poner los abrigos en la silla? (sobre la cama)

_____

6. ¿Van ustedes a tener un hijo? (tres hijos)

_____

9.2 Verbs that change meaning in the preterite

1 **Completar** Complete these sentences with the preterite tense of the verbs in parentheses.

1. Liliana no _____ (poder) llegar a la fiesta de cumpleaños de Esteban.

2. Las chicas _____ (conocer) a muchos estudiantes en la biblioteca.

3. Raúl y Marta no _____ (querer) invitar al padre de Raúl a la boda.

4. Lina _____ (saber) ayer que sus tíos se van a divorciar.

5. (Nosotros) _____ (poder) regalarle una bicicleta a Marina.

6. María _____ (querer) romper con su novio antes del verano.

2 **Traducir** Use these verbs to write sentences in Spanish.

conocer	querer
poder	saber

1. I failed to finish the book on Wednesday.

_____

2. Inés found out last week that Vicente is divorced.

_____

3. Her girlfriends tried to call her, but they failed to.

_____

4. Susana met Alberto's parents last night.

_____

5. The waiters managed to serve dinner at eight.

_____

6. Your mother refused to go to your brother's house.

_____

3 **Raquel y Ronaldo** Complete the paragraph with the preterite of the verbs in the word bank.

conocer	querer
poder	saber

El año pasado Raquel _____ al muchacho que ahora es su esposo, Ronaldo.
                                            1

Primero, Raquel no _____ salir con él porque él vivía (*was living*) en una ciudad
                                    2

muy lejos de ella. Ronaldo _____ convencerla durante muchos meses, pero no
                                          3

_____ hacerlo. Finalmente, Raquel decidió darle una oportunidad a Ronaldo.
            4

Cuando empezaron a salir, Raquel y Ronaldo _____ inmediatamente que eran el uno
                                                              5

para el otro (*they were made for each other*). Raquel y Ronaldo _____ comprar una
                                                                                    6

casa en la misma ciudad y se casaron ese verano.

Lección 9 Workbook Activities   **93**

9.3 Relative pronouns

1 **Relativamente** Complete the sentences with **que, quien**, or **quienes**.

1. La chica con _____ quiero ir a la fiesta se llama Luisa.

2. Julio es la persona _____ está planeando la fiesta.

3. Los amigos de Juan, _____ conozco de la escuela, van a ir a la fiesta.

4. María es la chica _____ cumple quince años.

5. La fiesta _____ está planeando Julio es un aniversario de bodas.

6. La ropa _____ quiero usar en la fiesta es muy elegante.

7. Los amigos con _____ voy a la fiesta son muy divertidos.

8. Luisa es la única amiga _____ no sé si va a ir a la fiesta.

2 **Fiesta sorpresa** Answer the questions using the words in parentheses.

> **modelo**
> ¿Qué es lo que está pasando aquí? (fiesta sorpresa)
> Lo que está pasando aquí es una fiesta sorpresa.

1. ¿Qué es lo que celebramos? (el cumpleaños de tu hermana)

_____

2. ¿Qué es lo que llevas de ropa? (vestido nuevo)

_____

3. ¿Qué es lo que hay en esa caja grande? (un regalo para tu hermana)

_____

4. ¿Qué es lo que estás comiendo? (pastel de chocolate)

_____

5. ¿Qué es lo que bailan los invitados? (salsa)

_____

6. ¿Qué es lo que beben los tíos Ana y Mauricio? (vino)

_____

3 **¿Que o lo que?** Complete the sentences with **que** or **lo que**.

1. El pastel de cumpleaños _____ me trajo mi abuela es delicioso.

2. _____ más le gusta a mi abuela es celebrar los cumpleaños de sus nietos.

3. Las fiestas _____ organiza mi abuela son muy divertidas.

4. _____ nos encanta de sus fiestas es que nos reímos mucho.

4 **Pronombres relativos** Complete the sentences with **que, quien, quienes,** or **lo que**.

1. Los vecinos _____ viven frente a mi casa nos invitaron a una fiesta

   en un salón de fiestas muy elegante.

2. _____ están celebrando es su aniversario de bodas.

3. Aurora y Ana, _____ son mis amigas de la escuela, van a ir también

   a la fiesta.

4. La fiesta _____ están organizando va a ser muy divertida.

5. Marcela y Luis, _____ son nuestros vecinos, están haciendo la comida.

6. Yo puedo usar el carro de mi hermano, a _____ se lo regalaron en Navidad.

5 **Mi amiga Natalia** Complete the paragraph with **que, quien, quienes,** or **lo que**.

Natalia, _____ es mi amiga, tuvo una gran idea. Natalia es la amiga
                        1

_____ más quiero de todas. _____ Natalia pensó es hacer una gran
              2   3

fiesta de Navidad con toda su familia. Su papá, a _____ ella quiere mucho, va a
                                                                  4

ayudarla con la fiesta. La fiesta _____ Natalia y su papá quieren hacer va a ser una
                                              5

fiesta muy especial. Natalia, _____ es muy organizada, ya tiene una lista de todas las
                                          6

cosas que tiene que hacer. Tiene dos amigas con _____ va a ir de compras. Ella
                                                                7

también tiene que estudiar para sus exámenes finales, _____ es muy importante. Pero
                                                                       8

sus amigas, _____ no tenemos exámenes finales, la estamos ayudando. Además dos
                        9

amigos de su padre, a _____ Natalia llama tíos, también la están ayudando. Todos los
                                  10

miembros de su familia, _____ son los invitados, van a pasarlo muy bien.
                                    11

¡_____ Natalia necesita de regalo de Navidad son unas vacaciones!
        12

6 **Una fiesta** Write a paragraph about a party. Be sure to use **que, lo que, quien,** and **quienes**.

_____

_____

_____

_____

_____

_____

_____

_____

_____

_____

9.4 ¿Qué? and ¿cuál?

1 **¿Qué o cuál?** Complete these sentences with **qué, cuál,** or **cuáles.**

1. ¿_____ estás haciendo ahora?

2. ¿_____ gafas te gustan más?

3. ¿_____ prefieres, el vestido largo o el corto?

4. ¿Sabes _____ de éstos es mi disco favorito?

5. ¿_____ es un departamento de hacienda?

6. ¿_____ trajiste, las de banana o las de limón?

7. ¿_____ auto compraste este año?

8. ¿_____ es la tienda más elegante del centro?

2 **Muchas preguntas** Complete the sentences with interrogative words or phrases.

1. ¿_____ de esas muchachas es tu novia?

2. ¿_____ es una *vendetta*?

3. ¿_____ años cumple tu mamá este año?

4. ¿_____ pusiste las fotos de la boda?

5. ¿_____ te dijo esa mentira?

6. ¿_____ te regalaron ese vestido tan hermoso?

7. ¿_____ empieza el partido de tenis?

8. ¿_____ de estos dulces te gustan más?

9. ¿_____ pudiste terminar la tarea esa noche?

10. ¿_____ te llevó tu esposo para celebrar su aniversario?

3 **¿Cuál es la pregunta?** Write questions that correspond to these responses. Use each word or phrase from the word bank only once.

¿a qué hora?	¿cuál?	¿cuándo?	¿de dónde?	¿qué?
¿adónde?	¿cuáles?	¿cuántos?	¿dónde?	¿quién?

1. _____

La camisa que más me gusta es ésa.

2. _____

Hoy quiero descansar durante el día.

3. _____

Mi profesora de matemáticas es la señora Aponte.

Workbook

4. _____

Soy de Buenos Aires, Argentina.

5. _____

Mis gafas favoritas son las azules.

6. _____

El pastel de cumpleaños está en el refrigerador.

7. _____

La fiesta sorpresa empieza a las ocho en punto de la noche.

8. _____

El restaurante cierra los lunes.

9. _____

Hay ciento cincuenta invitados en la lista.

10. _____

Vamos a la fiesta de cumpleaños de Inés.

4 **Síntesis** Research the life of a famous person who has had a stormy personal life, such as Elizabeth Taylor or Henry VIII. Write a brief biography of the person, including the following information:

- When was the person born?
- What was that person's childhood like?
- With whom did the person fall in love?
- Who did the person marry?
- Did he or she have children?
- Did the person get divorced?
- Did the person go to school, and did he or she graduate?
- How did his or her career or lifestyle vary as the person went through different stages in life?

_____

_____

_____

_____

_____

_____

_____

PREPARACIÓN

Lección 10

1   **El cuerpo humano**   Label the parts of the body.

1. _____

2. _____

3. _____

4. _____

5. _____

6. _____

7. _____

8. _____

2   **¿Adónde vas?**   Fill in each blank with the place that matches the description.

la clínica	el dentista	el hospital
el consultorio	la farmacia	la sala de emergencia

1. tienes que comprar aspirina _____

2. tienes un dolor de muelas _____

3. te rompes una pierna _____

4. te debes hacer un examen médico _____

5. te van a hacer una operación _____

6. te van a poner una inyección _____

3   **Las categorías**   List these terms with the appropriate category.

antibiótico	gripe	radiografía
aspirina	infección	receta
congestionado	operación	resfriado
dolor de cabeza	pastilla	tomar la temperatura
estornudos	poner una inyección	tos
fiebre		

Síntoma: _____

Enfermedad: _____

Diagnóstico: _____

Tratamiento (*Treatment*): _____

4   Oraciones completas Complete the sentences with the correct words.

alérgica	embarazada	hueso	receta
caerse	farmacia	inyección	salud
duele	fiebre	radiografía	síntomas

1. La señora Gómez va a tener un hijo en septiembre. Está _____.

2. Manuel tiene la temperatura muy alta. Tiene _____.

3. A Rosita le recetaron un antibiótico y le van a poner una _____.

4. A Pedro le cayó una mesa en el pie. El pie le _____ mucho.

5. Mi tía estornuda mucho durante la primavera. Es _____ al polen.

6. Tienes que llevar la _____ a la farmacia para que te vendan (*in order for them to sell you*) la medicina.

7. Le tomaron una _____ de la pierna para ver si se le rompió.

8. Los _____ de un resfriado son los estornudos y la tos.

5   Doctora y paciente Choose the logical sentences to complete the dialogue.

DOCTORA ¿Qué síntomas tienes?

1. PACIENTE _____
a. Tengo tos y me duele la cabeza.
b. Soy muy saludable.
c. Me recetaron un antibiótico.

2. DOCTORA _____
a. ¿Cuándo fue el accidente?
b. ¿Te dio fiebre ayer?
c. ¿Dónde está la sala de emergencia?

3. PACIENTE _____
a. Fue a la farmacia.
b. Me torcí el tobillo.
c. Sí, mi esposa me tomó la temperatura.

4. DOCTORA _____
a. ¿Estás muy congestionado?
b. ¿Estás embarazada?
c. ¿Te duele una muela?

5. PACIENTE _____
a. Sí, me hicieron una operación.
b. Sí, estoy mareado.
c. Sí, y también me duele la garganta.

6. DOCTORA _____
a. Tienes que ir al consultorio.
b. Es una infección de garganta.
c. La farmacia está muy cerca.

7. PACIENTE _____
a. ¿Tengo que tomar un antibiótico?
b. ¿Debo ir al dentista?
c. ¿Qué indican las radiografías?

8. DOCTORA _____
a. Sí, eres alérgico.
b. Sí, te lastimaste el pie.
c. Sí, ahora te lo voy a recetar.

GRAMÁTICA

10.1 The imperfect tense

1 **El imperfecto** Complete the sentences with the correct forms of the verbs in parentheses.

1. Antes, la familia Álvarez _____ (cenar) a las ocho de la noche.

2. De niña, yo _____ (cantar) en el Coro de Niños de San Juan.

3. Cuando vivían en la costa, ustedes _____ (ser) muy felices.

4. Mis hermanas y yo _____ (jugar) en un equipo de béisbol.

5. La novia de Raúl _____ (tener) el pelo rubio en ese tiempo.

6. Antes de tener la computadora, (tú) _____ (escribir) a mano (*by hand*).

7. (Nosotros) _____ (creer) que el concierto era el miércoles.

8. Mientras ellos lo _____ (buscar) en su casa, él se fue a la universidad.

2 **Oraciones imperfectas** Create sentences with the elements provided. Use the correct imperfect tense forms of the verbs.

1. mi abuela / ser / muy trabajadora y amable

_____

2. tú / ir / al teatro / cuando vivías en Nueva York

_____

3. ayer / haber / muchísimos pacientes en el consultorio

_____

4. (nosotros) / ver / tu casa desde allí

_____

5. ser / las cinco de la tarde / cuando llegamos a San José

_____

6. ella / estar / muy nerviosa durante la operación

_____

3 **No, pero antes...** Answer the questions negatively, using the imperfect tense.

> **modelo**
> ¿Juega Daniel al fútbol?
> No, *pero antes jugaba.*

1. ¿Hablas por teléfono? _____

2. ¿Fue a la playa Susana? _____

3. ¿Come carne Benito? _____

4. ¿Te trajo tu novio? _____

5. ¿Conduce tu mamá? _____

Workbook

4 **¿Qué hacían?** Write sentences about what the people in the drawings were doing yesterday at three o'clock in the afternoon. Use the subjects provided.

1. tú

_____

_____

_____

2. Rolando

_____

_____

_____

3. Pablo

_____

_____

_____

4. Lilia y yo

_____

_____

_____

5 **Antes y ahora** Javier is thinking about his childhood—how things were then and how they are now. Write two sentences saying what Javier used to do and what he does now.

> **modelo**
>
> vivir en casa / vivir en la residencia estudiantil
>
> Antes vivía en casa.
>
> Ahora vivo en la residencia estudiantil.

1. jugar al fútbol con mis primos / jugar en el equipo de la universidad

_____

_____

2. escribir las cartas a mano / escribir mensajes electrónicos en la computadora

_____

_____

3. ser gordito (*chubby*) / ser delgado

_____

_____

4. tener a mi familia cerca / tener a mi familia lejos

_____

_____

5. estudiar en mi habitación / estudiar en la biblioteca

_____

_____

6. conocer personas de mi ciudad / conocer personas de todo (*the whole*) el país

_____

_____

10.2 Constructions with se

1 **¿Qué se hace?** Complete the sentences with verbs from the word bank. Use impersonal constructions with **se**.

caer	hablar	recetar	vender
dañar	poder	servir	vivir

1. En Costa Rica _____ español.

2. En las librerías _____ libros y revistas.

3. En los restaurantes _____ comida.

4. En los consultorios _____ medicinas.

5. En el campo _____ muy bien.

6. En el mar _____ nadar y pescar.

2 **Los anuncios** Write advertisements or signs for the situations described. Use impersonal constructions with **se**.

1. "Está prohibido fumar".

2. "Vendemos periódicos".

3. "Hablamos español".

4. "Necesitamos enfermeras".

5. "No debes nadar".

6. "Estamos buscando un auto usado".

3 **Pronombres** Complete the sentences with the correct indirect object pronouns.

1. Se _____ perdieron las maletas a Roberto.

2. A mis hermanas se _____ cayó la mesa.

3. A ti se _____ olvidó venir a buscarme ayer.

4. A mí se _____ quedó la ropa nueva en mi casa.

5. A las tías de Ana se _____ rompieron los vasos.

6. A Isabel y a mí se _____ dañó el auto.

4 **El verbo correcto** Choose the correct form of the verb in parentheses, then rewrite each sentence.

1. A Marina se le (cayó, cayeron) la bolsa.

_____

2. A ti se te (olvidó, olvidaron) comprarme la medicina.

_____

3. A nosotros se nos (quedó, quedaron) los libros en el auto.

_____

4. A Ramón y a Pedro se les (dañó, dañaron) el proyecto.

_____

5 **Eso pasó** Create sentences using the elements provided and impersonal constructions with **se**. Use the preterite tense of the verbs.

> **modelo**
>
> (a Raquel) / olvidar / comer antes de salir
> *Se le olvidó comer antes de salir.*

1. (a tu hermana) / perder / las llaves del auto

_____

2. (a ustedes) / olvidar / ponerse las inyecciones

_____

3. (a ti) / caer / los papeles del médico

_____

4. (a Marcos) / romper / la pierna cuando esquiaba

_____

5. (a mí) / dañar / la cámara durante el viaje

_____

6 **¿Qué pasó?** Answer the questions, using the phrases in parentheses.

> **modelo**
>
> ¿Qué le pasó a Roberto? (quedar los libros en casa)
> *Se le quedaron los libros en casa.*

1. ¿Qué les pasó a Pilar y a Luis? (dañar el coche)

_____

2. ¿Qué les pasó a los padres de Sara? (romper la botella de vino)

_____

3. ¿Qué te pasó a ti? (perder las llaves de la casa)

_____

4. ¿Qué les pasó a ustedes? (quedar las toallas en la playa)

_____

5. ¿Qué le pasó a Hugo? (olvidar estudiar para el examen)

_____

10.3 Adverbs

1 **Adjetivos y adverbios** Complete the sentences by changing the adjectives in the first sentences into adverbs in the second.

1. Los conductores son lentos. Conducen _____.

2. Esa doctora es amable. Siempre nos saluda _____.

3. Los autobuses de mi ciudad son frecuentes. Pasan por la parada _____.

4. Rosa y Julia son chicas muy alegres. Les encanta bailar y cantar _____.

5. Mario y tú hablan un español perfecto. Hablan español _____.

6. Los pacientes visitan al doctor de manera constante. Lo visitan _____.

7. Llegar tarde es normal para David. Llega tarde _____.

8. Me gusta trabajar de manera independiente. Trabajo _____.

2 **Adverbios** Complete the sentences with adverbs and adverbial expressions from the word bank. Use each term once.

a menudo	casi
a tiempo	por lo menos
bastante	pronto

1. Tito no es un niño muy sano. Se enferma _____.

2. El doctor Garrido es muy puntual. Siempre llega al consultorio _____.

3. Mi madre visita al doctor con frecuencia. Se chequea _____ una vez cada año.

4. Fui al doctor el año pasado. Tengo que volver _____.

5. Llegué tarde al autobús, y _____ tuve que ir al centro caminando.

6. El examen fue _____ difícil.

3 **Más adverbios** Complete the sentences with the adverbs or adverbial phrases that correspond to the words in parentheses.

1. Van a conciertos _____ (*frequently*) y consiguen asientos muy buenos.

2. El accidente fue _____ (*quite*) grave, pero al conductor no se le rompió ningún hueso.

3. Irene y Vicente van a comer _____ (*less*) porque quieren estar más delgados.

4. Silvia y David _____ (*almost*) se cayeron de la motocicleta cerca de su casa.

5. Para aprobar (*pass*) el examen, tienes que contestar _____ (*at least*) el 75% de las preguntas.

6. Mi mamá _____ (*sometimes*) se tuerce el tobillo cuando camina mucho.

Lección 10 Workbook Activities   **105**

4 **Háblame de ti** Answer the questions using the adverbs and adverbial phrases that you learned in this lesson. Do not repeat the adverb or adverbial phrase of the question. Then, say how long ago you last did each activity.

> **modelo**
>
> ¿Vas siempre a la playa?
> No, a veces voy a la playa. Hace cuatro meses que no voy a la playa.

1. ¿Tú y tus amigos van al cine con frecuencia?

_____

2. ¿Comes comida japonesa a menudo?

_____

3. ¿Llegas tarde a tu clase de español?

_____

4. ¿Te enfermas con frecuencia?

_____

5. ¿Comes carne?

_____

5 **Síntesis** Think of a summer in which you did a lot of different things on vacation or at home. State the activities that you used to do during that summer; mention which of those things you still do in the present. How often did you do those activities then? How often do you do them now? How long ago did you do some of those things? Create a "photo album" of that summer, using actual photographs if you have them, or drawings that you make. Use your writing about the summer as captions for the photo album.

_____

_____

_____

_____

_____

_____

_____

_____

_____

_____

¡VIVAN LOS PAÍSES HISPANOS!

Suramérica II

1 **El mapa** Answer the questions in the map with complete sentences.

1. ¿Cuál es uno de los sitios turísticos más visitados de este país?

_____

2. ¿Por qué es especial el lago Titicaca?

_____

3. ¿Qué elemento es esencial en la dieta diaria de la población de este país?

_____

5. ¿Cuáles son los deportes que se practican en las montañas nevadas de la cordillera de los Andes?

_____

4. ¿Qué pasó con el tango durante los años 30?

_____

2 **Palabras desordenadas** Unscramble the words about Argentina, Chile, Uruguay, Paraguay, and Bolivia, using the clues.

1. ODNETOVEMI _____

(capital de Uruguay)

2. ANACFIRA _____

(una de las raíces del tango)

3. TOORVPOAVCI _____

(una característica del tango en un principio)

4. ÚIAUZG _____

(cataratas que se forman en la frontera entre Brasil, Argentina y Paraguay)

5. EPIIROM _____

(lo que fundaron los hijos del dios Sol cuando emergieron del lago Titicaca, según la mitología inca)

6. ILRARADLAP _____

(uno de los platos más conocidos en Uruguay y Argentina)

7. AGÍRNUA _____

(la moneda que se usa en Paraguay)

8. AZALACBA _____

(el material que se usa para hacer la taza en donde se bebe mate)

9. IOENVRNI _____

(tipo de deportes que son el esquí y el snowboard)

10. YAGPUARA _____

(río que divide el Gran Chaco)

3 Palabras cruzadas (*crossed*) Write a description of each of the words that are formed horizontally. Then, write a question that corresponds to the word that is formed vertically in bold letters.

1. _____
2. _____
3. _____
4. _____
5. _____
6. _____
7. _____
8. _____
9. _____
10. _____

¿ _____ ?

			M	e	n	d	o	z	a		
		b	o	m	b	i	l	l	a		
	P	a	r	a	n	á					
p	e	s	o	■	a	r	g	e	n	t	i	n	o
			n	a	v	e	g	a	b	l	e
	B	o	l	i	v	i	a				
	P	o	r	t	i	l	l	o			
	a	s	a	d	o						
	p	o	r	t	e	ñ	o				
B	u	e	n	o	s	■	A	i	r	e	s

4 ¿Qué se hace? Read each statement and choose the logical response.

____ 1. En Chile se practican

____ 2. El lago Titicaca está en

____ 3. En Argentina se baila

____ 4. La mitología inca cuenta que

____ 5. En Uruguay y en Argentina se come

____ 6. En Paraguay se visitan

____ 7. La moneda que se usa en Paraguay es

____ 8. En Uruguay y Argentina se bebe

a. su imperio surgió del lago Titicaca.

b. los Andes de Bolivia y Perú.

c. mate con una bombilla metálica.

d. las famosas cataratas de Iguazú.

e. el guaraní.

f. deportes de invierno.

g. tango, baile de raíces africanas y europeas.

h. asado, parrillada y chivito.

Workbook

PREPARACIÓN

1 **La tecnología** Fill in the blanks with the correct terms.

1. Para multiplicar y dividir puedes usar _____.

2. Para hacer videos de tu familia puedes usar _____.

3. Cuando vas a un sitio web, lo primero (*the first thing*) que ves es _____.

4. Cuando alguien te llama, te deja un mensaje en _____.

5. La red de computadoras y servidores más importante del mundo es _____.

6. Para poder ver muchos programas de TV distintos, tienes que tener _____.

2 **Eso hacían** Match a subject from the word bank to each verb phrase. Then write complete sentences for the pairs using the imperfect.

algunos jóvenes estadounidenses	el conductor del autobús	el mecánico de Jorge
el auto viejo	la impresora nueva	el teléfono celular

1. manejar lentamente por la nieve

_____

2. imprimir los documentos muy rápidamente

_____

3. revisarle el aceite al auto todos los meses

_____

4. sonar insistentemente, pero nadie contestarlo

_____

5. no arrancar cuando llover

_____

6. navegar en Internet cuando ser niños

_____

3 **La computadora** Label the drawing with the correct terms.

1. _____

2. _____

5. _____

3. _____

4. _____

6. _____

7. _____

4   **Preguntas** Answer the questions with complete sentences.

1. ¿Para qué se usa la impresora?

_____

2. ¿Para qué se usan los frenos del coche?

_____

3. ¿Qué se usa para enviar documentos?

_____

4. ¿Qué se usa para manejar el carro?

_____

5. ¿Qué se usa para cambiar los canales del televisor?

_____

6. ¿Para qué se usan las llaves del carro?

_____

_____

5   **Mi primer día manejando** Complete the paragraph with terms from the word bank using the appropriate tense of each verb.

accidente	camino	licencia de	parar	taller mecánico
aceite	entré	conducir	policía	tráfico
arrancar	estacionar	llanta	revisar	velocidad
calle	lento	lleno	subir	máxima

Después de dos exámenes, conseguí mi _____ para poder manejar legalmente
                                              1
por primera vez. Estaba muy emocionado cuando _____ al carro de mi papá. El
                                                         2
tanque estaba _____, el _____ lo revisaron el día
                      3   4
anterior (previous) en el _____. El carro y yo estábamos listos para
                                   5
_____. Primero salí por la _____ en donde está
          6   7
mi casa. Luego llegué a un área de la ciudad donde había mucha gente y también mucho

_____. Se me olvidó _____ en el semáforo,
          8   9
que estaba amarillo, estuve cerca de tener un _____. Sin saberlo,
                                                       10
_____ en la autopista (highway). La _____ era de 70
          11   12
millas (miles) por hora, pero yo estaba tan nervioso que iba mucho más _____, a
                                                                              13
10 millas por hora. Vi un carro de la _____ y tuve miedo. Por eso volví a casa y
                                             14
_____ el carro en la calle. ¡Qué aventura!
          15

GRAMÁTICA

11.1 The preterite and the imperfect

1 **¿Pretérito o imperfecto?** Complete the sentences correctly with imperfect or preterite forms of the verbs in parentheses.

1. Claudia _____ (escribir) un mensaje por Internet cuando la llamó Miguel.

2. El conductor estacionaba su auto cuando _____ (chocar) conmigo.

3. Mariela cruzaba la calle cuando el semáforo _____ (cambiar) a verde.

4. (Yo) _____ (estar) mirando la televisión cuando llegaron mis hermanos.

5. Mientras el mecánico _____ (revisar) el aceite, yo entré a comprar una soda.

6. Tú _____ (quedarse) en el auto mientras Rolando llenaba el tanque.

7. Cuando Sandra llegó al café, Luis _____ (leer) el periódico.

8. Antes el auto no _____ (funcionar), pero ayer el mecánico lo arregló.

2 **Antes y ayer** Complete each pair of sentences by using the imperfect and preterite forms of the verbs in parentheses.

(bailar)

1. Cuando era pequeña, Sara _____ ballet todos los lunes y miércoles.

2. Ayer Sara _____ ballet en el recital de la universidad.

(escribir)

3. El viernes pasado, (yo) le _____ un mensaje de texto a mi papá.

4. Antes (yo) le _____ mensajes por correo electrónico.

(ser)

5. El novio de María _____ guapo, inteligente y simpático.

6. El viaje de novios _____ una experiencia inolvidable (*unforgettable*).

(haber)

7. _____ una fiesta en casa de Maritere el viernes pasado.

8. Cuando llegamos a la fiesta, _____ mucha gente.

(ver)

9. El lunes _____ a mi prima Lisa en el centro comercial.

10. De niña, yo _____ a Lisa todos los días.

3 **¿Qué pasaba?** Look at the drawings, then complete the sentences, using the preterite or imperfect.

1. Cuando llegué a casa anoche, las

niñas _____.

2. Cuando empezó a llover, Sara

_____.

3. Antes de irse de vacaciones, la señora

García _____.

4. Cada verano, las chicas

_____.

4 **El pasado** Decide whether the verbs in parentheses should be in the preterite or the imperfect. Then rewrite the sentences.

1. Ayer Clara (ir) a casa de sus primos, (saludar) a su tía y (comer) con ellos.

_____

2. Cuando Manuel (vivir) en Buenos Aires, (conducir) mucho todos los días.

_____

3. Mientras Carlos (leer) las traducciones (*translations*), Blanca (traducir) otros textos.

_____

4. El doctor (terminar) el examen médico y me (recetar) un antibiótico.

_____

5. La niña (tener) ocho años y (ser) inteligente y alegre.

_____

6. Rafael (cerrar) todos los programas, (apagar) la computadora y (irse).

_____

5 **¡Qué diferencia!** Complete this paragraph with the preterite or the imperfect of the verbs in parentheses.

La semana pasada (yo) _____ (llegar) a la universidad y me di cuenta (*realized*)
1

de que este año va a ser muy diferente a los anteriores. Laura y yo _____ (vivir)
2

con Regina, pero la semana pasada (nosotras) _____ (conocer) a nuestra
3

nueva compañera de cuarto, Gisela. Antes Laura, Regina y yo _____ (tener)
4

un apartamento muy pequeño, pero la semana pasada, (nosotras) _____
5

(ver) el apartamento nuevo: es enorme y tiene mucha luz. Antes de vivir con Gisela, Laura y yo

no _____ (poder) leer el correo electrónico desde la casa, pero ayer Gisela
6

_____ (conectar) su computadora a Internet y todas _____
7   8

(leer) nuestros mensajes. Antes (nosotras) siempre _____ (caminar) hasta la
9

biblioteca para ver el correo, pero anoche Gisela nos _____ (decir) que podemos
10

compartir su computadora. ¡Qué diferencia!

6 **¿Dónde estabas?** Write questions and answers with the words provided. Ask where these people were when something happened.

modelo

Elena ⟶ Ricardo / salir a bailar // cuarto / dormir la siesta
¿Dónde estaba Elena cuando Ricardo salió a bailar?
Elena estaba en el cuarto. Dormía la siesta.

1. María ⟶ (yo) / llamar por teléfono // cocina / lavar los platos

_____

_____

2. (tú) ⟶ Teresa y yo / ir al cine // casa / leer una revista

_____

_____

3. tu hermano ⟶ empezar a llover // calle / pasear en bicicleta

_____

_____

4. ustedes ⟶ Luisa / venir a casa // estadio / jugar al fútbol

_____

_____

5. Ana y Pepe ⟶ (tú) / saludarlos // supermercado / hacer las compras

_____

_____

Workbook

7   **El diario de Laura** Laura has just found a page from her old diary. Rewrite the page in the past tense, using the preterite and imperfect forms of the verbs as appropriate.

Querido diario:

Estoy pasando el verano en Córdoba; es un lugar muy divertido. Salgo con mis amigas todas las noches hasta tarde. Bailo con nuestros amigos y nos divertimos mucho. Durante la semana trabajo: doy clases de inglés. Los estudiantes son alegres y se interesan mucho por aprender. El día de Navidad conocí a un chico muy simpático que se llama Francisco. Me llamó al día siguiente (*next*) y nos vemos todos los días. Me siento enamorada de él. Creo que va a venir a Boston para estar conmigo. Tenemos que buscar trabajo allí, pero estamos muy emocionados.

Laura

_____

_____

_____

_____

_____

_____

_____

_____

_____

8   **Pretérito e imperfecto** Rewrite the paragraph, using the preterite or imperfect forms of the verbs in parentheses as appropriate.

Ayer mi hermana y yo (ir) a la playa. Cuando llegamos, el día (estar) despejado con mucho sol, y nosotras (estar) muy contentas. A las doce (comer) unos sándwiches de almuerzo. Los sándwiches (ser) de jamón y queso. Luego (descansar) y (nadar) en el mar. Mientras (nadar), (ver) a las personas que (practicar) el esquí acuático. (Parecer) muy divertido, así que (decidir) probarlo. Mi hermana (ir) primero, mientras yo la (mirar). Luego (ser) mi turno. Las dos (divertirse) mucho esa tarde.

_____

_____

_____

_____

_____

_____

_____

_____

11.2 Por and para

1 **Para éste o por aquello** Complete the sentences with **por** or **para** as appropriate.

1. Pudieron terminar el trabajo _____ haber empezado (*having begun*) a tiempo.

2. Ese fax es _____ enviar y recibir documentos de la compañía.

3. Elsa vivió en esa ciudad _____ algunos meses hace diez años.

4. Mi mamá compró esta computadora portátil _____ mi papá.

5. Sales _____ Argentina mañana a las ocho y media.

6. Rosaura cambió la blusa blanca _____ la blusa rosada.

7. El señor López necesita el informe _____ el 2 de agosto.

8. Estuve estudiando toda la noche _____ el examen.

9. Los turistas fueron de excursión _____ las montañas.

10. Mis amigos siempre me escriben _____ correo electrónico.

2 **Por muchas razones** Complete the sentences with the expressions in the word bank.

por aquí	por eso
por ejemplo	por fin

1. Ramón y Sara no pudieron ir a la fiesta anoche; _____ no los viste.

2. Buscaron el vestido perfecto por mucho tiempo, y _____ lo encontraron en esa tienda.

3. Creo que va a ser difícil encontrar un navegador GPS _____.

4. Pídele ayuda a uno de tus amigos, _____, a Miguel, a Carlos o a Francisco.

5. Miguel y David no saben si podemos pasar _____ en bicicleta.

6. El reproductor de DVD no está conectado, y _____ no funciona.

3 **Por y para** Complete the sentences with **por** or **para**.

1. Fui a comprar frutas _____ (*instead of*) mi madre.

2. Fui a comprar frutas _____ (*to give to*) mi madre.

3. Rita le dio dinero _____ (*in order to buy*) la cámara digital.

4. Rita le dio dinero _____ (*in exchange for*) la cámara digital.

5. La familia los llevó _____ (*through*) los Andes.

6. La familia los llevó _____ (*to*) los Andes.

4 **Escribir oraciones** Write sentences in the preterite, using the elements provided and **por** or **para**.

> **modelo**
>
> (tú) / salir en el auto / ¿? / Córdoba
> *Saliste en el auto para Córdoba.*

1. Ricardo y Emilia / traer un pastel / ¿? / su prima

_____

2. los turistas / llegar a las ruinas / ¿? / barco

_____

3. (yo) / tener resfriado / ¿? / el frío

_____

4. mis amigas / ganar dinero / ¿? / viajar a Suramérica

_____

5. ustedes / buscar a Teresa / ¿? / toda la playa

_____

6. el avión / salir a las doce / ¿? / Buenos Aires

_____

5 **Para Silvia** Complete the paragraph with **por** and **para**.

Fui a la agencia de viajes porque quería ir _____ Mendoza
                                                    1

_____ visitar a mi novia, Silvia. Entré _____ la puerta y
        2   3

Marta, la agente de viajes, me dijo: "¡Tengo una oferta excelente _____ ti!"
                                                                          4

Me explicó que podía viajar en avión _____ Buenos Aires
                                              5

_____ seiscientos dólares. Podía salir un día entre semana,
        6

_____ ejemplo, lunes o martes. Me podía quedar en una pensión en Buenos
        7

Aires _____ quince dólares _____ noche. Luego viajaría
          8   9

_____ tren a Mendoza _____ encontrarme con Silvia.
        10   11

"Debes comprar el pasaje _____ el fin de mes", me recomendó Marta. Fue la
                                12

oferta perfecta _____ mí. Llegué a Mendoza y Silvia vino a la estación
                      13

_____ mí. Traje unas flores _____ ella. Estuve en
        14   15

Mendoza _____ un mes y _____ fin Silvia y yo nos
              16   17

comprometimos. Estoy loco _____ ella.
                                  18

11.3 Stressed possesive adjectives and pronouns

1 **Esas cosas tuyas** Fill in the blanks with the possessive adjectives as indicated.

1. Ana nos quiere mostrar unas fotos _____ (*of hers*).

2. A Lorena le encanta la ropa _____ (*of ours*).

3. Los turistas traen las toallas _____ (*of theirs*).

4. El mecánico te muestra unos autos _____ (*of his*).

5. El sitio web _____ (*of his*) es espectacular.

6. ¿Quieres probar el programa de computación _____ (*of ours*)?

7. Roberto prefiere usar la computadora _____ (*of mine*).

8. Ese ratón _____ (*of yours*) es el más moderno que existe.

2 **¿De quién es?** Complete the sentences with possessive adjectives.

1. Ésa es mi computadora. Es la computadora _____.

2. Vamos a ver su sitio web. Vamos a ver el sitio web _____.

3. Aquéllos son mis archivos. Son los archivos _____.

4. Quiero usar el programa de él. Quiero usar el programa _____.

5. Buscamos nuestra impresora. Buscamos la impresora _____.

6. Ésos son los discos compactos de ella. Son los discos compactos _____.

7. Tienen que arreglar tu teclado. Tienen que arreglar el teclado _____.

8. Voy a usar el teléfono celular de ustedes. Voy a usar el teléfono celular _____.

3 **Los suyos** Answer the questions. Follow the model.

> **modelo**
> ¿Vas a llevar tu cámara de video?
> Sí, voy a llevar la mía.

1. ¿Prefieres usar tu calculadora? _____

2. ¿Quieres usar nuestro navegador GPS? _____

3. ¿Guardaste los archivos míos? _____

4. ¿Llenaste el tanque de su auto? _____

5. ¿Manejó Sonia nuestro auto? _____

6. ¿Vas a comprar mi televisor? _____

Workbook

4 **Los pronombres posesivos** Replace the question with one using **de** to clarify possession. Then answer the question affirmatively, using a stressed possessive pronoun.

> modelo
>
> ¿Es suyo el teléfono celular? (de ella)
>
> *¿Es de ella el teléfono celular? Sí, es suyo.*

1. ¿Son suyas las gafas? (de usted)

_____

2. ¿Es suyo el estéreo? (de Joaquín)

_____

3. ¿Es suya la impresora? (de ellos)

_____

4. ¿Son suyos esos reproductores de MP3? (de Susana)

_____

5. ¿Es suyo el coche? (de tu mamá)

_____

6. ¿Son suyas estas calculadoras? (de ustedes)

_____

5 **Síntesis** Tell the story of a romantic couple you know. Use the preterite and the imperfect to tell their story, what happened between them and when. Use stressed possessive adjectives and pronouns as needed to talk about their families and their difficulties.

_____

_____

_____

_____

_____

_____

_____

_____

_____

_____

_____

_____

PREPARACIÓN

Lección 12

1 **Los aparatos domésticos** Answer the questions with complete sentences.

> *modelo*
>
> Julieta quiere calentar comida rápidamente. ¿Qué tiene que usar Julieta?
> Julieta tiene que usar el horno de microondas.

1. La ropa de Joaquín está sucia. ¿Qué necesita Joaquín?

_____

2. Clara lavó la ropa. ¿Qué necesita Clara ahora?

_____

3. Los platos de la cena están sucios. ¿Qué se necesita?

_____

4. Rita quiere hacer hielo (*ice*). ¿Dónde debe poner el agua?

_____

2 **¿En qué habitación?** Label these items as belonging to **la cocina, la sala,** or **la alcoba**.

1. el lavaplatos _____

5. la almohada _____

2. el sillón _____

6. el refrigerador _____

3. la cama _____

7. la mesita de noche _____

4. el horno _____

8. el sofá _____

3 **¿Qué hacían?** Complete the sentences, describing the domestic activity in each drawing. Use the imperfect tense.

1. Ramón _____

2. Rebeca _____

3. Mi tío Juan _____

4. Isabel _____

4 **Una es diferente** Fill in the blank with the word that doesn't belong in each group.

1. sala, plato, copa, vaso, taza _____

2. cuchillo, altillo, plato, copa, tenedor _____

3. horno, balcón, patio, jardín, garaje _____

4. pared, estante, pintura, vecino, cuadro _____

5. alcoba, sala, comedor, estufa, oficina _____

6. lavadora, escalera, secadora, lavaplatos, refrigerador _____

5 **Crucigrama** Complete the crossword puzzle.

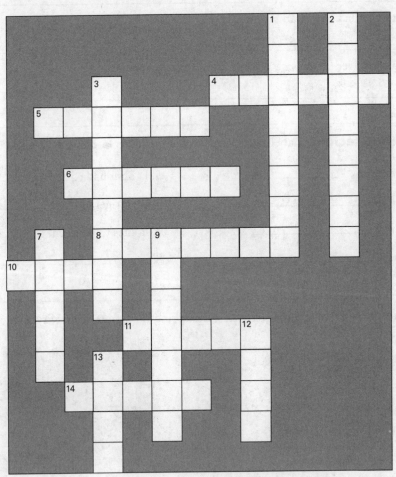

Horizontales

4. El hombre que vive al lado de tu casa.

5. Julieta habló con Romeo desde su _____.

6. sillón, mesa, cama o silla

8. Lo que pones cuando necesitas luz.

10. Lo que usas para tomar vino.

11. Usas estas cosas para tomar agua o soda.

14. Lo que usas cuando hace frío de noche.

Verticales

1. Lo que usas para ir de un piso a otro.

2. obras (*works*) de Picasso, de Goya, etc.

3. pagar dinero cada mes por vivir en un lugar

7. _____ de microondas

9. Si vas a vivir en otro lugar, vas a _____.

12. Donde se pueden sentar tres o cuatros personas.

13. Lo que usas para tomar el café.

GRAMÁTICA

12.1 Usted and ustedes commands

1   **Háganlo así** Complete the commands, using the verbs in parentheses.

Usted

1. (lavar) _____ la ropa con el nuevo detergente.

2. (salir) _____ de su casa y disfrute del aire libre.

3. (decir) _____ todo lo que piensa hacer hoy.

4. (beber) No _____ demasiado en la fiesta.

5. (venir) _____ preparado para pasarlo bien.

6. (volver) No _____ sin probar la langosta de Maine.

Ustedes

7. (comer) No _____ con la boca abierta.

8. (oír) _____ música clásica en casa.

9. (poner) No _____ los codos (*elbows*) en la mesa.

10. (traer) _____ un regalo a la fiesta de cumpleaños.

11. (ver) _____ programas de televisión educativos.

12. (conducir) _____ con precaución (*caution*) por la ciudad.

2   **Por favor** Give instructions to a person cleaning a house by changing the verb phrases into **usted** commands.

> **modelo**
> sacudir la alfombra
> *Sacuda la alfombra, por favor.*

1. venir a la casa

_____

2. traer la aspiradora

_____

3. arreglar el coche

_____

4. bajar al sótano

_____

5. apagar la estufa

_____

    Lección 12 Workbook Activities   **121**

3   **Para emergencias** Rewrite the paragraph, replacing **debe** + *verb* with **usted** commands.

Querido huésped:

Debe leer estas instrucciones para casos de emergencia. En caso de emergencia, debe tocar la puerta antes de abrirla. Si la puerta no está caliente, debe salir de la habitación con cuidado (*carefully*). Al salir, debe doblar a la derecha por el pasillo y debe bajar por la escalera de emergencia. Debe mantener la calma y debe caminar lentamente. No debe usar el ascensor durante una emergencia. Debe dejar su equipaje en la habitación en caso de emergencia. Al llegar a la planta baja, debe salir al patio o a la calle. Luego debe pedir ayuda a un empleado del hotel.

Querido huésped:

_____

_____

_____

_____

_____

_____

_____

_____

_____

_____

_____

4   **Lo opuesto** Change each command to say the opposite.

> **modelo**
> Recéteselo a mi hija.
> *No se lo recete a mi hija.*

1. Siéntense en la cama. _____

2. No lo limpie ahora. _____

3. Lávenmelas mañana. _____

4. No nos los sirva. _____

5. Sacúdalas antes de ponerlas. _____

6. No se las busquen. _____

7. Despiértenlo a las ocho. _____

8. Cámbiesela por otra. _____

9. Pídanselos a Martín. _____

10. No se lo digan hoy. _____

12.2 The present subjunctive

1 **Oraciones** Complete the sentences with the present subjunctive of the verb in parentheses.

1. Es bueno que ustedes _____ (comer) frutas, verduras y pescado.

2. Es importante que Laura y yo _____ (estudiar) para el examen de física.

3. Es urgente que el doctor te _____ (mirar) la rodilla y la pierna.

4. Es malo que los niños no _____ (leer) mucho de pequeños (*when they are little*).

5. Es mejor que (tú) les _____ (escribir) un mensaje antes de llamarlos.

6. Es necesario que (yo) _____ (pasar) por la casa de Mario por la mañana.

2 **El verbo correcto** Complete the sentences with the present subjunctive of the verbs provided.

almorzar	hacer	poner	traducir	venir
conducir	ofrecer	sacar	traer	ver

1. Es necesario que (yo) _____ a casa temprano para ayudar a mi mamá.

2. Es bueno que (la universidad) _____ muchos cursos por semestre.

3. Es malo que (ellos) _____ justo antes de ir a nadar a la piscina.

4. Es urgente que (Lara) _____ estos documentos legales.

5. Es mejor que (tú) _____ más lento para evitar (*avoid*) accidentes.

6. Es importante que (ella) no _____ la pintura en la mesa.

7. Es bueno que (tú) _____ las fotos para verlas en la fiesta.

8. Es necesario que (él) _____ la casa antes de comprarla.

9. Es malo que (nosotros) no _____ la basura todas las noches.

10. Es importante que (ustedes) _____ los quehaceres domésticos.

3 **El subjuntivo en las oraciones** Rewrite these sentences using the present subjunctive of the verbs in parentheses.

1. Mi padre dice que es importante que yo (estar) contenta con mi trabajo.

_____

2. Rosario cree que es bueno que la gente (irse) de vacaciones más a menudo.

_____

3. Creo que es mejor que Elsa (ser) la encargada del proyecto.

_____

4. Es importante que les (dar) las gracias por el favor que te hicieron.

_____

5. Él piensa que es malo que muchos estudiantes no (saber) otras lenguas.

_____

6. El director dice que es necesario que (haber) una reunión de la facultad.

_____

4 **Es necesario** Write sentences using the elements provided and the present subjunctive of the verbs.

> **modelo**
>
> malo / Roberto / no poder / irse de vacaciones
> Es malo que Roberto no pueda irse de vacaciones.

1. importante / Nora / pensar / las cosas antes de tomar la decisión

_____

2. necesario / (tú) / entender / la situación de esas personas

_____

3. bueno / Clara / sentirse / cómoda en el apartamento nuevo

_____

4. urgente / mi madre / mostrarme / los papeles que llegaron

_____

5. mejor / David / dormir / antes de conducir la motocicleta

_____

6. malo / los niños / pedirles / tantos regalos a sus abuelos

_____

5 **Sí, es bueno** Answer the questions using the words in parentheses and the present subjunctive.

> **modelo**
>
> ¿Tiene Marcia que terminar ese trabajo hoy? (urgente)
> Sí, es urgente que Marcia termine ese trabajo hoy.

1. ¿Debemos traer el pasaporte al aeropuerto? (necesario)

_____

2. ¿Tienes que hablar con la dueña del apartamento? (urgente)

_____

3. ¿Debe Manuel ir a visitar a su abuela todas las semanas? (bueno)

_____

4. ¿Puede Ana llamar a Cristina para darle las gracias? (importante)

_____

5. ¿Va Clara a saber lo que le van a preguntar en el examen? (mejor)

_____

12.3 Subjunctive with verbs of will and influence

1 **Preferencias** Complete the sentences with the present subjuntive of the verbs in parentheses.

1. Rosa quiere que tú _____ (ver) el sofá para la sala.

2. La mamá de Susana prefiere que ella _____ (estudiar) medicina.

3. Miranda insiste en que Luisa _____ (ser) la candidata a vicepresidenta.

4. Rita y yo deseamos que nuestros padres _____ (viajar) a Panamá.

5. A Eduardo no le importa que nosotros _____ (salir) esta noche.

6. La agente de viajes nos recomienda que _____ (quedarnos) en ese hotel.

2 **Compra una casa** Read the following suggestions for buying a house. Then write a note to a friend, repeating the advice and using the present subjunctive of the verbs.

> Antes de comprar una casa:
> - Se aconseja tener un agente inmobiliario (*real estate*).
> - Se sugiere buscar una casa en un barrio seguro.
> - Se insiste en mirar los baños, la cocina y el sótano.
> - Se recomienda comparar precios de varias casas antes de decidir.
> - Se aconseja hablar con los vecinos del barrio.

Te aconsejo que tengas un agente inmobiliario. _____

_____

_____

_____

_____

_____

_____

3 **Los pronombres** Write sentences using the elements provided and the present subjunctive. Replace the indirect objects with indirect object pronouns.

> **modelo**
> (a ti) / Simón / sugerir / terminar la tarea luego
> *Simón te sugiere que termines la tarea luego.*

1. (a Daniela) / José / rogar / escribir esa carta de recomendación

_____

2. (a ustedes) / (yo) / aconsejar / vivir en las afueras de la ciudad

_____

3. (a ellos) / la directora / prohibir / estacionar su carro frente a la escuela

_____

4. (a mí) / (tú) / sugerir / alquilar un apartamento en el barrio

_____

4 **¿Subjuntivo o infinitivo?** Write sentences using the elements provided. Use the subjunctive of the verbs when required.

1. Marina / querer / yo / traer / la compra a casa

_____

2. Sonia y yo / preferir / buscar / la información en Internet

_____

3. el profesor / desear / nosotros / usar / el diccionario

_____

4. ustedes / necesitar / escribir / una carta al consulado

_____

5. (yo) / preferir / Manuel / ir / al apartamento por mí

_____

6. Ramón / insistir en / buscar / las alfombras de la casa

_____

5 **Síntesis** Imagine that you are going away for the weekend and you are letting some of your friends stay in your house. Write instructions for your houseguests asking them to take care of the house. Use formal commands, the phrases **Es bueno, Es mejor, Es importante, Es necesario,** and **Es malo,** and the verbs **aconsejar, pedir, necesitar, prohibir, recomendar, rogar,** and **sugerir** to make sure that your house is in perfect shape when you get home.

_____

_____

_____

_____

_____

_____

_____

_____

_____

_____

¡VIVAN LOS PAÍSES HISPANOS!

América Central I

1 **El mapa** Identify in the map the names of the principal cities, rivers, lakes, and mountains of Guatemala, Honduras, and El Salvador.

2 **Sopa de letras** Find terms about Guatemala, Honduras, or El Salvador in the grid. Circle them in the puzzle, and write the words to complete these sentences.

1. Moneda de Honduras: _____

2. La Libertad es una

_____ de El Salvador.

3. Ropa tradicional de los guatemaltecos:

_____

4. Antigua Guatemala es famosa por su

_____ colonial hermosa.

5. La capital de Honduras es _____.

6. En el Parque Nacional Montecristo hay muchas

especies de plantas y animales como las orquídeas

y los _____ araña.

E	R	G	F	I	O	W	T
S	P	L	A	Y	A	D	E
L	O	L	E	N	R	Q	G
F	C	X	Z	B	Q	A	U
T	L	B	V	A	U	D	C
E	H	U	I	P	I	L	I
G	M	B	N	O	T	P	G
U	O	J	K	P	E	Q	A
C	N	D	L	A	C	W	L
I	O	K	L	R	T	X	P
L	S	E	H	T	U	F	A
L	E	M	P	I	R	A	A
R	A	P	O	N	A	M	R

3 **Palabras cruzadas** (*crossed*) Write a description of each of the words that are formed horizontally. Then, write a sentence describing the word that is formed vertically in bold.

1. _____
2. _____
3. _____
4. _____
5. _____
6. _____
7. _____
8. _____
9. _____
10. _____
11. _____
   _____.

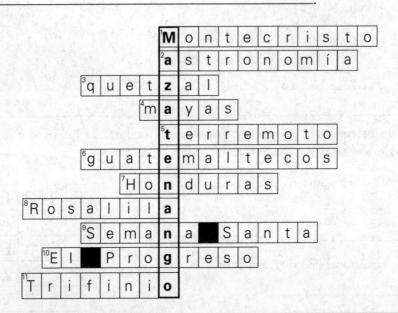

¹**M** o n t e c r i s t o
²**a** s t r o n o m í a
³q u e t **z** a l
⁴**m** a y a s
⁵**t** e r r e m o t o
⁶g u a t **e** m a l t e c o s
⁷H o **n** d u r a s
⁸R o s a l i l **a**
⁹S e m a **n** a ▪ S a n t a
¹⁰E l ▪ P r o **g** r e s o
¹¹T r i f i n i **o**

4 **Las fotos** Label the photos. Specify the location.

1. _____   2. _____   3. _____

REPASO   # Lecciones 9–12

1 **¿Por o para?** Complete the answers with **por** or **para**. Then write questions that correspond to the answers.

1. _____

   Trabajo _____ mi padre en la tienda.

2. _____

   Pasamos _____ la casa de Javier y Olga.

3. _____

   Ayer compré una blusa _____ mi hermana.

4. _____

   Ana estudia italiano _____ Internet.

2 **¿Pretérito o imperfecto?** Complete the sentences with the preterite or imperfect of the verbs in parentheses as appropriate.

1. Todos los años Mariana _____ (viajar) a San Francisco con sus padres.

2. El año pasado, ella _____ (enfermarse) durante el viaje.

3. Sus padres no _____ (saber) qué hacer. Entonces se detuvieron en un hospital público para

   ver qué enfermedad _____ (tener) ella.

4. Ese día, el doctor _____ (estar) almorzando cuando ellos _____ (llegar) a la sala

   de emergencias.

5. "Es apenas un resfriado", _____ (decir) el médico mientras la enfermera _____

   (ir) por la medicina para Mariana.

3 **Hágalo ahora** Write sentences using the words provided. Use **usted** and **ustedes** commands and the subjects indicated.

1. (ustedes) / ayudarlos a traer las compras _____

2. (usted) / poner la mesa _____

3. (ustedes) / sacudir las mantas _____

4. (usted) / limpiar la cocina y el baño _____

5. (ustedes) / barrer la sala _____

6. (usted) / no ensuciar los sillones _____

4 El subjuntivo Rewrite the sentences using the words in parentheses. Use the subjunctive of the verbs.

> **modelo**
> Ellos tienen muchos problemas. (ser malo)
> *Es malo que ellos tengan muchos problemas.*

1. Toma la medicina para sus alergias. (ser necesario / María) _____

_____

2. Las mujeres ven al doctor todos los años. (ser importante) _____

_____

3. Los pacientes hacen ejercicio. (la enfermera / sugerir) _____

_____

4. El paciente entra al consultorio. (el doctor / esperar) _____

_____

5 ¿Qué o cuál? Complete these sentences with **qué**, **cuál**, or **cuáles**.

1. ¿_____ es tu celebración favorita?

2. ¿_____ le vas a regalar a Patricia para su cumpleaños?

3. Para la fiesta de año nuevo, ¿_____ vestido debo llevar: el blanco o el rojo?

4. Mañana hay dos fiestas. ¿A _____ vas a ir?

5. ¿_____ sorpresa le tienen preparada a Martín para su graduación?

6. ¿_____ tipo de pastel tuvieron en la boda?

7. ¿_____ son nuestros asientos en la fiesta de fin de año?

8. ¿_____ quieres hacer para tu despedida de soltera (*bachelorette party*)?

6 La vida de ayer y de hoy Describe what people's lives were like in the early 1800s and what they are like now. Mention the things that people used to do and the things they do now (you may want to use adverbs like **siempre, nunca,** and **a veces**). Then mention the things that people should do to ensure quality of life in the future (you may want to use phrases like **es importante que**… and **es necesario que**…).

_____

_____

_____

_____

_____

_____

PREPARACIÓN

1 **La naturaleza** Complete the sentences with the appropriate nature-related words.

1. La luna, las estrellas, el sol y las nubes están en el _____.

2. El _____ es un lugar donde no llueve y hace mucho calor.

3. Una montaña que tiene un cráter es un _____.

4. La región llana (*flat*) que hay entre dos montañas es un _____.

5. La _____ es un bosque tropical, lo que significa que está cerca del ecuador.

6. Para ir de excursión por las montañas, es importante seguir un _____.

2 **Problema y solución** Match each problem with its solution. Then write a sentence with each pair, saying how we can solve the problem.

Problemas	Soluciones
1. la deforestación de los bosques	controlar las emisiones de los coches
2. la erosión de las montañas	plantar árboles y plantas
3. la falta (*lack*) de recursos naturales	reciclar los envases y las latas
4. la contaminación del aire en las ciudades	prohibir que se corten (*cut*) los árboles en algunas regiones

> **modelo**
> la extinción de plantas y animales / proteger las especies en peligro
> **Para resolver el problema de la extinción de plantas y animales,**
> **tenemos que proteger las especies en peligro.**

1. _____

2. _____

3. _____

4. _____

3 **Sinónimos y antónimos** Fill in the blanks with the correct verbs from the word bank.

conservar	dejar de	mejorar
contaminar	evitar	reducir

1. gastar ≠ _____   4. usar más ≠ _____

2. permitir ≠ _____   5. continuar ≠ _____

3. hacerse mejor = _____   6. limpiar ≠ _____

Workbook

4 **Nuestra madre** Fill in the blanks with the correct terms. Then, use the word formed vertically to complete the final sentence.

1. El lugar donde vivimos es nuestro medio _____.
2. Un bosque tiene muchos tipos de árboles y _____.
3. Un volcán tiene un _____ en la parte de arriba.
4. Cuando el cielo está despejado, no hay ni una _____.
5. Las _____ son rocas (*rocks*) más pequeñas.
6. Un _____ es un animal que vuela (*flies*).
7. La _____ es el estudio de los animales y plantas en su medio ambiente.
8. Por la noche se ven las _____.
9. El salmón es un tipo de _____.
10. El satélite que se ve desde la Tierra es la _____.

Todas estas cosas forman parte de la _____.

5 **Carta al editor** Complete the letter to the editor with items from the word bank.

árboles	deforestación	mejorar	reducir
conservar	dejar de	población	resolver
contaminación	evitar	recurso natural	respiramos

Creo que la _____ del aire en nuestra ciudad es un problema que se tiene
                        1

que _____ muy pronto. Cada día hay más carros que contaminan el aire que
        2

nosotros _____. Además, la _____ en las regiones cerca de la ciudad
            3   4

elimina una gran parte del oxígeno que los _____ le proveían (*provided*) a la
                                              5

_____ de la ciudad. Creo que es importante _____ las condiciones
        6   7

de las calles para que las personas puedan montar en bicicleta para ir al trabajo. Así, todos pueden

_____ el petróleo, que es un _____ que no va a durar (*last*) para
        8   9

siempre. El uso de bicicletas en la ciudad es una de las mejores ideas para _____
                                                                              10

el uso de los carros. Debemos _____ pensar que el carro es un objeto
                                11

absolutamente necesario, y buscar otras maneras de transportarnos. Quizás algún día podamos

_____ los problemas que nos causa la contaminación.
        12

GRAMÁTICA

13.1 The subjunctive with verbs of emotion

1 **Emociones** Complete the sentences with the subjunctive of the verbs in parentheses.

1. A mis padres les molesta que los vecinos (quitar) _____ los árboles.

2. Julio se alegra de que (haber) _____ muchos pájaros en el jardín de su casa.

3. Siento que Teresa y Lola (estar) _____ enfermas de gripe.

4. Liliana tiene miedo de que sus padres (decidir) _____ mudarse a otra ciudad.

5. A ti te sorprende que la deforestación (ser) _____ un problema tan grande.

6. Rubén espera que el gobierno (mejorar) _____ las leyes que protegen la naturaleza.

2 **Es así** Combine each pair of sentences, using the subjunctive.

> **modelo**
> Los gobiernos no se preocupan por el calentamiento global. Es terrible.
> **Es terrible que los gobiernos no se preocupen por el calentamiento global.**

1. Muchos ríos están contaminados. Es triste.

_____

2. Algunas personas evitan reciclar. Es ridículo.

_____

3. Los turistas no recogen la basura. Es una lástima.

_____

4. La gente destruye el medio ambiente. Es extraño.

_____

3 **Ojalá...** Form sentences, using the elements provided. Start the sentences with **Ojalá que**.

1. los países / conservar sus recursos naturales

_____

2. este sendero / llevarnos al cráter del volcán

_____

3. la población / querer cambiar las leyes de deforestación

_____

4. mi perro / gustarle ir de paseo por el bosque

_____

5. las personas / reducir el uso de los carros en las ciudades

_____

6. los científicos (*scientists*) / saber resolver el problema de la contaminación

_____

4 **Lo que sea** Change the subject of each second verb to the subject in parentheses. Then complete the new sentence with the new subject, using the subjunctive.

> **modelo**
>
> Pablo se alegra de ver a Ricardo. (su madre)
> Pablo se alegra de que *su madre vea a Ricardo.*

1. Me gusta salir los fines de semana. (mi hermana)

Me gusta que _____.

2. José y tú esperan salir bien en el examen. (yo)

José y tú esperan que _____.

3. Es ridículo contaminar el mundo en que vivimos. (la gente)

Es ridículo que _____.

4. Carla y Patricia temen separarse por el sendero. (sus amigos)

Carla y Patricia temen que _____.

5. Te molesta esperar mucho al ir de compras. (tu novio)

Te molesta que _____.

6. Es terrible usar más agua de la necesaria. (las personas)

Es terrible que _____.

7. Es triste no saber leer. (Roberto)

Es triste que _____.

8. Es una lástima encontrar animales abandonados. (los vecinos)

Es una lástima que _____.

5 **Emociones** Form sentences using the elements provided and the present subjunctive.

1. Rosa / alegrarse / sus amigos / reciclar los periódicos y los envases

_____

2. los turistas / sorprenderse / el país / proteger tanto los parques naturales

_____

3. (nosotros) / temer / la caza / poner en peligro de extinción a muchos animales

_____

4. la población / sentir / las playas de la ciudad / estar contaminadas

_____

5. las personas / esperar / el gobierno / desarrollar nuevos sistemas de energía

_____

6. a mi tía / gustar / mi primo / recoger y cuidar animales abandonados

_____

7. mis vecinos / tener miedo / el gobierno / abrir una fábrica cerca

_____

13.2 The subjunctive with doubt, disbelief, and denial

1 **No es probable** Complete the sentences with the subjunctive of the verbs in parentheses.

1. No es verdad que Raúl _____ (ser) un mal excursionista.

2. Es probable que Tito y yo _____ (ir) a caminar en el bosque nacional.

3. Claudia no está segura de que Eduardo _____ (saber) dónde estamos.

4. No es seguro que el trabajo nos _____ (llegar) antes del viernes.

5. Es posible que Miguel y Antonio _____ (venir) a visitarnos hoy.

6. No es probable que esa compañía les _____ (pagar) bien a sus empleados.

2 **Es posible que pase** Rewrite the sentences, using the words in parentheses.

> **modelo**
>
> Hay mucha contaminación en las ciudades. (probable)
> **Es probable que haya mucha contaminación en las ciudades.**

1. Hay muchos monos en las selvas de la región. (probable)

_____

2. El agua de esos ríos está contaminada. (posible)

_____

3. Ese sendero nos lleva al lago. (quizás)

_____

4. El gobierno protege todos los peces del océano. (imposible)

_____

5. La población reduce el uso de envases. (improbable)

_____

6. El desierto es un lugar mejor para visitar en invierno. (tal vez)

_____

3 **¿Estás seguro?** Complete the sentences with the indicative or subjunctive form of the verbs in parentheses.

1. No dudo que Manuel _____ (ser) la mejor persona para hacer el trabajo.

2. El conductor no niega que _____ (tener) poca experiencia por estas calles.

3. Ricardo duda que Mirella _____ (decir) siempre toda la verdad.

4. Sé que es verdad que nosotros _____ (deber) cuidar el medio ambiente.

5. Lina no está segura de que sus amigos _____ (poder) venir a la fiesta.

6. Claudia y Julio niegan que tú _____ (querer) mudarte a otro barrio.

7. No es probable que ella _____ (buscar) un trabajo de secretaria.

Lección 13 Workbook Activities **135**

4 **¿Es o no es?** Choose the correct phrase in parentheses to rewrite each sentence, based on the verb.

1. (Estoy seguro, No estoy seguro) de que a Mónica le gusten los perros.

_____

2. (Es verdad, No es verdad) que Ramón duerme muchas horas todos los días.

_____

3. Rita y Rosa (niegan, no niegan) que gaste mucho cuando voy de compras.

_____

4. (No cabe duda de, Dudas) que el aire que respiramos está contaminado.

_____

5. (No es cierto, Es obvio) que a Martín y a Viviana les encanta viajar.

_____

6. (Es probable, No hay duda de) que tengamos que reciclar todos los envases.

_____

5 **Oraciones nuevas** Rewrite the sentences, using the words in parentheses. Use the indicative or subjunctive form as appropriate.

1. Las matemáticas son muy difíciles. (no es cierto)

_____

2. El problema de la contaminación es bastante complicado. (el presidente no niega)

_____

3. Él va a terminar el trabajo a tiempo. (Ana duda)

_____

4. Esa película es excelente. (mis amigos están seguros)

_____

5. El español se usa más y más cada día. (no cabe duda)

_____

6. Lourdes y yo podemos ir a ayudarte esta tarde. (no es seguro)

_____

7. Marcos escribe muy bien en francés. (el maestro no cree)

_____

8. Pedro y Virginia nunca comen carne. (no es verdad)

13.3 The subjunctive with conjunctions

1 **Las conjunciones** Complete the sentences with the subjunctive form of the verbs in parentheses.

1. Lucas debe terminar el trabajo antes de que su jefe (*boss*) _____ (llegar).

2. ¿Qué tenemos que hacer en caso de que _____ (haber) una emergencia?

3. Ellos van a limpiar su casa con tal de que (tú) _____ (quedarse).

4. No puedo ir al museo a menos que Juan _____ (venir) por mí.

5. Alejandro siempre va a casa de Carmen sin que ella lo _____ (invitar).

6. Tu madre te va a prestar dinero para que te _____ (comprar) un coche usado.

7. No quiero que ustedes se vayan sin que tu esposo _____ (ver) mi computadora nueva.

8. Pilar no puede irse de vacaciones a menos que (ellos) le _____ (dar) más días en el trabajo.

9. Andrés va a llegar antes de que Rocío y yo _____ (leer) el correo electrónico.

10. Miguel lo va a hacer con tal que tú se lo _____ (revisar).

2 **¿Hasta cuándo?** Your gossipy coworker is always in everyone else's business. Answer his questions in complete sentences, using the words in parentheses.

1. ¿Hasta cuándo vas a ponerte ese abrigo? (hasta que / el jefe / decirme algo)

_____

2. ¿Cuándo va Rubén a buscar a Marta? (tan pronto como / salir de clase)

_____

3. ¿Cuándo se van de viaje Juan y Susana? (en cuanto / tener vacaciones)

_____

4. ¿Cuándo van ellos a invitarnos a su casa? (después de que / nosotros / invitarlos)

_____

5. ¿Hasta cuándo va a trabajar aquí Ramón? (hasta que / su esposa / graduarse)

_____

6. ¿Cuándo puede mi hermana pasar por tu casa? (cuando / querer)

_____

7. ¿Hasta cuándo vas a tomar las pastillas? (hasta que / yo / sentirme mejor)

_____

8. ¿Cuándo va Julia a reciclar estos envases? (tan pronto como / regresar del almuerzo)

_____

3 **Siempre llegas tarde** Complete this conversation, using the subjunctive and the indicative as appropriate.

MARIO Hola, Lilia. Ven a buscarme en cuanto (yo) _____ (salir) de clase.

LILIA Voy a buscarte tan pronto como la clase _____ (terminar), pero no quiero esperar como ayer.

MARIO Cuando iba a salir, (yo) me _____ (encontrar) con mi profesora de química, y hablé con ella del examen.

LILIA No quiero esperarte hasta que _____ (ser) demasiado tarde para almorzar otra vez.

MARIO Hoy voy a estar esperándote en cuanto (tú) _____ (llegar) a buscarme.

LILIA Después de que (yo) te _____ (recoger), podemos ir a comer a la cafetería.

MARIO En cuanto (tú) _____ (entrar) en el estacionamiento, me vas a ver allí, esperándote.

LILIA No lo voy a creer hasta que (yo) lo _____ (ver).

MARIO Recuerda que cuando (yo) te _____ (ir) a buscar al laboratorio la semana pasada, te tuve que esperar media hora.

LILIA Tienes razón. ¡Pero llega allí tan pronto como (tú) _____ (poder)!

4 **Síntesis** Write an opinion article about oil spills (**los derrames de petróleo**) and their impact on the environment. Use verbs and expressions of emotion, doubt, disbelief, denial, and certainty that you learned in this lesson to describe your own and other people's opinions about the effects of oil spills on the environment.

_____

_____

_____

_____

_____

_____

_____

_____

PREPARACIÓN   **Lección 14**

---

1 **El dinero** Complete the sentences with the correct banking-related words.

1. Necesito sacar dinero. Voy al _____.

2. Quiero ahorrar para comprar una casa. Pongo el dinero en una _____.

3. Voy a pagar, pero no quiero pagar al contado ni con tarjeta de crédito. Voy a usar un _____.

4. Cuando uso un cheque, el dinero sale de mi _____.

5. Para cobrar un cheque a mi nombre, lo tengo que _____ por detrás.

6. Para ahorrar, pienso _____ $200 en mi cuenta de ahorros todos los meses.

---

2 **¿Qué clase (*kind*) de tienda es ésta?** You are running errands, and you can't find the things you need. Fill in the blanks with the names of the places that should carry these items.

1. ¿No tienen manzanas? ¿Qué clase de _____ es ésta?

2. ¿No tienen una chuleta de cerdo? ¿Qué clase de _____ es ésta?

3. ¿No tienen detergente? ¿Qué clase de _____ es ésta?

4. ¿No tienen dinero? ¿Qué clase de _____ es éste?

5. ¿No tienen diamantes (*diamonds*)? ¿Qué clase de _____ es ésta?

6. ¿No tienen estampillas? ¿Qué clase de _____ es éste?

7. ¿No tienen botas? ¿Qué clase de _____ es ésta?

8. ¿No tienen aceite vegetal? ¿Qué clase de _____ es éste?

---

3 **¿Cómo pagas?** Fill in the blank with the most likely form of payment for each item.

al contado	a plazos
gratis	con un préstamo

1. un refrigerador _____

2. una camisa _____

3. un coche nuevo _____

4. las servilletas en un restaurante _____

5. una computadora _____

6. un vaso de agua _____

7. una hamburguesa _____

8. una cámara digital _____

9. la universidad _____

10. unos sellos _____

Workbook

4 Tu empresa Fill in the blanks with the type of store each slogan would promote.

1. "Compre aquí para toda la semana y ahorre en alimentos para toda la familia". _____

2. "Deliciosos filetes de salmón en oferta especial". _____

3. "Recién (*Just*) salido del horno". _____

4. "Naranjas y manzanas a dos dólares el kilo". _____

5. "Tráiganos su ropa más fina. ¡Va a quedar como nueva!" _____

6. "51 sabrosas variedades para el calor del verano". _____

7. "¡Reserva el pastel de cumpleaños de tu hijo hoy!" _____

8. "Un diamante es para siempre". _____

9. "Salchichas, jamón y chuletas de cerdo". _____

10. "Arréglese las uñas y péinese hoy por un precio económico". _____

5 Cómo llegar Identify the final destination for each set of directions.

1. De la Plaza Sucre, camine derecho en dirección oeste por la calle Comercio. Doble a la derecha en la calle La Paz hasta la calle Escalona. Doble a la izquierda y al final de la calle va a verlo. _____

2. Del banco, camine en dirección este por la calle Escalona. Cuando llegue a la calle Sucre, doble a la derecha. Siga dos cuadras hasta la calle Comercio. Doble a la izquierda. El lugar queda al cruzar la calle Bella Vista. _____

3. Del estacionamiento de la calle Bella Vista, camine derecho por la calle Sta. Rosalía hasta la calle Bolívar. Cruce la calle Bolívar, y a la derecha en esa cuadra la va a encontrar. _____

4. De la joyería, camine por la calle Comercio hasta la calle Bolívar. Doble a la derecha y cruce la calle Sta. Rosalía, la calle Escalona y la calle 2 de Mayo. Al norte en esa esquina la va a ver. _____

Plaza Bolívar Farmacia Joyería
Plaza Sucre Iglesia Zapatería
Banco Terminal Café Primavera
Casa de la Cultura Escuela Estacionamiento (*parking lot*)

GRAMÁTICA

14.1 The subjunctive in adjective clauses

1 **El futuro de las computadoras** Complete the paragraph with the subjunctive of the verbs in parentheses.

¿Alguna vez ha pensado en un programa de computadora que _____ (escribir)
₁

las palabras que usted le _____ (decir)? En nuestra compañía queremos
₂

desarrollar un programa que _____ (poder) reconocer la voz (*voice*) de
₃

las personas en varias lenguas. Así, todos van a poder escribir con la computadora ¡sin tocar el

teclado! Para desarrollar un programa de reconocimiento (*recognition*) del habla, primero hay que

enseñarle algunas palabras que se _____ (decir) con mucha frecuencia en esa
₄

lengua. Luego el programa tiene que "aprender" a reconocer cualquier (*any*) tipo de pronunciación

que _____ (tener) las personas que _____ (usar) el
₅ ₆

programa. En el futuro, va a ser normal tener una computadora que _____
₇

(reconocer) el habla de su usuario. Es posible que hasta (*even*) algunos aparatos domésticos

_____ (funcionar) con la voz de su dueño.
₈

2 **¿Esté o está?** Complete the sentences with the indicative or the subjunctive of the verbs in parentheses.

(ser)

1. Quiero comprar una falda que _____ larga y elegante.

2. A Sonia le gusta la falda que _____ verde y negra.

(estar)

3. Nunca visitaron el hotel que _____ en el aeropuerto.

4. No conocemos ningún hotel que _____ cerca de su casa.

(quedar)

5. Hay un banco en el edificio que _____ en la esquina.

6. Deben poner un banco en un edificio que _____ más cerca.

(tener)

7. Silvia quiere un apartamento que _____ balcón y piscina.

8. Ayer ellos vieron un apartamento que _____ tres baños.

(ir)

9. Hay muchas personas que _____ a Venezuela de vacaciones.

10. Raúl no conoce a nadie que _____ a Venezuela este verano.

3 **No es cierto** Rewrite the sentences to make them negative, using the subjuntive where appropriate.

1. Ricardo conoce a un chico que estudia medicina.

_____

2. Laura y Diego cuidan a un perro que protege su casa.

_____

3. Maribel y Lina tienen un pariente que escribe poemas.

_____

4. Los González usan coches que son baratos.

_____

5. Mi prima trabaja con unas personas que conocen a su padre.

_____

6. Gregorio hace un plato venezolano que es delicioso.

_____

4 **¿Hay alguno que sea así?** Answer these questions positively or negatively, as indicated. Use the subjunctive where appropriate.

1. ¿Hay algún buzón que esté en la calle Bolívar?

Sí, _____.

2. ¿Conoces a alguien que sea abogado de inmigración?

No, _____.

3. ¿Ves a alguien aquí que estudie contigo en la universidad?

Sí, _____.

4. ¿Hay alguna panadería que venda pan caliente (*hot*) cerca de aquí?

No, _____.

5. ¿Tienes alguna compañera que vaya a ese gimnasio?

Sí, _____.

6. ¿Conoces a alguien en la oficina que haga envíos a otros países?

No, _____.

5 **Une las frases** Complete the sentences with the most logical endings from the word bank. Use the indicative or subjunctive forms of the infinitive verbs as appropriate.

abrir hasta las doce de la noche	quererlo mucho	siempre decirnos la verdad
no dar direcciones	ser cómoda y barata	tener muchos museos

1. Rolando tiene una novia que _____.

2. Todos buscamos amigos que _____.

3. Irene y José viven en una ciudad que _____.

4. ¿Hay una farmacia que _____?

Workbook

14.2 Familiar (tú) commands

1 **Haz papel** Read the instructions for making recycled paper from newspaper. Then use familiar commands to finish the e-mail in which Paco explains the process to Marisol.

> hacer un molde con madera y tela (*fabric*)
>
> romper el papel de periódico en trozos (*pieces*) pequeños
>
> poner el papel en un envase con agua caliente
>
> preparar la pulpa con una licuadora (*blender*)
>
> volver a poner la pulpa en agua caliente
>
> empezar a poner la pulpa en un molde que deje (*lets*) salir el agua
>
> quitar el molde y dejar (*leave*) el papel sobre la mesa
>
> poner una tela encima del papel
>
> planchar el papel
>
> usar el papel

A Marisol	De Paco	Asunto Cómo reciclar papel

Para reciclar papel de periódico, _____

_____

_____

_____

_____

_____

¡Ya sabes cómo reciclar!
Hasta luego, Paco

2 **Díselo** Your friends are traveling to Costa Rica. Give them advice based on the cues provided using familiar commands.

> **modelo**
> Ramón / comprarte una camiseta en Costa Rica
> Ramón, *cómprame una camiseta en Costa Rica.*

1. David / quedarse unos días en San José

_____

2. Laura / no salir muy tarde

_____

3. Patricia / probar la comida típica de Costa Rica

_____

4. Isabel / no olvidar comer un helado en el parque del centro

_____

5. Cecilia / tener cuidado al cruzar las calles

_____

6. Simón / aprender a bailar en Costa Rica

_____

Workbook

3 **Planes para el verano** Rewrite this paragraph from a travel website. Replace the **usted** commands with familiar commands.

Este verano, descubra la ciudad de Panamá. Camine por las calles y observe la arquitectura de la ciudad. La catedral es un edificio que no puede dejar de visitar. Visite las ruinas en Panamá Viejo y compre artesanías *(crafts)* del país. Vaya a un restaurante de comida panameña y no se olvide de probar un plato popular. Conozca el malecón *(seafront)* y respire el aire puro del mar. Explore el Canal de Panamá y aprenda cómo funciona. Súbase a un autobús colorido y vea cómo vive la gente local. ¡Disfrute Panamá!

Verano en la ciudad de Panamá

_____

_____

_____

_____

_____

_____

_____

4 **¿Te ayudo?** Imagine that you are a child asking one of your parents these questions. Write his or her positive and negative answers in the form of familiar commands.

> modelo
> ¿Tengo que traer leche y pan?
> Sí, trae leche y pan. / No, no traigas leche y pan.

1. ¿Puedo pedir una pizza en el restaurante?

_____

2. ¿Debo ir a la panadería a comprar pan?

_____

3. ¿Tengo que hacer las diligencias?

_____

4. ¿Debo buscar a mi hermano después de la escuela?

_____

5. ¿Tengo que venir a casa después de clase el viernes?

_____

6. ¿Puedo cuidar al perro este fin de semana?

_____

14.3 Nosotros/as commands

1 **Hagamos eso** Rewrite these sentences, using the **nosotros/as** command forms of the verbs in italics.

> **modelo**
> Tenemos que *terminar* el trabajo antes de las cinco.
> **Terminemos el trabajo antes de las cinco.**

1. Hay que *recoger* a los niños hoy.

_____

2. Tenemos que *ir* al dentista esta semana.

_____

3. Debemos *depositar* el dinero en el banco.

_____

4. Podemos *viajar* a Perú este invierno.

_____

5. Queremos *salir* a bailar este sábado.

_____

6. Deseamos *invitar* a los amigos de Ana.

_____

2 **¡Sí! ¡No!** You and your roommate disagree about everything. Write affirmative and negative **nosotros/as** commands for these actions.

> **modelo**
> abrir las ventanas
> tú: **Abramos las ventanas.**
> tu compañero/a: **No abramos las ventanas.**

1. pasar la aspiradora hoy

tú: _____

tu compañero/a: _____

2. poner la televisión

tú: _____

tu compañero/a: _____

3. compartir la comida

tú: _____

tu compañero/a: _____

4. hacer las camas todos los días

tú: _____

tu compañero/a: _____

3 **Como Lina** Everyone likes Lina and wants to be like her. Using **nosotros/as** commands, write sentences saying what you and your friends should do to follow her lead.

1. Lina compra zapatos italianos en el centro.

_____

2. Lina conoce la historia del jazz.

_____

3. Lina se va de vacaciones a las montañas.

_____

4. Lina se corta el pelo en la peluquería de la calle Central.

_____

5. Lina hace pasteles para los cumpleaños de sus amigas.

_____

6. Lina no sale de fiesta todas las noches.

_____

7. Lina corre al lado del río todas las mañanas.

_____

8. Lina no gasta demasiado dinero en ropa.

_____

4 **El préstamo** Claudia is thinking of everything that she and her fiancé, Ramón, should do to buy an apartment. Write what she will tell Ramón, using **nosotros/as** commands for verbs in the infinitive. The first sentence is done for you.

Podemos pedir un préstamo para comprar un apartamento. Debemos llenar este formulario cuando solicitemos el préstamo. Tenemos que ahorrar dinero todos los meses hasta que paguemos el préstamo. No debemos cobrar los cheques que nos lleguen; debemos depositarlos en la cuenta corriente. Podemos depositar el dinero que nos regalen cuando nos casemos. Le debemos pedir prestado a mi padre un libro sobre cómo comprar una vivienda. Queremos buscar un apartamento que esté cerca de nuestros trabajos. No debemos ir al trabajo mañana por la mañana; debemos ir al banco a hablar con un empleado.

Pidamos un préstamo para comprar un apartamento. _____

_____

_____

_____

_____

_____

_____

_____

¡VIVAN LOS PAÍSES HISPANOS!

América Central II

1 **El mapa** Write three features of each country in the blanks provided.

1. Nicaragua

_____

_____

_____

2. Costa Rica

_____

_____

_____

3. Panamá

_____

_____

2 **Palabras desordenadas** Unscramble the words about places in Nicaragua, Costa Rica, or Panamá, using the clues.

1. STARPNANEU _____
   (ciudad de Costa Rica)

2. VZNEANRTEÓ _____
   (río en Costa Rica que está cerca de
   San José)

3. EATAPARZ _____
   (isla en el lago de Nicaragua)

4. ASARTBÁA _____
   (serranía en Panamá)

5. ARANADG _____
   (ciudad de Nicaragua)

6. ONLCAITÁT _____
   (uno de los océanos que conecta el Canal
   de Panamá)

7. AGAMUNA _____
   (capital de Nicaragua)

8. AUSCTNEAGA _____
   (cordillera que está en Costa Rica)

3 **Las fotos** Write a complete sentence about each photo. Identify each person and their country of origin.

1. _____

2. _____

3. _____

4 **Palabras cruzadas** (*crossed*) Complete this crossword puzzle based on the clues provided.

Horizontales

3. En 1948 en Costa Rica se disolvió el _____.

6. Costa Rica es una nación _____.

7. _____ es un país con un área de 130.370 km².

11. Costa Rica abolió la _____ de muerte en 1970.

12. El _____ de Panamá se construyó en 1903.

13. Ernesto Cardenal es poeta, _____ y sacerdote católico.

14. La capital de Nicaragua es _____ .

15. Ernesto Cardenal cree en el poder de la _____ .

Verticales

1. Nicaragua, Costa Rica y Panamá están en _____.

2. La isla de _____ es de Panamá.

4. Las _____ tradicionales tienen dibujos geométricos.

5. Óscar _____ fue presidente de su país.

7. Arias ganó el Premio _____ de la Paz en 1987.

8. _____ es una ciudad de Costa Rica.

9. Los kunas viven en las islas _____ de Panamá.

10. La moneda de Panamá es el _____ .

5 **El Canal de Panamá** Write why you think the *Canal de Panamá* is important.

El Canal de Panamá es importante porque… _____

_____

_____

_____

PREPARACIÓN

1 Lo opuesto Fill in the blanks with the terms that mean the opposite of the descriptions.

1. sedentario _____

2. con cafeína _____

3. fuerte _____

4. adelgazar _____

5. comer en exceso _____

6. con estrés _____

7. con (*with*) _____

8. fuera (*out*) de forma _____

2 Vida sana Complete the sentences with the correct terms.

1. Antes de correr, es importante hacer ejercicios de _____ para calentarse.

2. Para dormir bien por las noches, es importante tomar bebidas _____.

3. Para desarrollar músculos fuertes, es necesario _____.

4. Una persona que es muy sedentaria y ve mucha televisión es un _____.

5. _____ es bueno porque reduce la temperatura del cuerpo.

6. Para aliviar el estrés, es bueno hacer las cosas tranquilamente y sin _____.

7. Cuando tienes los músculos tensos, lo mejor es que te den un _____.

8. Las personas que dependen de las drogas son _____.

3 Completar Look at the drawings. Complete the sentences with the correct forms of the verbs from the word bank.

(no) apurarse	(no) hacer ejercicios de estiramiento
(no) consumir bebidas alcohólicas	(no) llevar una vida sana

1. Isabel debió _____.

2. Mi prima prefiere _____.

3. A Roberto no le gusta _____.

4. Ana va a llegar tarde y tiene que _____.

4 **¿Negativo o positivo?** Categorize the terms in the word bank according to whether they are good or bad for one's health.

buena nutrición	entrenarse	llevar vida sedentaria
colesterol	fumar	ser un drogadicto
comer comida sin grasa	hacer ejercicios de estiramiento	ser un teleadicto
comer en exceso	hacer gimnasia	sufrir muchas presiones
consumir mucho alcohol	levantar pesas	tomar vitaminas
dieta equilibrada	llevar vida sana	

Positivo para la salud   **Negativo para la salud**

_____ _____
_____ _____
_____ _____
_____ _____
_____ _____
_____ _____
_____ _____

5 **El/La instructor(a)** You are a personal trainer, and your clients' goals are listed below. Give each one a different piece of advice, using familiar commands and expressions from **Preparación**.

1. "Quiero adelgazar". _____

2. "Quiero tener músculos bien definidos". _____

3. "Quiero quemar grasa". _____

4. "Quiero respirar sin problemas". _____

5. "Quiero correr una maratón". _____

6. "Quiero engordar un poco". _____

6 **Los alimentos** Write whether these food categories are rich in **vitaminas, minerales, proteínas,** or **grasas.**

1. carnes _____
2. agua mineral _____
3. mantequilla _____
4. frutas _____

5. huevos _____
6. aceite _____
7. vegetales _____
8. cereales enriquecidos (*fortified*) _____

GRAMÁTICA

15.1 Past participles used as adjectives

1 **Oraciones** Complete the sentences with the correct past participle forms of these verbs.

1. Estoy haciendo ejercicio en una bicicleta _____ (prestar).

2. Dame la botella _____ (abrir) de vitaminas.

3. La comida está _____ (hacer) con mucha grasa.

4. Lee la tabla de nutrición _____ (escribir) en los alimentos.

5. ¿Está la mesa _____ (poner) para la cena?

6. Voy a pagar el gimnasio con el dinero que tengo _____ (ahorrar).

7. Porque estoy a dieta tengo muchos dulces _____ (guardar).

8. Estoy muy contenta con mis kilos _____ (perder).

9. Todos los días hago mis ejercicios _____ (preferir).

10. No puedo caminar porque tengo el tobillo _____ (torcer).

2 **Las consecuencias** Complete the sentences with **estar** and the correct past participle.

> **modelo**
>
> La señora Gómez cerró la farmacia.
> La farmacia *está cerrada*.

1. Julia resolvió sus problemas de nutrición. Sus problemas _____.

2. Antonio preparó su bolsa del gimnasio. Su bolsa _____.

3. Le vendimos las vitaminas a José. Las vitaminas _____.

4. El doctor le prohibió comida con grasa. La comida con grasa _____.

5. El maestro habló para confirmar la clase de ejercicios. La clase de ejercicios _____.

6. Carlos y Luis se aburrieron de ir al gimnasio. Carlos y Luis _____.

3 **¿Cómo están?** Label each drawing with a complete sentence, using the nouns provided with **estar** and the past participle of the verbs.

1. pavo / servir _____   2. cuarto / desordenar _____

3. cama / hacer _____   4. niñas / dormir _____

4 **El misterio** Complete this paragraph with the correct past participle forms of the verbs in the word bank. Use each verb only once.

| abrir | desordenar | hacer | poner | romper |
| cubrir | escribir | morir | resolver | sorprender |

El detective llegó al hotel con el número de la habitación _____ en un papel.
                                                                          1
Entró en la habitación. La cama estaba _____ y la puerta del baño estaba
                                                          2
_____. Vio a un hombre que parecía estar _____ porque
          3   4
no movía ni un dedo. El hombre tenía la cara _____ con un periódico y no tenía
                                                      5
zapatos _____. El espejo estaba _____ y el baño estaba
              6   7
_____. De repente, el hombre se levantó y salió corriendo sin sus
          8
zapatos. El detective se quedó muy _____ y el misterio nunca fue
                                              9
_____.
      10

5 **Preguntas personales** Write short paragraphs answering these two questions. Use past participles as often as possible.

1. ¿Estás preocupado/a por estar en buena forma?

_____

_____

_____

2. ¿Estás interesado/a en seguir una dieta equilibrada?

_____

_____

_____

_____

15.2 The present perfect

1 **¿Qué han hecho?** Complete each sentence with the present perfect of the verb in parentheses.

> **modelo**
>
> Marcos y Felipe **han hecho** (hacer) sus tareas de contabilidad.

1. Gloria y Samuel _____ (comer) comida francesa.

2. (Yo) _____ (ver) la última película de ese director.

3. Pablo y tú _____ (leer) novelas de García Márquez.

4. Liliana _____ (tomar) la clase de química.

5. (Nosotros) _____ (ir) a esa lavandería antes.

6. Tú le _____ (escribir) un mensaje electrónico al profesor.

2 **¿Qué han hecho esta tarde?** Write sentences that say what these people have done this afternoon. Use the present perfect.

1. Ricardo

_____

2. Víctor

_____

3. (tú)

_____

4. (yo)

_____

5. Claudia y yo

_____

3 Ha sido así Rewrite the sentences, replacing the subject with the one in parentheses.

1. Hemos conocido a varios venezolanos este año. (tú)

_____

2. Gilberto ha viajado por todos los Estados Unidos. (yo)

_____

3. ¿Has ido al museo de arte de Boston? (ustedes)

_____

4. Paula y Sonia han hecho trabajos muy buenos. (Virginia)

_____

5. He asistido a tres conferencias de ese autor. (los estudiantes)

_____

6. Mi hermano ha puesto la mesa todos los días. (mi madre y yo)

_____

4 Todavía no Rewrite the sentences to say that these things have not yet been done. Use the present perfect.

> **modelo**
> Su prima no va al gimasio.
> *Su prima todavía no ha ido al gimnasio.*

1. Pedro y Natalia no nos dan las gracias.

_____

2. Los estudiantes no contestan la pregunta.

_____

3. Mi amigo Pablo no hace ejercicio.

_____

4. Esas chicas no levantan pesas.

_____

5. Tú no estás a dieta.

_____

6. Rosa y yo no sufrimos muchas presiones.

_____

15.3 The past perfect

1 **Vida nueva** Complete this paragraph with the past perfect forms of the verbs in parentheses.

Antes del accidente, mi vida _____ (ser) tranquila y sedentaria. (Yo) Nunca antes
                                     1

_____ (mirar) tanto la televisión y _____ (comer) en exceso.
        2   3

Nunca me _____ (pasar) nada malo. El día en que pasó el accidente, mis amigos
                  4

y yo nos _____ (encontrar) para ir a nadar en un río. (Nosotros) Nunca
                 5

antes _____ (ir) a ese río. Cuando llegamos, entré de cabeza al río. (Yo) No
              6

_____ (ver) las rocas que estaban debajo del agua. Me di con las rocas en la
        7

cabeza. Mi hermana, que _____ (ir) con nosotros al río, me sacó del agua. Todos
                                  8

mis amigos se _____ (quedar) fuera del agua. Entre todos me llevaron al hospital. En
                      9

el hospital, los médicos me dijeron que yo _____ (tener) mucha suerte. (Yo) No me
                                                    10

_____ (lastimar) la espalda demasiado, pero tuve que hacer terapia (*therapy*) física por
        11

muchos meses. (Yo) Nunca antes _____ (preocuparse) por estar en buena forma, ni por
                                         12

ser fuerte. Ahora hago gimnasia y soy una persona activa, flexible y fuerte.

2 **Nunca antes** Rewrite the sentences to say that these people had never done these things before.

> **modelo**
> Julián se compró un coche nuevo.
> Julián nunca antes se había comprado un coche nuevo.

1. Tu novia fue al gimnasio por la mañana.

_____

2. Carmen corrió en la maratón de la ciudad.

_____

3. Visité los países de Suramérica.

_____

4. Los estudiantes escribieron trabajos de veinte páginas.

_____

5. Armando y Cecilia esquiaron en los Andes.

_____

6. Luis y yo tenemos un perro en casa.

_____

7. Condujiste el coche de tu papá.

_____

8. Ramón y tú nos prepararon la cena.

_____

3 **Ya había pasado** Combine the sentences, using the preterite and the past perfect.

> **modelo**
>
> Elisa pone la televisión. Jorge ya se ha despertado.
> *Cuando Elisa puso la televisión, Jorge ya se había despertado.*

1. Lourdes llama a Carla. Carla ya ha salido.

_____

2. Tu hermano vuelve a casa. Ya has terminado de cenar.

_____

3. Llego a la escuela. La clase ya ha empezado.

_____

4. Ustedes nos buscan en casa. Ya hemos salido.

_____

5. Salimos a la calle. Ya ha empezado a nevar.

_____

6. Ellos van a las tiendas. Las tiendas ya han cerrado.

_____

7. Lilia y Juan encuentran las llaves. Raúl ya se ha ido.

_____

8. Preparas el almuerzo. Yo ya he comido.

_____

4 **Rafael Nadal** Write a paragraph about the things that Rafael Nadal had achieved by age 18. Use the phrases from the word bank with the past perfect. Start each sentence with **Ya**. The first one has been done for you.

empezar a jugar al tenis profesionalmente	jugar en torneos del Grand Slam
ganar un torneo Masters Series	recibir miles de dólares
ingresar a la lista de los 100 mejores jugadores de la ATP	ser el campeón (*champion*) de la Copa Davis

Cuando tenía 18 años, Rafael Nadal ya había empezado a jugar al tenis profesionalmente. _____

_____

_____

_____

_____

_____

PREPARACIÓN   Lección 16

1 El anuncio Answer the questions about this help-wanted ad, using complete sentences.

> **EMPRESA MULTINACIONAL BUSCA:**
> • Contador   • Gerente   • Secretario
> Salarios varían según la experiencia. Seguro (*Insurance*) de salud, plan de jubilación 401(k), dos semanas de vacaciones.
> Enviar currículum y carta de presentación por fax o por correo electrónico para concertar (*schedule*) una entrevista con el Sr. Martínez.

1. ¿Cuántos puestos hay?

_____

2. ¿Cuáles son los sueldos?

_____

3. ¿Qué beneficios ofrece la empresa?

_____

4. ¿Qué deben enviar los aspirantes?

_____

5. ¿Quién es el señor Martínez?

_____

6. ¿Dice el anuncio que hay que llenar (*fill out*) una solicitud?

_____

2 Vida profesional Complete the paragraph with items from the word bank.

| anuncio | aspirante | currículum | entrevista | éxito | profesión | renunciar |
| ascenso | beneficios | empresa | entrevistadora | obtener | puesto | salario |

Vi el _____1 en el periódico. Se necesitaban personas que hablaran español e inglés para un _____2 de editor en una pequeña _____3 que se encontraba en el centro de la ciudad. Preparé mi _____4 con mucha atención y lo envié por fax. Esa tarde me llamó la _____5, que se llamaba Patricia Pineda. Me dijo que el _____6 que ofrecían no era demasiado alto, pero que los _____7, como el seguro de salud y el plan de jubilación, eran excelentes. Era una buena oportunidad para _____8 experiencia. Me pidió que fuera a la oficina al día siguiente para hacerme una _____9. Había otro _____10 en la sala de espera cuando llegué. Me puse un poco nerviosa. Ese día decidí _____11 a mi trabajo anterior (*previous*) y desde entonces ejerzo (*I practice*) la _____12 de editora. ¡He tenido mucho _____13!

3 **Una es diferente** Fill in the blanks with the words that don't belong in the groups.

1. ocupación, reunión, oficio, profesión, trabajo _____

2. pintor, psicólogo, maestro, consejero _____

3. arquitecta, diseñadora, pintora, bombera _____

4. invertir, currículum, corredor de bolsa, negocios _____

5. sueldo, beneficios, aumento, renunciar, ascenso _____

6. puesto, reunión, entrevista, videoconferencia _____

4 **Las ocupaciones** Fill in the blanks with the profession of the person who would make each statement.

1. "Decido dónde poner los elementos gráficos de las páginas de una revista".

_____

2. "Ayudo a las personas a resolver sus problemas. Hablan conmigo y buscamos soluciones".

_____

3. "Defiendo a mis clientes y les doy consejos legales".

_____

4. "Investigo las cosas que pasan y escribo artículos sobre los eventos".

_____

5. "Les doy clases a los niños en la escuela".

_____

6. "Hago experimentos y publico los resultados en una revista".

_____

5 **¿Quién lo usa?** Label each drawing with the profession associated with the objects.

1. _____   2. _____

3. _____   4. _____

GRAMÁTICA

16.1 The future tense

1 **Preguntas** Answer the questions with the future tense and the words in parentheses.

> **modelo**
> ¿Qué vas a hacer hoy? (los quehaceres)
> Haré los quehaceres.

1. ¿Cuándo vamos a jugar al fútbol? (el jueves)

_____

2. ¿Cuántas personas va a haber en la clase? (treinta)

_____

3. ¿A qué hora vas a venir? (a las nueve)

_____

4. ¿Quién va a ser el jefe de Delia? (Esteban)

_____

5. Cuándo va a salir Juan? (en una hora)

_____

6. ¿Quiénes van a estar en la fiesta? (muchos amigos)

_____

2 **A los 30 años** Some friends in their late teens are talking about what they think they will be doing when they turn 30 years old. Complete the conversation with the correct form of the verbs in parentheses.

LETI Cuando tenga 30 años, _____ (ser) una arqueóloga famosa.
Para entonces, _____ (haber) descubierto unas ruinas indígenas
muy importantes.

SERGIO Yo _____ (tener) un programa de viajes en la televisión. Mi cámara
de video y yo _____ (visitar) lugares hermosos y muy interesantes.

SUSI Entonces (tú) _____ (venir) a visitarme a mi restaurante de comida
caribeña que _____ (abrir) en Santo Domingo, ¿verdad? El Sabor
Dominicano _____ (tener) los mejores platos tradicionales y otros
creados (*created*) por mí.

SERGIO Claro que sí, _____ (ir) a comer las especialidades y
_____ (recomendarlo) a mis telespectadores (*viewers*). También (tú y
yo) _____ (poder) visitar a Leti en sus expediciones.

LETI Sí, Susi _____ (cocinar) platos exóticos en medio de la selva y todos
_____ (disfrutar) de su deliciosa comida.

Workbook

3   **Será así** Rewrite each sentence to express probability. Each new sentence should start with a verb in the future tense.

> **modelo**
>
> Creemos que se llega por esta calle.
> *Se llegará por esta calle.*

1. Es probable que sea la una de la tarde.

_____

2. Creo que ellas están en casa.

_____

3. Estamos casi seguros de que va a nevar hoy.

_____

4. ¿Crees que ella tiene clase ahora?

_____

5. Es probable que ellos vayan al cine luego.

_____

6. Creo que estamos enfermos.

_____

4   **Fin de semana entre amigos** Rosa, one of your friends, is telling you about some of the activities she has planned for this weekend. Write complete sentences to describe each image. Then keep using the future tense to write two activities that you will do this weekend.

sábado por la mañana / nosotros   después / ustedes   mientras / yo

1. _____   2. _____   3. _____

_____   _____

por la noche / Julio, Lisa y Cata   domingo por la mañana / yo   domingo por la tarde / nosotros

4. _____   5. _____   6. _____

_____   _____

7. _____

8. _____

16.2 The conditional tense

1 **¿Lo haría?** Rosa is not happy with her current job. What would happen if she looked for a new job? Complete the sentences with the conditional forms of the verbs in parentheses.

1. Rosa _____ (buscar) trabajo en los anuncios del periódico, pero no

   _____ (encontrar) nada.

2. Entonces, ella le _____ (preguntar) a un amigo.

3. Él le _____ (aconsejar) que busque oportunidades de trabajo en Internet.

4. Rosa _____ (solicitar) un puesto relacionado con su profesión.

5. Ella _____ (llevar) la solicitud de trabajo a la empresa.

6. En la compañía, ella se _____ (entrevistar) con el gerente.

7. El gerente _____ (hablar) del puesto.

8. Rosa _____ (preguntar) sobre el salario y sobre los beneficios.

9. Alguno de los dos no _____ (estar) de acuerdo (*agree*).

10. Rosa _____ (tener) que buscar trabajo en otro lugar.

2 **La entrevista** You are talking to a friend about a possible job interview. Write a paragraph explaining what you would do if you were granted an interview.

buscar información sobre la empresa	tener el currículum
saber lo que hace la compañía	hablar sobre mi carrera
llenar la solicitud de trabajo	(no) reír muy fuerte
vestirse de forma profesional	decir mi salario ideal
(no) ponerse sombrero	hacer preguntas sobre los beneficios
llegar temprano a la entrevista	(no) comer nada en la reunión
saludar al / a la entrevistador(a)	finalmente, dar las gracias al / a la entrevistador(a)

Buscaría información sobre la empresa. _____

_____

_____

_____

_____

_____

_____

_____

Workbook

3 **Los buenos modales** (*manners*) Rewrite these commands as polite requests, using the conditional.

> **modelo**
>
> Termina el trabajo hoy antes de irte.
> **¿Terminarías el trabajo hoy antes de irte, por favor?**

1. Lleva mi currículum al entrevistador. _____   4. Dame un aumento de sueldo. _____

_____   _____

2. Llama a Marcos esta tarde. _____   5. Ven a trabajar el sábado y el domingo. _____

_____   _____

3. Escucha la videoconferencia. _____   6. Búscame en la oficina a las seis. _____

_____   _____

4 **¿Sería así?** Change the sentences into questions that express conjectures. Use the conditional tense.

> **modelo**
>
> Natalia recibió un aumento de sueldo. (tener éxito su proyecto)
> **¿Tendría éxito su proyecto?**

1. Natalia se durmió en la videoconferencia de hoy. (estar cansada)

_____

2. El jefe de Natalia le habló. (despedir su jefe a Natalia)

_____

3. Natalia se fue a su casa. (renunciar Natalia a su puesto)

_____

4. Natalia obtuvo un aumento de sueldo. (estar loco su jefe)

_____

5 **Eso pensamos** Write sentences using the conditional of the verbs in parentheses.

> **modelo**
>
> Nosotros decidimos que (ustedes / tener tiempo) para estar en la reunión.
> **Nosotros decidimos que ustedes tendrían tiempo para estar en la reunión.**

1. Yo pensaba que (mi jefe / estar enojado) porque llegué tarde a la reunión.

_____

2. Beatriz dijo que (en la reunión / presentar al nuevo empleado).

_____

3. Marta y Esther creían que (en la reunión / hablar del aumento) en los sueldos de los empleados.

_____

4. Mi jefe dijo que (el gerente / tener buenas noticias) del éxito de la compañía.

_____

16.3 The past subjunctive

1 **Si pudiera** Complete the sentences with the past subjunctive of the verbs in parentheses.

1. El arqueólogo se alegró de que todos _____ (hacer) tantas preguntas.

2. Mi madre siempre quería que yo _____ (estudiar) arquitectura.

3. Te dije que cuando _____ (ir) a la entrevista, deberías llevar tu currículum.

4. Tal vez no fue una buena idea que nosotros le _____ (escribir) esa carta.

5. Era una lástima que su esposo _____ (tener) que trabajar tanto.

6. Luisa dudaba que ese empleo _____ (ser) su mejor alternativa.

7. Era probable que Francisco _____ (llevarse) mal con sus jefes.

8. Laura buscaba músicos que _____ (saber) tocar el saxofón.

9. Ustedes no estaban seguros de que el reportero _____ (conocer) al actor.

10. Fue extraño que Daniela y tú _____ (solicitar) el mismo (*same*) trabajo.

2 **Sería más feliz** Álex is talking to himself about the things that would make him happier. Complete his statements with the past subjunctive form of the verbs in parentheses. Then draw a portrait of yourself and write five sentences describing things that would make you happier. Try to use as many singular and plural forms as you can.

Álex

Sería (*I would be*) más feliz si...

1. (yo) _____ (ver) a Maite todos los días cuando regresemos a Quito.

2. mis papás _____ (venir) a Ecuador a visitarme.

3. Maite _____ (querer) hacer un viaje conmigo.

4. (yo) _____ (tener) una computadora más moderna.

5. mis nuevos amigos y yo _____ (viajar) juntos otra vez.

Sería más feliz si...

6. _____

7. _____

8. _____

9. _____

10. _____

3 **Lo contrario** Complete the second sentences to say the opposite of the first ones.

> **modelo**
>
> Nadie dudaba que el candidato era muy bueno.
> Nadie *estaba seguro de que el candidato fuera muy bueno.*

1. Nadie dudaba de que el ascenso de Miguel fue justo (*fair*).

No estabas seguro de que _____.

2. Era obvio que todos los participantes sabían usar las computadoras.

No fue cierto que _____.

3. Raquel estaba segura de que las reuniones no servían para nada.

Pablo dudaba que _____.

4. Fue cierto que Rosa tuvo que ahorrar mucho dinero para invertirlo.

No fue verdad que _____.

5. No hubo duda de que la videoconferencia fue un desastre (*disaster*).

Tito negó que _____.

6. No negamos que los maestros recibieron salarios bajos.

La directora negó que _____.

4 **El trabajo** Complete the paragraph with the past subjunctive, the preterite, or the imperfect of the verbs in parentheses as appropriate.

MARISOL ¡Hola, Pepe! Me alegré de que (tú) _____₁_____ (conseguir) el trabajo de arquitecto.

PEPE Sí, aunque fue una lástima que (yo) _____₂_____ (tener) que renunciar a mi puesto anterior.

MARISOL No dudé de que _____₃_____ (ser) una buena decisión cuando lo supe.

PEPE No estaba seguro de que este puesto _____₄_____ (ser) lo que quería, pero resultó ser muy bueno.

MARISOL Estoy segura de que (tú) _____₅_____ (hacer) muy bien la entrevista.

PEPE Me puse un poco nervioso, sin que eso _____₆_____ (afectar) mis respuestas.

MARISOL Sé que ellos necesitaban a alguien que _____₇_____ (tener) tu experiencia.

PEPE Era cierto que ellos _____₈_____ (necesitar) a muchas personas para la oficina nueva.

¡VIVAN LOS PAÍSES HISPANOS!

España

1   **El mapa de España** Fill in the blanks with the name of the city or geographical feature.

1. _____
2. _____
3. _____
4. _____
5. _____
6. _____
7. _____
8. _____

2   **Lugares** Write the words to complete these sentences about Spanish places. Then circle them on the grid (horizontally, diagonally, and vertically).

1. España está en _____.

2. _____ tiene un área de 505.370 km^2.

3. _____, _____, _____ y _____ son ciudades importantes de España.

4. En Valencia hay un pequeño pueblo llamado _____.

5. En España se encuentran las islas _____ y _____.

6. El Museo del Prado está en _____.

A	M	T	K	I	P	M	Y	T	B	U	Ñ	O	L	O
D	B	A	L	E	A	R	E	S	U	R	A	Z	I	P
E	R	G	D	P	L	R	H	B	M	V	A	A	N	N
C	A	N	A	R	I	A	S	B	R	A	G	R	U	Y
U	Z	K	C	S	I	N	B	A	L	L	I	V	E	S
Y	S	A	D	A	O	D	C	L	P	E	I	E	S	A
T	L	X	P	Ñ	I	X	Z	E	S	N	P	U	P	E
A	Z	O	G	A	R	A	Z	A	D	C	C	R	A	L
X	T	A	Z	O	L	G	A	R	A	I	V	O	Ñ	A
E	R	B	A	R	C	E	L	O	N	A	K	P	A	B
P	Ñ	E	S	P	O	Ñ	O	L	K	Ñ	H	A	Z	D

3 **Palabras cruzadas** (*crossed*) Write one letter in each blank. Then answer the final question using the words formed vertically.

1. región de España donde está Buñol
2. Hay muchas cafeterías donde la gente pasa el tiempo.
3. Salamanca es famosa por su arquitectura antigua, como estos edificios de estilo gótico.
4. moneda que se usa en España
5. baile con raíces (*roots*) judías (*Jewish*), árabes y africanas
6. islas españolas del mar Mediterráneo
7. la profesión de Goya y El Greco
8. capital de España
9. la obra más famosa de Diego Velázquez
10. museo español famoso

El festival de Buñol se llama: _____.

4 **Las fotos** Label each photo.

1. _____

2. _____

3. _____

4. _____

1 **¿Subjuntivo o indicativo?** Write sentences, using the elements provided and either the subjunctive or the indicative, depending on the cues and context.

1. Jorge / esperar / su madre / conseguir un trabajo pronto

_____

2. (nosotros) / no negar / trabajar más de ocho horas diarias / ser duro

_____

3. ser imposible / Marisa y Rubén / ayudar con el nuevo proyecto

_____

4. ustedes / alegrarse / Natalia / regresar a nuestra oficina

_____

5. ser cierto / el jefe / ganar mucho dinero

_____

2 **¡Que sí! ¡Que no!** Your mother and father disagree on the things that you and the family should do. Write positive and negative informal commands for the subjects indicated.

1. comer en casa (nosotros)

_____

2. estudiar por las noches (tú)

_____

3. visitar a la abuela (nosotros)

_____

4. comprar un coche nuevo (tú)

_____

5. limpiar la casa (nosotros)

_____

3 **Las conjunciones** Use the subjunctive or the indicative of the verbs in parentheses.

1. Debes hacer gimnasia todas las semanas, a menos que (querer) _____ engordar.
2. Gabriela nunca hace ejercicios de estiramiento cuando (ir) _____ al gimnasio.
3. Siempre me ducho después de que (levantar) _____ pesas.
4. A Martín y a su novia les recomiendan estar a dieta para que (llevar) _____ una vida sana.
5. Con tal de que Susana (estar) _____ en forma, yo pagaría por sus clases de ejercicios aeróbicos.
6. Mi hermana aumenta de peso en cuanto (dejar) _____ de entrenar.

4 **Hemos dicho** Complete the dialogues with the present perfect or the past perfect as appropriate.

DARÍO Marcela, ¿ _____ (ir) al supermercado últimamente?
1

MARCELA No, las últimas dos semanas _____ (estar) muy ocupada y no _____
2   3
(hacer) ninguna compra.

DARÍO ¡Nunca te _____ (ver) tan ocupada en tu vida!
4

JOSÉ Debo ir al banco. Hace días que tengo un cheque y no lo _____ (cobrar) todavía.
5

MIGUEL Yo nunca cobro los cheques. Hasta hoy, siempre los _____ (depositar) en mi
6
cuenta de ahorros.

JOSÉ De todas maneras es un poco tarde y probablemente el banco _____ (cerrar) sus
7
puertas. Iré a cobrar el cheque mañana.

IRMA ¡Estamos perdidas en la ciudad otra vez, Sonia! Yo nunca antes _____ (estar)
8
perdida en la ciudad.

SONIA Antes de venir aquí, yo _____ (preparar) un plan de viaje… ¡para no perderme!
9

IRMA Cuando salimos, mi tía ya me _____ (dar) unas direcciones escritas, pero las
10
olvidé en mi escritorio. ¡Qué mala suerte!

5 **Ecología** Complete the sentences with the conditional of the verbs in parentheses.

1. Me _____ (gustar) hacer algo para evitar la contaminación del agua.

2. (Nosotros) _____ (poder) comenzar por reciclar los periódicos.

3. La deforestación en exceso _____ (tener) consecuencias terribles en nuestra provincia.

4. A José le _____ (interesar) estar en un grupo de protección del medio ambiente, pero

   primero _____ (querer) investigar un poco al respecto.

5. Mis hermanos dicen que _____ (ir) a otro país para estudiar ecología.

6 **El extranjero** Write a paragraph, keeping in mind the indicative and subjunctive moods.

• Describe what you like and dislike about living in your town. What would you recommend to
someone new to your town?

• What would your childhood have been like if you had grown up in a Spanish-speaking country?

• Finally, mention where you will live in the future and why.

_____

_____

_____

_____

_____

_____

_____